Fundamentalism

& Gender,

1875 to the Present

Yale University Press

Fundamentalism

& Gender,

1875 to the Present

Margaret Lamberts Bendroth

New Haven and London

Published with assistance from the Louis Stern Memorial
Fund.

Designed by Deborah Dutton.
Set in Primer text and Helvetica display type by Rainsford
Type, Danbury, Connecticut.
Printed in the United States of America by Edwards Brothers,
Inc., Ann Arbor, Michigan.

Library of Congress Cataloging-in-Publication Data

Bendroth, Margaret Lamberts, 1954–
    Fundamentalism and gender, 1875 to the present /
Margaret Lamberts Bendroth.
        p.   cm.
    Includes bibliographical references and index.
    ISBN 0-300-05593-5 (alk. paper)
    1. Women in fundamentalist churches—History. 2. Sex
role—Religious aspects—Christianity—History of
doctrines—20th century. 3. Fundamentalism. 4. Modernist-
fundamentalist controversy. 5. Feminism—Religious
aspects—Christianity—History of doctrines—
20th century. 6. Woman (Christian theology)—History
of doctrines—20th century. I. Title.
BX7800.F864B46   1993
277.3'082'082—dc20   93-13546
                                                     CIP

A catalogue record for this book is available from the British
Library.
The paper in this book meets the guidelines for permanence
and durability of the Committee on Production Guidelines for
Book Longevity of the Council on Library Resources.
10 9 8 7 6 5 4 3 2 1

To Norman

Contents

Acknowledgments

This book would not have been possible without the generous support of the Evangelical Scholarship Initiative, a program of the Pew Foundation. I am particularly indebted to Nathan Hatch, Mary Stewart Van Leeuwen, Eleanore Stump, and Michael Hamilton for their faith in this project, even before it had begun. The Institute for the Study of American Evangelicals, through the kind ministrations of Daryl Hart, also provided financial assistance and ready access to the Billy Graham Center Archives.

Friends and colleagues also donated time, energy, and numerous lunch hours on my behalf. Virginia Lieson Brereton proved a valuable critic, ally, and friend along the way. I am grateful to Elizabeth Nordbeck for her mentorship and encouragement, to Mike Hamilton for his timely suggestions and graceful criticisms, and to Mark Noll for his insightful and gentle reading of this manuscript.

I am also grateful for the help and support of librarians and archivists. Robert Shuster and his staff at the Billy Graham Center Archives in Wheaton, Illinois, and the staff at the American Baptist Historical Society in Rochester, New York, were very helpful at the earliest stages. The library staff at Northwestern College in Roseville, Minnesota, and William Darr at Grace College, Winona Lake, Indiana, graciously provided access to their collections. John Beauregard at Gordon College and Mary MacGregor at Park Street Church also proved invaluable allies in my search for materials.

I also owe a great debt to my advisor, Timothy Smith, for his faith in my future as a scholar, even when, at least in my mind, this faith appeared to be a considerable leap in the dark. With patience and skill he taught me to think and to rethink; by example and through many hours of painstaking editing, he also introduced me to the craft and discipline of writing. He is an example and an inspiration, both as a scholar and as a true Christian humanist.

Thanks are also due for the help and encouragement of my parents and siblings, many of whom were thoughtful enough to live in cities with good manuscript collections. I appreciated their home-cooked meals, late-night conversations, and the hospitality of their pets, some of whom generously shared their sleeping quarters with me.

My deepest gratitude goes to Norman, my husband and fellow traveler, who shared my joy in creating this book. I do not stretch the truth to say that without him, none of this would have been possible. These chapters grew between chauffeuring excursions to nursery school and kindergarten, during bouts of chicken pox and strep, and in long weeks of separation. I write surrounded by the loving artwork and creative disorder of my children. In more ways than I could name, this book is as much theirs as mine. To those three, Norman, Nathan, and Anna, I give my deepest love and gratitude.

Fundamentalism

& Gender,

1875 to the Present

Introduction

The popular image of contemporary evangelicalism is deeply antifeminist. And, it seems, rightly so. In the 1970s the "total womanhood" advocated by Marabel Morgan, as well as the political agenda of groups like Concerned Women for America, rallied religious conservatives in opposition to feminism. As the core constituency of the New Right in the 1980s, fundamentalists and their neo-evangelical cousins won a large share of public credit (or blame) for defeating the equal rights amendment.

That position appears only to have strengthened. By the end of the 1980s, the pro-family message of James Dobson's "Focus on the Family" radio program reached 970 radio stations, and his books had sold more than six million copies. At the time of this writing, organized opposition to feminism is attracting new attention. In January 1989 the newly formed Council on Biblical Manhood and Womanhood issued the Danvers Statement, a conservative manifesto that decried "feminist egalitarianism" and framed relationships between the sexes in terms of the "loving, humble leadership of redeemed husbands, and the intelligent, willing support of that leadership by redeemed wives."[1]

But the new round of controversy generated by the Danvers Statement suggests that support for its conservative ideology is far from widespread. Polls and literature surveys have evidenced growing popular acceptance of the evangelical feminist movement, especially within the younger generation. James Hunter's study of evangelical college students has unearthed relatively strong support for feminist ideals of egalitarian marriage and shared child-rearing.[2] Though evangelicals often describe the ideal marriage as one of masculine "headship" and feminine submission, it is doubtful how much they carry this into practice. Judith Stacey has concluded that these marriages are in fact a "patriarchy of the last gasp," supporting her observation that the use of hierarchical language often masks the relative lack of rigid structure in most successful evangelical marriages.[3]

Sociological evidence suggests that the antifeminist image is in fact a stereotype, glossing over some deep conflicts within evangelical ranks over the nature of women's role in family and society. The issue is far from settled: gender issues remain a central battlefield in the "culture war" waged by conservatives, not only against secular culture, but among themselves.[4]

Since the 1970s the ideological debate over the role of women has ranged toward two opposite poles, one defending feminism and another condemning it wholeheartedly. Although arguments are often cast in terms of disagreement over biblical interpretation, the real issue goes much deeper. Both traditionalists and evangelical feminists have accused the other side of one unforgivable sin: thoughtless capitulation to the secular standards of American culture. While conservatives accuse the feminists within evangelical ranks of simply parroting the agenda of secular women's groups, they have come under equally strong attack for idealizing a model every bit as secular, the postindustrial nuclear family of the 1950s. With the stakes for ideological purity raised this high, the prospects for immediate resolution are slight.[5]

Feminism, it seems fair to say, has inspired as much confusion among evangelicals as outright opposition. And thus it seems more profitable to ask not which side in the controversy will or should win, but why the conflict continues. If modern evangelicalism is not inherently antifeminist, then what is the source of energy behind the incessant debates over feminism and women's role, and what purpose do these arguments serve?

This question, which is essentially a historical one, raises larger issues about the nature of evangelicalism itself, especially its roots in the twentieth-century fundamentalist movement. For the debate over gender roles is far more than an endless parlor game evangelicals play to stave off more important matters; it is central to questions about the survival of conservative religious values within modern secular culture, of maintaining a visibly distinctive tradition that is still socially relevant. It touches on the common twentieth-century problem of attaching meaning to the fact of human gender in a society where arbitrary roles seem unnecessary—and ever more elusive. Thus it is not surprising that the debate generates such heated energy among evangelicals or that it seems so far from resolution.

Gender issues stood at the heart of fundamentalist desire to be different. In the late nineteenth century the movement emerged in decisive reaction to conventional Victorian piety, demanding heartfelt conversion and a life of godly service. From the start fundamentalists doubted the sentimental faith in "womanhood" that all but exonerated half the human race from the original sin of Adam. Evangelical Protestants of the previous century elevated women as the keepers of morality and assumed conversely that men had no natural aptitude for religion. Women maintained the private sphere of home, and by extension, church, while men managed the public world of business and politics, relatively free of moral entanglements. Fundamentalists, however, allowed no special favors when it came to sin.

In fact, they ultimately reversed the Victorian formula. By the 1920s fundamentalists had adopted the belief that it was men, not women, who had the true aptitude for religion. In 1946, evangelist John R. Rice condemned the old Victorian piety about sainted womanhood as "a lie out of Hell." It is a "wicked, hellish, ungodly, satanic teaching," he declared, "that by nature men are not as good, that by nature women are . . . [more] inclined toward God and morality."[6] In fundamentalist culture, women became the more psychologically vulnerable sex, never to be trusted with matters of doctrine, and men stronger both rationally and spiritually, divinely equipped to defend Christian orthodoxy from its enemies within and without.

The social and theological forces that unseated women from their superior position and defined religious orthodoxy as a masculine enterprise are complex, and rooted in the history of fundamentalism, a movement often misunderstood, and notoriously difficult to define. For the sake of clarity, a brief digression is necessary.

Defining Fundamentalism

In its proper historical sense, the term *fundamentalist* describes a coalition of conservative, predominantly Calvinist, Protestants that emerged from within a broader, more ecumenical evangelical culture in the late nineteenth century. Known largely for their unrelenting attacks against evolution, they were committed to a militant defense of orthodoxy against what they saw as liberalizing influences in Protestant institutions. Rather than accommodate the Christian message to intellectual trends in modern scholarship, they adhered to what they held as elemental truths of the "faith once delivered."

The five "fundamentals" (hence the name "fundamentalist") included, first of all, the virgin birth of Christ, a doctrine foundational to the deity of Christ. Fundamentalists also held to the substitutionary atonement, elevating Christ as more than an example of humanity at its best, but one whose death was actual payment for human sin. They defended the bodily resurrection of Christ, as well as the supernatural reality of miracles. Fundamentalists also held to an inerrant Scripture, without factual or scientific error. Most, but not all, were dispensational premillennialists, which meant that they saw human history only in terms of decline and expected a literal Second Coming of Christ. Many fundamentalists often displayed an anti-intellectual attitude toward biblical scholarship and academic theology, even though the movement itself was never as rural or backward as its detractors made it out to be. Although its message resonated with the cultural Christianity of the American South, it began as a northern, urban phenomenon, socially rooted in the lower middle classes. After the 1920s, many Southern Baptists did ally with fundamentalism, though they remained divided about the fundamentalist label, even to the present day.[7]

Fundamentalists differentiated themselves, for reasons both social and theological, from pentecostal and holiness groups. Although all shared much in common, especially in their antipathy to "worldliness," fundamentalists emphatically rejected the pentecostal emphasis on spiritual gifts, especially the experience of "spirit baptism" or tongues, as a requisite of conversion. They taught instead that these gifts ceased immediately after their outpouring at Pentecost and would not resume until after Christ's Second Coming. Although many holiness and pentecostal groups may rightly assume the fundamentalist label, the two groups parted ways decisively in regard to the "woman question." For the purposes of my argument, I have chosen to differentiate the main body of fundamentalists from their charismatic conservative brethren. For although to outsiders they appeared nearly indistinguishable, fundamentalists abhorred the use of women preachers in holiness churches almost as vehemently as they opposed the practice of speaking in tongues.[8]

The term *evangelical* refers to the historic tradition in American Protestantism that was broadly orthodox and active in social and missionary outreach. After the 1920s, this coalition fragmented and the label took on a confusing array of interpretations. *Neo-evangelical* is a term describing a group within post–World War II fundamentalism which tried to bring the movement out of its intellectual isolation and to broaden its evangelistic appeal. Although in a historic sense, most Protestant denominations still hold rightful title to the evangelical label, it is most often applied to those who are culturally and theologically conservative, the modern-day heirs of fundamentalism. For clarity's sake, they are best referred to as "new evangelicals," though the term *evangelical* is often used interchangeably.[9]

Fundamentalism has deeply influenced twentieth-century American religious expression. Its powerful language of alienation and its critique of moral laxity in the wider culture have resonated across the Protestant spectrum. Groups as ethnically diverse as Southern Baptists, Missouri Synod Lutherans, and the Christian Reformed have adopted much of its rhetoric and shared many of its goals, if not all the fine points of fundamentalist theology. The rock-hard certainties of fundamentalist and evangelical faith have in fact stood well against doctrinal drift and confusion and show few signs of losing their appeal. Though marginalized by intellectuals and almost entirely misunderstood by journalists, conservative religion continues to attract new followers. As Garry Wills has commented, "No group making up a fifth of the population can safely be ignored by anyone trying to understand America."[10]

Men, Women, and Fundamentalism

Fundamentalist attitudes about gender provide a key to understanding fundamentalism's internal development and its interaction with the dominant forces of American culture. As Laurence Moore has pointed out, fundamentalists were not naturally social "outsiders." Nearly all of the movement's early leadership was white, male, middle-class, well-educated, and Protestant.[11] Fundamentalist militancy grew from more than just its rejection by intellectual elites, although this did elicit considerable anger.[12] A significant element of this militancy was generated in the masculine persona that fundamentalists identified as the true hallmark of the Christian warrior. Fundamentalist leaders were men determined to stop the spread of liberal and secularizing trends in a society once defined by Christian values. And they were men making their livelihood in a social institution that was predominantly female in membership and, fundamentalists believed, in its watered-down doctrine. Masculine language and comradery became a common rallying point for those who chose to do battle with the devil in modern Babylon.

Gender is a powerful means of orienting world and self. In the Middle Ages, for example, male monks symbolized their renunciation of the world by self-consciously leaving behind their masculine power and adopting a female state of "lowliness."[13] In the twentieth century, fundamentalist men, who saw their world as dangerously "feminized," sought other-worldliness through assertive masculinity. "The world," wrote Presbyterian Clarence Macartney, "is a proud, cold, haughty, attractive, but heartless woman." Just as the seductive Salome won the heart of Herod, he warned, "when the world dances before a soul, the voice of the true preacher sounds fainter and fainter." The world might scoff at righteous zeal, but the true man stood for his faith without compromising an inch.[14]

Fundamentalism was born in an era of anxiety over gender roles. By the close of the nineteenth century, woman suffragists and social reformers had stretched the traditional boundaries of the feminine sphere to the breaking point. Their "domestic feminism" elevated women as homemakers for the entire nation, responsible for both private and public standards of morality. Middle-class males confronted this challenge to their leadership in the family and public sphere at the same time that the business world was rapidly professionalizing, narrowing the path of individual initiative. Thus, while applauding women's strides toward equality, religious and secular leaders began to worry that the "new woman" was creating an increasingly passive type of manhood. The Protestant churches, already numerically dominated by women, felt the crisis most keenly and responded with urgency.

As chapter 1 describes, fundamentalism emerged from a revivalist tradition that, especially by the turn of the century, was deeply concerned with winning the hearts of men. Its early leaders were popular evangelists who strove to convince middle-class males that religion was more than a sentimental haven for their wives and sisters. In an intellectual culture that was retreating from a specifically Christian identity, early fundamen-

talists upheld allegiance to orthodox Christianity as a cause which demanded a special inner bravery. Evangelists also held forth the promise
of spiritual power over sin, a teaching borrowed from the Victorious Life,
or Keswick, movement in British evangelicalism. The form of piety this
movement generated made religious faith a new arena of purposeful striv-
ing and invigorating challenge.

Still, early fundamentalism was far from a masculine enclave, for like
most religious movements it attracted large numbers of women. Its pragmatic bent allowed and even encouraged numerous opportunities for
female evangelists and preachers. In its aggressive spirit, early fundamentalism in fact closely resembled many of the missionary and reform
efforts gaining popularity among women in the late nineteenth century;
crossover between these two rising groups of "outsiders," women and
fundamentalists, was not uncommon.

Fundamentalism's continuing attraction for women ensured that gender questions would arise over and over. Promoting any kind of religion
as a masculine enterprise was a difficult, if not impossible, task when
women responded so readily to its call.

But by the early twentieth century, fundamentalism was beginning
to define itself in opposition to feminist trends elsewhere in evangelical
Protestantism. Chapter 2 deals with two related developments in fundamentalist theology, the doctrine of biblical inerrancy and dispensational
premillennialism. These two doctrinal innovations gave clearest expression
to a rising suspicion that "woman's religion" was basically incompatible
with the defense of orthodoxy.

In the late nineteenth century, leaders of women's missionary and
temperance groups had begun to press for greater power in the denominations they served. Although only a minority wished for ordination privileges, most agreed that the time was ripe for fuller representation of
women in deliberative bodies and wider access to the pulpit. The standard
defense of these rights was a biblical argument that depended heavily on
a nonliteral, thematic reading of the Pauline prescriptions used to silence
women since apostolic times. Like the popular evangelicalism of its day,
this argument was basically Wesleyan and perfectionist in its approach.
Its adherents argued that all of the biblical restrictions on feminine leadership were temporary, swept away by the atoning death and resurrection
of Christ, when all the world began its final movement toward the perfect
consummation.

The Princeton theologians who championed the inerrancy of Scripture placed themselves squarely at odds with such reasoning. They opposed feminist biblical scholarship, codified in the *Woman's Bible* Elizabeth Cady Stanton issued in 1895, and the popular evangelical understandings of troubling Bible passages on women's role. The inerrancy doctrine simply demanded much more serious attention to the divine intent behind each literal word of Scripture. But the arguments went farther than that. Ultimately, fundamentalist biblicists defended their belief, not only as doctrinally correct, but as the inherently more masculine choice. In this sense, early fundamentalism began to define itself as a theological alternative to evangelical feminism.

The logic of dispensational premillennialism, the system of biblical interpretation which most fundamentalists adhered to, also clashed with perfectionist interpretations of the Bible. Dispensational teaching placed women squarely under the curses God instituted after Adam and Eve sinned in the Garden of Eden. Thus womankind, like the rest of humanity, waited for Christ's Second Coming to lift the penalty of sin brought on by the Fall; in the meantime, dispensationalists argued, attempts to end their subordination were doomed to failure.

In the first wave of fundamentalism, which lasted until the end of World War I, this understanding of women's spiritual position did not directly affect their status. Strict prohibitions against women speaking would have been impossible to enforce, as well as unwise, given the great need to evangelize the world before its rapidly approaching end. Still, by the early twentieth century, fundamentalism had a clear theological rationale for opposing feminine leadership in home and church. Indeed, its basic orientation was increasingly inimical to any requests for change in women's status. Dispensationalism was a system that depended heavily on notions of order and obedience. It defined sin as "disorder" and rebellion against God's rule as a latter-day sign of religious apostasy and social anarchy. In fact, the Greek word for "dispensation," adherents explained, was "oikoumene," freely translated as the "ordering of a household." In the growing chaos of twentieth-century domestic and social life, and especially in the religious turmoil of the 1920s, this understanding would assume special relevance and practicality.

Matters came to a head in the 1920s, when conservative men clashed directly with liberal women. During that decade fundamentalists found themselves painfully retreating from positions of leadership in northern

Presbyterian and Baptist circles, just as women were beginning to achieve new visibility there. Little of this was by feminine design, however, since women's inclusion on denominational boards and committees signalled a loss of independent power in female missionary organizations. Still, women's apparently rising status contrasted markedly with declining fundamentalist prestige.

As chapter 3 argues, the ensuing encounters between laywomen and fundamentalists unearthed growing suspicions of feminine disloyalty and drastically reshaped some long-held gender stereotypes. During the 1920s fundamentalist men began to take on the role as guardians of orthodoxy and women lost their standing as the morally superior sex, becoming not just morally but psychologically inferior to men. By the 1930s these assumptions about masculinity and femininity had begun to shape the roles both sexes filled in fundamentalist institutions and in the family, issues discussed separately in two following chapters.

After the 1920s came a period of sorting-out, as fundamentalists attempted the difficult task of lining up practice with the strict implications of their doctrine. The movement, as always, depended on the willing participation of its predominantly female constituency. But the resulting numerical imbalance created some potentially awkward contradictions between strict standards of female subordination and relatively permissive customs. Although fundamentalist doctrine prohibited women from teaching doctrine, the practical necessities of evangelism demanded their skills in religious education, Bible teaching, and foreign missions. Women's participation implied a social cost that fundamentalists would not always be willing to pay. Not only did much of their activity seem to conflict with prohibitions against women in teaching roles, it visibly contradicted the image of fundamentalist orthodoxy as a predominantly masculine exercise. Fundamentalists and neo-evangelicals thus remained deeply ambivalent about the women in their ranks, dependent on their support but wary of its inherent risks.

The final two chapters, both covering the period from the end of the 1920s through the 1950s, deal with the practical consequences of fundamentalist attitudes about femininity and masculinity. Chapter 4 examines questions of vocation in fundamentalist and neo-evangelical institutions. After losing their denominational battles in the 1920s, fundamentalists channeled their energy into building a separate subculture, hesitantly transforming themselves from sect to institutionalized church.

Male fundamentalists invested heavily in protecting and expanding the minister's role, an occupation with declining prestige in secular American society. This meant drawing it along more combative lines, as an aggressive evangelist rather than a pencil-pushing church administrator; and it meant protecting the ministry from undue female intrusion.

These concerns heavily influenced the role of women, especially in post–World War II fundamentalism. Entrepreneurial women found an expanding array of opportunities in the prospering fundamentalist empire of the 1930s and 1940s, especially in foreign missions and as Bible teachers; however, by the late 1940s, the preponderance of women working as missionaries and teaching Bible in fundamentalist churches had grown beyond the limits of acceptability. After World War II, fundamentalists and neo-evangelicals began to tighten restrictions against women teaching, arguing that their primary role was in the home, in strict subordination to their husbands.

Chapter 5 explores the fundamentalist version of American society's retreat to the nuclear family after World War II and its rising conservatism toward women's role. Fundamentalists were certainly not alone in emphasizing women's responsibility to the home or in worrying over the continuing absence of masculine leadership there. In one sense, their rhetorical excesses in defense of the home only writ large what most Americans implicitly believed. The modern age had eroded rigid Victorian sex roles without providing satisfying substitutes. By the 1950s the traditional family had become a battleground of competing expectations, far different from the idealized model of intimacy and stability most Americans cherished.

For fundamentalists, and neo-evangelicals as well, the prospect of failure here was unthinkable. They had long upheld morally grounded homes as the best proof of their separation from the world and the last Christian line of defense against the inherent disorder of secular systems. Not surprisingly, the stricter teaching about women's role in the late 1940s and 1950s centered on the need for order, an idea foundational to dispensationalist theology. The notion of a natural hierarchy in creation that governed the relations between the sexes encompassed the fundamentalists' existing assumptions about masculine strength and feminine weakness and theologically guaranteed masculine leadership in both home and church. Fundamentalists and neo-evangelicals embraced this new teaching with enthusiasm. After decades of ambiguity and unresolved tension, both sexes apparently found a measure of relief in the new emphasis on order and authority.

Indeed, despite its restrictive view of women's role, fundamentalism did continue to attract substantial numbers of female supporters. In one sense, the persistent presence of women in fundamentalism almost defies logic; though fundamentalist institutions provided opportunities for career-minded women, certainly similar openings existed elsewhere and in less restrictive surroundings. What then attracted women to fundamentalism? The answer lies outside of any strictly gender-based speculation. Women, like men, found in the fundamentalist movement a clear, though perhaps narrow, call to Christian vocation and a language of cultural critique that simplified the daunting range of choices in a secular lifestyle. Women perhaps especially appreciated the movement's high standards for family life, still the primary area of concern for most mid-twentieth-century women. Fundamentalist churches upheld women's role in the family and, even more important, provided a forum for like-minded women to air common fears and hopes for their children. In short, women's stake in the success of the fundamentalist movement was at least as strong as the ambitions which drove its masculine leadership.

All the same, the feminist movement came as a deep shock to evangelicals and fundamentalists, who among all Protestants were the most historically unprepared to deal with its demands. Secure in their religious and social subculture, they had easily ignored the protracted discussions of women's ordination that had roiled mainline denominations since the early twentieth century. Their attention was turned to the secular drama of war and economic upheaval, which they interpreted as clear signs of Christ's approaching second advent. Only after the World War II ended, relatively uneventfully for fundamentalists, did more pedestrian issues, among them women's ordination, begin to warrant sustained and serious concern.

The story of fundamentalist and neo-evangelical response to feminism in the 1960s and 1970s is still in the making, and I have chosen to deal with it briefly and suggestively. Because of theological and gender assumptions deeply rooted in their past, neo-evangelicals had no language of equality and no experience of feminine leadership. Not surprisingly, reactions toward feminism wavered between dogmatic rejection and perilously uncritical acceptance. The debates of the 1970s sounded suspiciously similar to fundamentalist deliberations of nearly a century before, especially as they touched on issues of biblical authority and interpretation. Yet in the feminist culture of the 1970s, masculinity was almost a discredited concept, heavily identified with negative, patriarchal associations. There would be no outward battle for supremacy between the sexes; evangelicalism would retain, almost by default, its traditional biases against female leadership, but without the aggressive use of masculine rhetoric, which had been so much a part of the earlier confrontation. Small wonder that the debate continues to build confusion and division, or that it persists, even after nearly thirty years of give-and-take; evangelicals have yet to look to their past for answers—or new questions.

Perhaps this book will raise some of those new questions. Many issues remain for further study. For example, my relatively narrow definition of fundamentalism does not chart the influence of fundamentalist thought and practice in related traditions, especially immigrant and holiness denominations. But the similarities are clearly present, judging from the widespread adoption of strict fundamentalist teaching on women's roles in groups historically more open to feminine leadership. Moreover, this study documents, but does not fully explore, some important points of encounter between fundamentalists and socially conservative Southern Baptists, especially through evangelists such as John R. Rice and his widely circulated periodical, the *Sword of the Lord*. Although I have attempted to balance the opinions of fundamentalist leaders against a wider background of practice in fundamentalist institutions, there are still many stories left to be told, especially those of the near-invisible ranks of women who pushed those organizations forward. Indeed, the real history of fundamentalism is perhaps still to be found in the countless women who lived out its doctrines from day to day. The historical resurrection of those lives is an important future task for scholars, one both rewarding and complex.

Chapter One

Revivalism and Masculinity in
Early Fundamentalism

Early fundamentalism was far from monolithic. It cannot trace its origins to a single event or a single founder; it formed no single organization or church body. Late-nineteenth-century fundamentalism was the drawing together of co-belligerents, united in their opposition to various forms of "modernism" but willing to disagree on less important matters.

The new coalition formed within the culture of American revivalism. Popular evangelists, with Dwight L. Moody as the foremost example, were among the movement's earliest leaders. Their emphasis on personal conversion and warnings against moral laxity gave fundamentalism its deep popular appeal and a powerful language of cultural critique.

The message of fundamentalist revivalism was primarily a masculine one. Of course, evangelists rarely sought to exclude or silence women, who remained intensely loyal supporters. But in late-nineteenth-century Protestant culture, feminine piety was something revivalists could almost take for granted; indeed, it was nearly approaching the level of a threat, as women gained social power for themselves by pointing out the moral irresponsibility of middle-class men. Consequently, revivalists directed their appeal at men, who seemed far more vulnerable to secular temptations and stood in much greater need of repentance and conversion. In this way, notions of Christian masculinity influenced the early strategy of protofundamentalist revivalism, as middle-class men sought to regain custodianship of religion, ultimately at the expense of women's exalted role in evangelical piety.

This did not occur without significant strain, however. Revivalism was only one manifestation of the fundamentalist ethos, and it often stood in direct conflict with its more rigid, authoritarian side. Revivalism was not antifeminist by nature, nor was fundamentalism necessarily; that fundamentalist proclivity has separate roots, which will be discussed in the next chapter. In its late-nineteenth-century social context, however, fundamentalist revivalism provided a base for the airing of masculine grievances against religious feminization that would in time become openly antifeminist in language and practice.

Historically, revivalism has been a democratizing force within American society. Since the eighteenth century, when itinerant evangelists challenged the authority of the established churches, popular religion has, on the whole, exalted the values of the common man.[1]

The same principle holds true in regard to sex roles. In the heat of revival fervor, nineteenth-century evangelists cared little for social conventions or ecclesiastical rules against women preachers: all stood equal at the foot of the Cross. The populist appeal and the millennial urgency of their message simply overshadowed secondary matters of social conduct. The attitude of Christian and Missionary Alliance founder A. B. Simpson was typical. Writing in 1893, he belittled the debate over women speaking as "a little side issue of a purely speculative character." Simpson encouraged his followers to "let the Lord manage the women," exhorting them instead to "turn your batteries against the common enemy."[2]

Though roughly egalitarian in their approach to sex roles, late-nineteenth-century revivalists helped construct the masculine persona that would later become a distinguishing feature of fundamentalism. The constant debt they owed to the women in their ranks often made the task a difficult one, but by the early twentieth century they were clearly successful in redefining religious fervor as a positive and forceful means of masculine expression.

Revivalists and Women

The revivalist tradition in evangelical Protestantism was deeply entwined with the spiritual and social emancipation of women. The religious awakenings before the Civil War, and their perfectionist vision of a Christian social order, inspired both the abolitionist and temperance movements. They also contributed to a rising sense of feminine mission; historians rightly credit them as early vehicles of feminist zeal. Critics of revivalist excess often bemoaned popular practices which encouraged women's public testimonies, and excoriated evangelist Charles Finney's inclusion of women in mixed prayer assemblies. But the enthusiasm was impossible to restrict. Separate women's benevolent and missionary societies, though firmly rooted in the ideology of "woman's sphere," gave women confidence and skill in enterprises that took them increasingly beyond the four walls of home.[3]

The revivals gave women new access to the larger world. In the early nineteenth century the economic changes of the industrial revolution had introduced a new ordering of reality into two separate public and private spheres, the first for men, the latter for women. This arrangement, which defined women's duties solely in terms of home responsibilities, brought decidedly mixed blessings. While the domestic ideal enshrined women as the moral arbiters of society, it denied them direct public influence. Indeed, women found their sphere steadily encroached upon, as public schools assumed responsibility for educating the young, the medical profession took over their care for the sick, and new industries arose year by year to manufacture and distribute all the household items women had traditionally made within the confines of home. Thus, as temperance leader Frances Willard reminisced in 1887, "We had no earthly redress open to us except to capture some of the territory" men controlled, "or else spy out a new world."[4]

The impetus of revivalistic fervor intensified these social sources of feminine restlessness. Women themselves often described a new sense of power from religious conversion, which they linked to an experience of "second blessing," an infusion of the Holy Spirit resulting in complete freedom from willful sin. In the 1850s, Phoebe Palmer, who propagated the doctrine in her well-known Tuesday Meetings for the Promotion of Holiness, instilled enthusiasm for service in countless other women and brought about a holiness revival in Wesleyan circles after the Civil War. The dynamic sense of freedom from sin transcended all literal arguments against female preachers, and a good many personal doubts as well. "What is impossible for woman," a Methodist woman exulted, "when the love of Jesus fills her soul?"[5]

The perfectionist theology of these antebellum revivals also unleashed women for service. Rooting women's subordination in humanity's sinfulness, perfectionists denied that it was normative; indeed, women's new power was a clear sign of the dawning new age.[6] Phoebe Palmer's well-known treatise, *The Promise of the Father*, published in 1859, linked women's emancipation with the approaching millennium. "The time is coming and now is," she declared, "when women's gifts, so long-entombed in the church, shall be resurrected" and "the last act in the great drama of man's redemption" would begin.[7]

By the post–Civil War era, separate women's organizations on behalf of missions and temperance had become an established means of channeling this energy. Although most of these groups were established after the war, their idealism was rooted in the antebellum revivals. They adroitly avoided male control, or even participation, with appeals to feminine prerogative that drew from an earlier generation's sense of feminine mission.[8] And men gave way readily. Joanna Moore, a founder of the Woman's American Baptist Home Missionary Society, traced her calling to a male missionary's appeal for women to minister in slave refugee camps during the Civil War. "What can a man do to help such a suffering mass of humanity?" this missionary entreated Moore's class at Rockford Female Seminary, "Nothing. Only a woman will do."[9]

Once they achieved this access to the public sphere, women chose to work as separately from masculine interference as possible. "Woman's mission" to society demanded a pure expression of uniquely feminine virtues. Moreover, in a culture which idealized the complementary roles of men and women, gender-segregated organizations allowed both sexes the maximum amount of freedom. "I believe not only that division of labor is, temporarily, a good thing," May Wright Sewall told a sympathetic audience at the National Council of Women in 1895, "but . . . it may, indeed, be regarded as permanently good." Yet, Frances Willard explained, this was never the final goal. "We need the stereoscopic view of truth," she wrote in 1889, "when woman's eye and man's together shall discern the perspective of the Bible's full-orbed revelation."[10]

Why Men Do Not Go to Church

Yet by the end of the nineteenth century it appeared that men, not women, were not holding up their end of the partnership. Religion had become an area of female prerogative, where many men found themselves distinctly uncomfortable. In the antebellum revivals, women had been the first to rise from the mourners' bench, and often as not, returned the following evening with husbands and sons reluctantly in tow. This situation afforded women unusual power, especially within their own families, but exacted a significant social cost. For all its short-term benefits to women, masculine indifference to religion clearly threatened Protestant hegemony in a rapidly secularizing, increasingly non-Protestant, American culture.

Thus both male and female observers noted the declining appeal of religion among middle-class men with alarm. In 1899 Baptist preacher Cortland Myers identified not women's suffrage but masculine passivity as "one of the burning questions of the hour."[11] The men must be won, all agreed, or society would fall into ruin. As General Brinkerhoff, a Christian Alliance spokesman, put it, "The great roaring train of the nineteenth century is rushing down the track of time [and] the young men are running this train. Unless the Lord interferes," he warned, "they will land us in perdition." While seminary faculties debated the Virgin Birth and the inerrancy of Scripture, the average clergymen faced a weekly "spiritual crisis," the predominance of women in the pews and the dearth of capable men.[12]

The late nineteenth century, known for its imperialistic ventures abroad and capitalist excesses at home, was in fact a period of rising insecurity for middle-class males. As Peter Filene argues, the bureaucratization of white-collar professions and the father's increasing absence from the home were signs that "the concept of manliness was suffering strain in all its dimensions." Urban middle-class culture seemed to allow fewer and fewer opportunities for masculine self-determination and patriarchal control. These changes signalled not so much a short-term crisis in gender roles as a slow reorientation of the meaning of masculinity. The closing of the frontier, the rise of pacifism, and declining opportunities for the self-made man in the urban business world made the quest for authentic manhood elusive and difficult.[13]

Masculinity seemed everywhere on the retreat. The success of women's causes—suffrage, temperance, and "social purity"—rebounded smartly on middle-class males. Temperance and suffrage leaders often bolstered their arguments for feminine influence by pointing out the moral failures of American men, alternately cajoling and scolding them for being "too busy making money" to care about social evils.[14] And men received the rebuke with remorse. Responding to the formation of the Woman's Christian Temperance Union in 1874, temperance leader J. G. Holland wearily advised his male followers to "be either humbly helpful or dumb. We who have dallied with this question . . . can only step aside with shame-faced humility while the great crusade goes on." "It is only natural that the matter should be taken out of [men's] hands by the other sex," a writer for the *Nation* admitted, "but it is unquestionably humiliating."[15]

While men were withdrawing from the action, women's place in evangelical Protestantism grew ever more secure. Missionary spokesman Arthur T. Pierson saw the "epiphany of women" in their astounding success with foreign missions and temperance.[16] Even the pulpit drew within their grasp, as the level of women's public influence in the churches slowly approached their numerical dominance there. Indeed, as the century of women drew to a close, the real question was where the men would go.

Women seemed to be advancing on all fronts, but especially in religious institutions. In 1904 when twenty-five Methodist women took their seats in the General Conference some churchmen's worst fears were realized: after more than two decades of controversy, the male leaders of the nation's largest denomination conceded their minority status. Opponents of the measure painted a grim future for male Methodists, especially the clergy. *Christian Advocate* editor James Buckley predicted that proportional representation in a General Conference of 600 delegates would add up to "400 women, 196 laymen, and 4 ministers."[17]

Religious leaders found cold comfort only in the extent of masculine apathy. As a Congregationalist minister reasoned, from the "complaint of school superintendents that fathers seem to care nothing about educational affairs" to the "lament of librarians over the small number of men's names on the list of those who draw books," conditions everywhere implied that "the fault lies with the men and not with the church."[18]

The search for the absent male crossed both theological and denominational barriers. The Presbyterian Brotherhood, authorized by the denomination in 1906, brought liberals and conservatives into common cause for "the better balancing of the church forces." The success of Presbyterian women's groups had made men "ashamed of themselves," one Brotherhood member confessed, "Now we are repenting."[19]

Interdenominational laymen's groups, drawing members across the theological spectrum, also rose in popularity. Most visible were the Young

Men's Christian Associations. Closely associated with mainstream revivalism through Dwight L. Moody, the YMCAs ministered to the whole man, body and soul. The largest of the laymen's organizations, the Men and Religion Forward Movement, was an interdenominational crusade with strong ties to the Social Gospel movement. Walter Rauschenbusch described it as a "front attack on that part of the enemy's lines which was supposed to be most impregnable—the men."[20] Though its early emphasis on missions attracted conservatives, the Men and Religion Forward ultimately championed a characteristically liberal social agenda. With its depiction of Jesus as the manly carpenter of Nazareth, the Social Gospel movement also aimed for masculine converts. Indeed, the rallying cry for liberals in the early twentieth century was the "brotherhood of man" and the "fatherhood of God."[21]

The Masculine Message of Fundamentalism

But the fundamentalists' appeal was particularly urgent—and effective. In fact, a Congregational minister's description of "what men like" reads like a script for the fundamentalist movement. "If men are to be as loyal to their church as they are to their college," he wrote, "they must be given a chance to fight for her, their hunger for truth must be fed with facts, and their fellowship must be based upon their service in and their devotion to a common cause."[22]

Of course, liberalism had no shortage of masculine rhetoric. The ideals of "muscular Christianity" transcended theological boundaries. But for fundamentalists, this language was a vehicle of protest against the religious status quo. It took particular hold in the twentieth century as a means of separation, a way to declare superiority over a domesticated faith that shunned open conflict with the world, the flesh, and the devil.

Fundamentalism claimed the most effective cure for ailing masculinity. Its defenders insisted that it alone offered the challenge men sought and that liberalism was a spineless alternative. "The only churches in America that have any considerable number of big hearted brainy men in them," Minnesota Baptist William Bell Riley maintained, "are those churches that stand . . . for biblical doctrines—the great verities of the good Word of God." "It is a mistake to suppose that men like to hear ministers discuss social, economical and political affairs in the pulpit," Moody Bible

Institute president James M. Gray insisted. Cortland Myers agreed, "Men will come only to hear the unvarnished truth, red hot from a courageous heart."[23]

By the 1920s, the movement had produced a charismatic set of masculine heroes, individualists who disdained bureaucracy and gloried in their social ostracism. A later generation reminisced fondly about the "old gentlemen's movement" led by the likes of William Jennings Bryan, William Bell Riley, and J. Gresham Machen. Their fearless example challenged lesser men, in their own religious circles, to engage the forces of apostasy without compromise.[24]

Revivalists and Men

This masculine tradition was rooted in the message of late-nineteenth-century urban revivalism. Beginning in the "prayer meeting revival" of 1857–1858, revivalists found a ready audience in the business culture of large cities. During this revival, sparked in part by a spectacular financial panic in the fall of 1857, businessmen sustained daily noon prayer meetings in cities up and down the East Coast, and into the Midwest.[25]

The Civil War was a proving ground for revivalists. Young Men's Christian Associations and the United States Christian Commission brought evangelical Christianity to the battlefields and launched not a few careers. Dwight L. Moody, and many of his future associates, received their first taste of full-time Christian work with the Christian Commission, an organization that mobilized more than 5,000 lay and clergy volunteers in charitable and evangelistic work in Union army camps and battlefields.

This enthusiasm carried over into the post–Civil War decades. Sandra Sizer has noted the "strong appeal to men" by revivalist Dwight L. Moody and his associate Ira Sankey. And, she writes, they were largely successful: "All reports testify that men thronged to the special meetings and to the general public ones."[26]

Moody, a successful businessman who began his evangelistic career with the Young Men's Christian Association, was a central figure in the early development of fundamentalism. Although he was never dogmatic in his own doctrinal positions, he brought together other fundamentalists who were. Indeed, a good part of his appeal was his formidable, yet personal, platform style. Moody never shied from sentimentalism, balancing it with a direct approach to the uncommitted in his audiences. As one admiring biographer put it, the great evangelist stood "boldly, manfully, and squarely" against the masculine retreat from religion. "Predominantly," the writer noted, "he was a benefactor of men."[27]

So much so in fact that a Chicago prostitute once denounced him as a "one-sided evangelist" for paying too much attention to young men ensnared by "harlots" and ignoring the women sinned against. "We need the comfort of Jesus as much as they," the woman protested in a letter Moody read from the platform. Although the evangelist accepted her chastisement with remorse, he did not attempt such work himself, nor did he engage in wholesale attempts at social reform; his entourage included a Woman's Evangelistic Committee to engage in home visitation and work with "fallen women"—traditionally female roles in urban evangelism.[28]

Many evangelists contrasted their combative occupation with the more feminized image of the church pastor. Moody represented a late Victorian masculine ideal, described by one admirer as a "broad-gage, noble, virile, whole-souled man."[29] His associates included two men with the title "Major" and Charles M. Morton, a Civil War amputee. Evangelists often complained of the jealousy of other pastors who did not possess their "personal magnetism" or ease in winning souls. And they decried the ministers' slavery to the endless round of church socials, normally engineered by women. "There are churches," William Biederwolf charged, "that will work to death 100 women at all sorts of secular and not infrequently questionable entertainments . . . and will not permit to stand in their pulpits a man who is notedly successful in winning souls for Jesus because, . . . he is an evangelist." Similarly, Baptist preacher A. J. Gordon complained that "the pulpit today is muzzled. [Pastors] dare not cry out against these growing evils for their salaries depend upon them."[30]

Evangelists saw themselves as rugged entrepreneurs who urged other young men to similar independence. And although Moody himself was far from a separatist fundamentalist, he did encourage his audiences to reject conventional piety. "I like men of decision," he urged. "Hundreds of thousands of men are thoroughly convinced, but they lack moral courage to come out and confess their sins."[31] Although the demands of true Christianity might be daunting, they promised greater rewards. "You never find men backsliding into Orthodoxy," Gordon observed. "On the contrary, one has to climb to get into this kind of faith. . . . If one gets tired of believing this he has only to close his Bible and shut his eyes and *slide*, and by the simple gravitation of human nature he lands among the liberals as certainly as a stone, loosed from the mountain side[,] lands in the valley."[32]

Men and "Victorious Christianity"

The evangelists' promise of a "Victorious Life," a doctrine borrowed from the British Keswick movement promising Christians power over willful sin, was another feature of revivalism that increased its appeal to a masculine audience. In 1871 Moody himself experienced this intense filling of the Holy Spirit and made it central to his message: the Christian life was not a set of moralistic precepts, but one with continual "power for service." The larger fundamentalist movement also adopted this emphasis on personal holiness and made it a characteristic feature of its piety.[33]

Conversion was not an easy passage for Victorian men. As one observer commented, "Men, in general, prefer being considered hardened sinners to being known as humble penitents."[34] The conversion process often highlighted the distance between male and female spheres, as women often gained new self-confidence and men were required to deny themselves the strengths of aggressive self-assertiveness that were essential to success in the business world. The stereotypical language of penitence and surrender in conversion narratives drew heavily from female vocabulary and experience, as Virginia Brereton has observed. The role of the submissive believer often afforded women a new sense of power and moral authority; however, it was the antithesis of nineteenth-century masculinity, which was characterized by boldness and self-mastery.[35]

But revivalism's emphasis on victory and power turned this self-negating experience into a dynamic, self-authenticating one. As Gordon declared, "A single man filled with the Holy Spirit, can of course do what a thousand cannot do without it. He is the strong man, the wise man, the effective man."[36] The holiness teachings adopted by fundamentalists denied the Wesleyan understanding that sanctification could rid believers entirely of sin; from their more Calvinist perspective, they taught that victory over sin demanded constant vigilance and unquestioning trust in the power of God's grace.[37]

Although this emphasis did not necessarily preclude a feminine audience, it undoubtedly increased the movement's masculine appeal. By the early twentieth century, men were prominent figures in the Victorious

Life conferences where the doctrines of sanctified living were propagated and taught. In 1922, one report noted that testimonial meetings were dominated by "the presence of young and older men." When the time came for public announcements of spiritual victory, "not a girl had a chance, for one after another stalwart, athletic young fellows sprang to their feet to tell what the Lord Jesus Christ was meaning to them."[38]

Businessmen testified to their new freedom from worry and tension often in terms borrowed from their secular occupations. Robertson McQuilkin received his victory over sin as a "definite and clear-cut business proposition, without any special emotion." J. Harvey Borton, leading a "businessmen's vespers" at a Victorious Life convention in 1918, described his clearheaded acceptance of the divine "offer" and its new power in his vocational life. "Last year I had the most difficult situation to cope with in [my] business," Borton testified, "but since I accepted Jesus Christ in his fullness he has just taken care of these things. . . . All I had to do was to use the common sense which he gave me, and then stand back and marvel at what he was going to do."[39]

Evangelists constantly reminded their audiences that conversion was an objective reality that need not be an emotional event. Decrying the artificial means of the "pocket-handkerchief preacher," Gordon observed with satisfaction that "our most effective revival preachers disparage all trust in frames and feelings[,] telling sinners to look to Christ on the cross, instead of searching for Christ in the heart."[40] Addressing the Winona Bible Conference in 1909, John Balcom Shaw observed that "virile preaching" aimed at the "sturdy and thoughtful" had replaced the "effusive, mushy, story-crammed, platitudinous" preaching of a past generation. "Instead of excitement," he noted, "there is a deep, quiet atmosphere, often a hush upon the assemblage, born not of agitation, but attention. So true is this that some critically opposed to evangelism have said that the speaker hypnotized the audience."[41]

The Victorious Life movement's emphasis on "power to serve" balanced out its passive imagery of self-surrender. It summoned men from churches encrusted with conservatism to a vigorous new form of spiritual conquest. As Grant Wacker argues, for higher life leaders "the problem with mainstream conservatism was not so much its austerity as its impotence, its lack of a supernaturally imparted vitality, its inability to inspire and to empower believers for Christian service."[42] As higher life spokesman W. B. Anderson reminded his audience, "Jesus Christ has never asked that man should make this living gift an emasculated human being, or that any of man's normal, vital members be cut off. [Christ came] not to destroy but to fulfill. He came not to curtail life but to release it."[43]

Laymen and the Bible Conference Movement

By the early twentieth century, evangelical religion was losing many of its feminine trappings. Evangelist Billy Sunday, a former White Sox second baseman, successfully used an athletic platform style and rugged language to convince male skeptics that Christianity was not a "pale, effeminate proposition." "Jesus was no ascetic," he reminded, but a "robust, red-blooded man" who lived life to the full.[44] H. L. Mencken testified to being "constantly struck by the great preponderance of males in the bull-ring devoted to the saved" at Sunday's crusades. "For six nights running," he recalled, "I sat directly beneath the gifted exhorter without seeing a single female convert."[45] By 1911, according to a Moody Bible Institute spokes-man, evangelists Gipsy Smith and A. C. Dixon were expressing misgivings about the "over-emphasis" on men in many crusades. Although many rejoiced over the increasing male attendance and the rate of conversion, their greater numbers were actually encouraging a "decline of pure and undefiled religion among the other sex," a development soon to attract the uneasy attention of fundamentalist leaders.[46]

The popular Bible conferences held annually at Winona Lake, Indiana, also demonstrate the growing link between revivalists and the masculine world of commerce. The Winona Lake conferences began in 1894 as part of the Chautauqua movement, which offered correspondence courses and a lecture series to the aspiring middle classes. By the early twentieth century the Winona conferences had become an annual gathering ground for fundamentalists from a wide range of denominations and traditions and a showcase for the rhetorical skills of the movement's leaders. Situated in a grove of trees on a quiet lake, Winona initially advertised itself as both a "tired mothers' paradise" and a wholesome environment, free of gambling houses or saloons, for harried husbands. Both the Chautauqua and the Bible conferences, which began in 1902, were the inspiration of a group of local "Christian businessmen," nearly all prominent merchants and bankers, engaged in "money-making altruism."[47]

As the summer home of Billy Sunday, Winona became a popular

meeting place for fundamentalist ministers, evangelists, and laymen. Speakers addressed a variety of practical topics, with advice for ministers and laymen a frequent theme. Indeed, most emphasized the necessity of presenting the gospel in ways that appealed to men of the world. "If you want to reach men," Presbyterian Brotherhood member Fred B. Smith advised in 1902, "say to them, 'This means the death sentence; are you ready to lay down your life?' This thrills them."[48] Methodist bishop Edwin Hughes used language oddly reminiscent of Phoebe Palmer's in his prediction that "when the modern layman comes back to that priesthood that was claimed and used by the Saviour's first disciples, the kingdom of God will spread with gracious rapidity and the Church will dwell in an unceasing Pentecost.[49]

Many fundamentalist leaders inveighed against male "secret societies" and lodges. Jonathan Blanchard, the first president of Wheaton College, an institution that trained hundreds of fundamentalist leaders, campaigned tirelessly against Masonry and Knights Templars, in the tradition of Charles Finney before him. These secret associations represented a form of competition for masculine attention. In 1912 evangelist George R. Stuart strove to convince his Winona Lake audience that Christianity offered far greater challenges to men than Masonry. "I am going to give you the grip tonight, I am going to give you the password," he declared. "I am going to initiate you into the greatest brotherhood you ever saw."[50]

Bible Schools and Women

Yet, despite the emphasis on masculine piety, turn-of-the-century revivalism did retain a good deal of its earlier feminist propensities. Arthur T. Pierson and A. J. Gordon were among the foremost defenders of women's right to preach, arguing that it was a sign of an approaching worldwide revival. A. B. Simpson listed "the ministry of women" as one of five necessary elements for his fledgling "Evangelical Missionary Alliance" in 1887.[51]

Many male evangelists shared the spotlight with highly capable women. Wives of prominent men, most notably Elizabeth Needham, Maria Gordon, and Helen Sunday, were gifted writers and organizers, clearly indispensable to their husbands' success but also renowned in their own right. Women occupied a prominent role in the early Christian and Missionary Alliance, not only as missionaries, but as organizers and leaders on the "home front." Billy Sunday's entourage included several highly visible female members. Grace Saxe, who often led women's meetings during crusades, was also a fixture at the Winona conferences. Virginia Asher, a talented soloist, attracted a loyal female following, especially among young businesswomen.[52]

Moody himself was a tireless supporter of women's Christian vocation. In 1873 he enlisted Emma Dryer to run the Chicago Bible Work at Moody Church, a program that formed the nucleus of the future Moody Bible Institute. Moody first envisioned the training school for women only, an early point of conflict with Dryer who believed it should be coeducational. The famous women's school Moody established at Northfield also testified to his personal zeal for women's education; in 1893 he began sponsoring conferences at Northfield for the Young Women's Christian Association, to complement work already being done among young men in the popular Students' Conferences at Holyoke. In 1894 Moody also established a Students' Aid Society to provide scholarships for promising young women, administered through the Ladies' Department at Moody. In 1900 an admiring female student concluded that "in the matter of women's work and sphere there was no one who was more progressive than Mr. Moody."[53]

Women in turn flocked to Moody Bible Institute and other Bible schools. The rapidly growing complex of fundamentalist Bible schools was a primary means of "training God's army" and furthering the cause of evangelism. The schools were coeducational and offered unique educational opportunities for both sexes. To young men with limited prospects, sometimes without a high school diploma, these schools provided an opportunity for professional status as an ordained minister. Young women, who dominated the schools numerically, gravitated toward other semiprofessional careers. The largest proportion of women chose foreign missions, a vocation that attracted only a few married men and, even more rarely, single male volunteers. Others became "assistant pastors," visiting parishioners and assisting the minister with secretarial duties. For many, the atmosphere was clearly exhilarating. Margaret Blake Robinson, an Irishwoman of feminist leanings, found her woman companions at Moody Bible Institute "seeking the truth with the free unfettered minds that the Holy Spirit imparts. The Moody Institute," she concluded, "drags no one into mental slavery."[54]

When they opened, most Bible institutes admitted women into ministerial programs, including courses in sermon preparation and delivery. It was not unusual for a woman student to win the yearly sermon prize: in 1921 Riley's periodical, *Christian Fundamentals in School and Church*, reprinted in full a first-place sermon written by a female student at Northwestern Bible Institute, Karen Gjelhaug.[55] Although most women preachers were not nationally known, their work provided valuable publicity for the fledgling schools. William Bell Riley's "girl evangelists" in the wilds of northern Minnesota established Sunday schools, preached, and pastored churches in the early years of Northwestern Bible Institute. The school gratefully acknowledged their work, commenting that "we have yet to know of . . . a church that was not delighted with them."[56]

But the experience of women in Bible schools suggests that though fundamentalists might countenance the occasional female preacher, they were not out to encourage the practice. The presence of women does not indicate a dramatic departure from a primary emphasis on the role of men. In most cases, Bible institutes aimed to train men for various forms of leadership. Moody, for example, apparently discarded his earlier vision of a women's Bible training school and by 1886 was calling for "gap-men" to reach the masses for Christ. In his famous "Farwell Hall Address," which outlined the goals of his fledgling school, Moody made no mention of women. As one account has noted, "Time and again he referred to training *men*."[57]

In fact, financial considerations often governed the choice to open degree programs to young women. As the schools matured and stabilized, they often closed ministerial courses and degrees to women, or instituted quotas on female students, a development discussed in chapter 4. Virginia Brereton suggests that the "advantages of Bible school education for women were unintended: they resulted as by-products from the nature and purposes of the institutions rather than from their ideology."[58]

Moreover, most agreed that women could only assume leadership as a stopgap measure, filling a post until a male preacher could be recruited. Jessie Van Booskirk, assistant superintendent at Northwestern, interpreted the biblical account of the prophet Deborah as a story "of Israel's failing strength [when] her manhood was at so low an ebb that God was obliged to call a woman." And while A. B. Simpson praised Deborah's forthright leadership, he qualified it with the observation that she "was wise enough to call [her male assistant] Barak to stand in the front, while she stood behind him, modestly directing his work."[59]

Protestant Women's Organizations and Fundamentalism

Such attitudes inspired little in the way of feminine protest, for in fact fundamentalist Bible schools represented only one option among many for aspiring female evangelists and missionaries. The work of women in the highly publicized Moody and Sunday crusades actually supplemented evangelistic endeavors women were already pursuing in their own independent organizations. The Woman's Christian Temperance Union, for example, successfully trained hundreds of female evangelists. In 1881 Sarepta M. I. Henry, the "national evangelist" of the WCTU, opened a Gospel Training Institute in Lake Bluff, Illinois, to equip women for public speaking. The WCTU also offered a four-year home study course, modelled after Chautauqua, to teach evangelistic skills.[60] "Women who had but lately found no wider sphere than the domestic or social circle," one temperance worker reminisced with satisfaction, "suddenly found themselves facing vast audiences." "The zeal and faithfulness of our women in pleading the gospel of temperance," agreed another, "[have] removed the prejudice against her occupying a pulpit, and now a woman is welcomed as an evangelist almost anywhere."[61] By the end of the century, women had ceased to be a rarity on a public platform; temperance workers regularly coopted church pulpits for messages they carefully described as "teaching" rather than preaching.[62]

Even more than temperance work, home and foreign missions gave women a distinctively feminine public voice. In the years between the Civil War and World War I, women published periodicals, developed educational curricula, and raised millions of dollars on behalf of "woman's mission" to the non-Christian world. A. J. Gordon's famous defense of "the ministry of women" in 1894, supporting the right of female missionaries to teach and preach at home as they did on the foreign field, actually summarized a case that many women had long considered closed. In their view, women's natural affinity for such work seemed ample proof of its propriety.[63]

Moreover, the training schools developed by women's groups actually served as prototypes for the fundamentalist Bible institutes founded by evangelists. The Baptist Missionary Training School in Chicago, formed by the Woman's Baptist Home Missionary Society in 1877, and the Methodist school, established in Chicago in 1885, both predated the founding of Moody Bible Institute in 1886. The women's training schools offered courses in Bible, as well as in organizing temperance associations, kindergartens, and Sunday schools. Classes were supplemented by daily forays into their city neighborhood. The Bible institutes, though basically similar, offered a more specialized curriculum revolving entirely around study of the English Bible and placed less emphasis on preparation for social service.[64]

Although women's evangelistic work and fundamentalist revivalism shared common goals and methods, there was often a whiff of competitiveness behind that similarity. Moody's complicated relationship with Frances Willard highlighted some of the difficulties these two groups encountered in joint enterprises. Hoping to enlist Willard, already a rising star in education and temperance work, as a co-worker, Moody asked her to assist with women's meetings in Boston in the early 1870s. Both soon found that city too small to encompass them. Moody, who disapproved of Mary Livermore, a Unitarian, on the Boston WCTU platform, urged Willard to form a women's "evangelical" Christian temperance union. Willard resisted his advice and ultimately left to pursue her temperance work independently. As she later explained, their differences went beyond the theological realm. She believed that her approach to evangelism and strategy for prohibition were incompatible with Moody's commitment to spiritual revival. "Mr. Moody views the temperance work from the standpoint of a revivalist," she wrote, "and so emphasizes the regeneration of men. But to me as a woman, there are other phases of it almost equally important to its success," addressing the needs of children and mothers, and, ultimately, giving women the ballot to end the evil once and for all.[65]

Fundamentalism thus forged relatively few connections with the burgeoning "women's culture" of nineteenth-century evangelical Protestantism, despite their obvious similarities of purpose. The relative absence of formal relationships between women's groups and fundamentalism is in fact somewhat curious. Women's work, like fundamentalism, was hardly a sentimental affair. Both were dynamic efforts propelled by revivalistic enthusiasm, and they embraced a similar identity as privileged "outsiders" within the Protestant mainstream.

But fundamentalism accommodated no independent, self-consciously feminine auxiliaries. Hoping to unite all true Christians in a single crusade, the movement was wary of dividing its energy. "Christ ordained no 'auxiliaries' nor 'annexes' for his Church," E. P. Marvin declared, "and if she is faithful she needs none." Though he saw their usefulness, he found it "a pity that the Church should need so much and such help!"[66] Moreover, emphasizing the level ground at the foot of the Cross, fundamentalists often rejected sentimental idealizations of women's religious superiority and favored a more pragmatic, even secular approach. "We have heard some preachers talk as though women were naturally better than men," James M. Gray complained in 1911, "but they need the same salvation as ourselves and, except they repent, they shall all likewise perish."[67]

Fundamentalists were simply not in search of feminine allies. There was nothing to be gained in breaching the gender-segregated network of women's organizations, for to do so would only strengthen the perception that men were incapable of religious leadership on their own. Fundamentalism was meant to appeal first, though not exclusively, to men.

This masculine identity was not an easy one to assume. In 1910 a newspaper account of a talk by William Bell Riley on "The Church and Men" noted that three-fourths of his audience was female, despite the sending of 2,000 invitations to the men of Minneapolis. Fundamentalists were never in a position to reject feminine support. Indeed, the popular appeal of early fundamentalism was shaped by two opposing forces: a desire to win the hearts of men, and the practical necessity of involving women.[68]

This dilemma framed the early history of the movement and remained an underlying concern for its male leadership. The pragmatic bent within early fundamentalism tolerated relatively open practice, even though, as the following chapter will discuss, fundamentalist doctrines of biblical inerrancy and dispensational premillennialism demanded a strict view of women's subordinate role. The result was an uneasy truce between two incompatible elements in fundamentalism itself, a tension not destined to survive the emotionally turbulent years after World War I.

Chapter
Two

The Roots of Antifeminism:
Early Fundamentalism's Search
for Order

The antipathy of many early fundamentalist leaders to feminism was deep, widespread, and well documented; indeed, the movement's literature is rife with strident antifeminist pronouncements, some of them bordering on outright misogyny.[1]

Less clear, however, are the origins of these attitudes and the extent of their practice within the movement. Certainly the turn of the century's general anxiety and confusion over changing gender roles contributed to fundamentalist antifeminism; but that alone does not explain the depth of emotion that surrounded gender issues well into the twentieth century; nor, on the other hand, does it account for the relatively positive attitude of other fundamentalist leaders, especially from within the revivalist ethos, toward their female co-workers.

The question of practice is even more difficult. Fundamentalist leaders were almost refreshingly frank in denouncing the social evils of their day, but their outspokenness did not necessarily entail an ability to translate their grievances into practice. And, given the preponderance of women in many fundamentalist schools and churches, it seems doubtful that they would be eager to do so.

The question behind this chapter, therefore, concerns the origin and development of antifeminism in fundamentalist theology. Fundamentalism certainly inclined toward masculine language and associations, but this relatively benign orientation rarely issued into antifeminist bias. The masculine persona of fundamentalist revivalism was cast in largely positive terms. Indeed it reflected to a large degree the optimistic, confident spirit of mainstream evangelicalism. Revivalists hoped to win men to their cause by emphasizing the inherent manliness of true, fervent Christianity. Although they often relegated women to a secondary role, they rarely argued for their subordination or exclusion.

Other strains in emergent fundamentalism, however, defined masculinity in more negative language, in opposition to things feminine. This was a sharp break with the evangelical past. Many early fundamentalist leaders clearly viewed women less as partners and more as a threat, a pernicious influence to be silenced and subordinated. Without serious restraints, they believed, women would only impede the quest for doctrinal purity, a pursuit that required the work of trustworthy men.

Antifeminism is most clearly evident in fundamentalism on the defensive, in pursuit of order. Throughout its history, the movement has held in tension two nearly opposing impulses, one to win the secular world through aggressive evangelism, and another to reject all worldly contacts through strict separation. Revivalism embodied much of this first strain, and two other doctrinal movements within fundamentalism, dispensational premillennialism and biblical inerrancy, have largely incorporated the latter.

None of these movements were airtight, for all assumed some rejection of the religious status quo, and to a degree all were invested in evangelistic outreach; but in regard to the woman question, they are relatively distinct. Especially in early fundamentalism, the strict views of inerrantists and dispensationalists on biblical teachings concerning women's role clashed uneasily with the more permissive standards of missionaries and evangelists.

Before the fundamentalist movement took clear institutional form, stricter precepts were usually subordinated to the pragmatic necessity of filling missionary rolls and reopening churches. Moreover, within their network of loosely affiliated prophetic conferences and Bible institutes, fundamentalist leaders would have been unable to enforce prohibitions against women evangelists, even if they had been willing to do so.[2]

But by the early twentieth century, the theological rationale for subordinating women—and elevating men—was firmly in place. And once the fundamentalist movement began charting its own separate path, as it would do after the 1920s, the difficult task of putting these beliefs into practice would begin.

Of course, fundamentalists were not the only Protestants to confront the perplexities of women's role during the late nineteenth century. In fact, without an organized female presence, they were relatively insulated from the rhetoric of sexual equality—and slow, haphazard changes in practice—that bedeviled mainstream Protestants for most of the twentieth century.[3]

In the major denominations, the ordination question demanded increasing amounts of time and attention. Methodists, who voted against ordaining Anna Howard Shaw in 1880, would confront the issue repeatedly in subsequent decades, until women received full ordination in 1956. Presbyterians also witnessed periods of struggle, beginning with a vote on women elders in 1920 and continuing into the 1950s, when ordination finally passed. Indeed, most major denominations struggled with issues of sexual equality for decades, well after most discarded official barriers to ordination in the 1950s.

Fundamentalists, operating largely outside denominational confines, had neither the obligation to resolve disputes nor the benefit of the ordered discussion these mitigating structures afforded. Without the possibility of direct confrontation or a definitive vote on issues surrounding women's leadership in the churches, their discussion had fewer prospects for immediate resolution—or limitations on debate. The woman question in fundamentalist circles, orchestrated by magazine editors, Bible school administrators, and prominent pulpiteers, was wide-ranging and often intensely personal.

The Bible and Gender

The central drama of the fundamentalist-modernist controversy in the early twentieth century was a conflict over the nature of biblical truth. For fundamentalists, all other debates over evolution, the conduct of foreign missions, or the coming millennium boiled down to a single principle: their insistence on the utter reliability of God's word.

More than simply an intramural debate among theologians, the controversy over scriptural authority held a wide and varied audience. Despite the growing atmosphere of spiritual crisis at the turn of the century, most Americans still looked to the ancient Word for answers to life's mysteries, both social and personal.

The fundamentalist defense of the Bible arose within the context of a wide-ranging, serious debate over the scriptural dimensions of women's role in the late nineteenth century. The suffrage issue inspired numerous pamphlets and articles, by clergymen and feminists alike, all claiming a biblical basis for or against women's right to vote. Similar questions about the nature of biblical authority pressed the established churches, as vocal women demanded the right to preach and be ordained.

In short, the popular religious culture that gave rise to fundamentalism was deeply concerned with matters of gender and Scripture. Even the most anticlerical feminists approached biblical matters with deep seriousness, most of them hoping to convince both enemies and friends that their cause was not inherently opposed to Christianity. Such efforts were inspired by necessity, for the vast majority of nineteenth-century Americans used biblical texts not as a gloss, but as a clear warrant for their own social and moral concerns. Fundamentalist biblicism occupied an important role in this broader debate, a role which significantly shaped its antifeminist orientation. It was the first time, but not the last, that feminist and fundamentalist exegesis of Scripture would lock in disagreement.

The biblical inerrancy movement, led by a cohort of Calvinist theologians from Princeton Theological Seminary, argued that the Bible stood without factual or scientific error. Their challenge to the academic science of biblical scholarship, known as the higher criticism, gave fundamentalism a strong critical edge against modernity; though the Princetonians were often reluctant to identify themselves as fundamentalists and rejected much of its theology, especially the literalistic approach of most dispensationalists, the larger movement adopted the views of Benjamin Warfield, A. A. Hodge, and J. Gresham Machen with enthusiasm.[4]

The Old School wing of the Presbyterian church, which the Princetonians represented, was known for its cultural conservatism. Before the Civil War, Charles Hodge and his Princeton colleagues Archibald Alexander and Samuel Miller, referring to themselves as an "Association of Gentlemen," not only condoned slavery from their hierarchical reading of Scripture but firmly opposed innovations in women's sphere. Slavery, at least as an abstract state, was neither moral nor immoral, Hodge argued in 1860, but a means of promoting the "general good" of society through the imposition of righteous order. "In this country," he reasoned, "we believe that the general good requires us to deprive the whole female sex of the right of self-government" because they are "incompetent to the proper discharge of the duties of citizenship." So slaves might be deprived of personal freedom because they were "incompetent to exercise it with safety to society." According to Hodge, arguing otherwise elevated reason above the authority of Scripture. "If we are wiser, better, more courageous than Christ and his apostles, let us say so," he warned; but the misguided attempts of abolitionists to wrest their arguments from Scripture would in the end "tear the Bible to pieces, or . . . extort, by violent exegesis, a meaning foreign to its obvious sense."[5]

In regard to women, Hodge promoted an ideal of "Ornamental Womanhood" and frowned on any activities that took women from their appointed role in the home. Even the genteel reform and benevolent societies popular among antebellum Presbyterian women met with his disapproval. The association prized its reputation for erudition and orthodoxy, prompting one historian to conclude that they lived "primarily from the neck up." And, it seems clear, the Princeton dons equated this aptitude for rationality with masculinity and viewed women as superfluous to its pursuit. As this critic concludes, "For the Association of Gentlemen male relationships were all-embracing, while women were at best, a female appendage to the central drama of life."[6]

The biblical inerrancy movement, led by the heirs of Hodge, Alexander, and Miller, had a similar orientation. It arose to defend an exclusively male interest in orthodox control of theological seminaries, none of which admitted women students. In 1904 the American Bible League made a direct appeal to "Christian laymen," warning of the higher criticism's encroaching power and calling on lay support to defeat it. The league itself, composed of seminary presidents and professors, aimed "to defend the Bible, but [also] to defend the men, and especially the young men" against the inroads of the higher criticism.[7]

Implicit in the league's rhetoric and strategy was a desire to elevate the status of its ministerial constituency. Their profession had suffered the brunt of rising modern religious skepticism, as well as powerful movements for laity rights within the established churches. In an age that increasingly valued specific expertise and empirical knowledge, the ministry was beginning to lose some of its intellectual status.[8] Thus, as president Francis Patton explained, "in the management of this controversy, you have to depend on the specialist[s].... They are the only ones that know anything about it." The esoteric science of textual and higher criticism was simply beyond the reach of even the most earnest Sunday school teachers, most of whom were women. "The main teaching of the school should be from the platform," W. E. Scofield urged. "Here is the opportunity for the Biblical expert, the pastor."[9]

The Princetonians also believed that their allegiance to the words of Scripture demanded a conservative stand on the woman question. Just as they rejected abolitionism for adhering to the "spirit of the age" rather than the literal teaching of Scripture on slavery, they eyed efforts to elevate the status of women with deep theological suspicion.

As Calvinists, they believed that the subordination of women was inherent in the created order. Calvin taught that Eve came from Adam's rib as his loving subordinate, not his equal; sin did not create inequality, but only intensified its effects, transforming women's appointed role into an onerous burden. Although Christ's atoning death and resurrection made women and men spiritual co-heirs, orthodox Calvinists were only guardedly optimistic about the possibilities of social amelioration in women's status.[10]

Warfield and his Princeton colleague Alexander McGill helped lead an effort to revive the New Testament order of deaconesses in the 1880s, largely because they believed this was the only female office the Bible condoned. McGill reminded the General Assembly that the innovation might relieve "the embarrassments we have had to stop [women] from preaching in Presbyterian churches."[11] Warfield continued to believe that Paul's prohibitions against women speaking in churches were "precise, absolute, and all-inclusive." "We may like what Paul says, or we may not like it," he concluded in 1920, "but there is no room for doubt in what he says."[12]

Feminists, of course, disagreed. Although they did not directly confront fundamentalists, who were not yet a visible, organized movement, their views clashed with the inerrancy doctrine in every respect. Since its inception, the women's rights movement had held strong views on the proper use of the Bible. In 1848, the Seneca Falls convention adopted a Declaration of Sentiments which listed "corrupt customs and interpretations of Scripture" as a fundamental roadblock to women's social and religious emancipation.[13] From the 1850s on, the woman's rights movement engaged in regular debate over the proper role of Scripture. Despite heated disagreements, most of its members came to endorse the views of Lucretia Mott and Lucy Stone, who argued that, if properly interpreted, the Bible offered full support for sexual equality.

But a determined radical core, led by Elizabeth Cady Stanton, pushed the debate to the limits of social acceptance. Stanton brought together a committee of feminist scholars who published a two-volume *Woman's Bible*, in 1895 and 1898. By then the book was far too radical for the increasingly centrist suffrage movement; in 1896 the National American Woman Suffrage Association publicly repudiated both Stanton and her unorthodox theology.

Still, the *Woman's Bible* touched on issues crucial for women in biblical scholarship. Without doubt, as Aileen Kraditor has suggested, radical feminists received the higher criticism from Europe "as a gift from heaven." Embracing rather than rejecting the spiritual crisis of their age, they capitalized on rising intellectual skepticism about the Bible's supernatural origins to raise difficult questions about its interpretation.[14]

More of a commentary than an actual rewriting of Scripture, the *Woman's Bible* gave a great deal of attention to the creation account in Genesis. Its authors all accepted the opinion of the higher critics that "no Christian theologian of to-day, with any pretensions to scholarship, claims that Genesis was written by Moses." Interpreting this book's early chapters as "myth and fable," they praised Eve's natural curiosity and independence, characterizing her as "a woman fearless of death" in pursuit of wisdom. Adam's conduct was simply "to the last degree dastardly," for he stood idly by during Eve's temptation, and then "whined" about the unfairness of his punishment.[15]

The contributors to the *Woman's Bible* were not so eager to debunk Genesis as they were to reinterpret its masculine and feminine typologies. They rejected with disgust the "petty surgical operation" that brought forth Eve from Adam's rib, as well as the entire second chapter of Genesis, which they believed was added by conspiring males. Instead, the commentators argued, the sexes were inherently equal, reflecting a divine image that embodied that highest qualities of both genders.[16]

Most feminists insisted that the church was a male-dominated institution that rightfully belonged to women. Matilda Joslyn Gage charged popular religion with being "essentially masculine" in its form and function, twisting Scripture and exalting one "central error, a belief in a trinity of masculine gods."[17] "The Church is spiritually and actually a womanly institution," Lucinda Chandler wrote in the *Woman's Bible*, "and this is recognized by the unvarying expression 'Mother Church.' Yet man monopolizes all offices of distinction and of leadership, and receives the salaries for material support."[18]

The radical wing of the women's rights movement was also deeply anticlerical. In 1854, the convention adopted a resolution authored by William Lloyd Garrison that the clergy were their most "determined opposition," spreading biblical teachings "intensely inimical to the equality of woman with man." In 1880 Sara Andrews Spencer introduced another resolution castigating the "unauthorized theocratic tyranny" of the ministerial establishment and urging women to resist this "odious form of religious persecution."[19] Feminists, led by Stanton, often contrasted their own physical and intellectual heartiness with the "small, thin, shadowy" physiques of their opponents. Gage characterized Rev. Craven, the antagonist in a Presbyterian controversy over women in the pulpit, as a bony, balding man, "a resurrected mummy in whom all the sympathies of humanity had died out." Others delighted in belittling these symbols of religious authority. Susan B. Anthony, responding to an address by Howard University president W. W. Patton on "Woman and Skepticism," remarked to the divine that "your mother, if you have one, should lay you across your knee and give you a good spanking for that sermon." She and Elizabeth Cady Stanton left the room laughing before Patton had a chance to respond.[20]

Certainly the *Woman's Bible*, and its anticlerical rhetoric, possessed a relatively minor audience. Yet, in a general sense, it was not a profound departure from standard interpretations of scriptural passages on women's role. By the turn of the century, the defense of women's right to preach and teach also depended on a nonliteral, thematic interpretation of Scripture, sensitive to the cultural conditions that gave rise to Paul's prohibitions against female leadership. Although most evangelicals had not yet encountered the higher criticism, they had long ago adopted historicist understandings of its teaching. Advocates of women preachers, many from Wesleyan and holiness traditions, emphasized the example of Christ and explained Paul's words as idiosyncratic and temporary. Citing the practical benefits of women's work, Kate Tannatt Woods warned against absolutizing "one dyspeptic utterance" into an unbending rule. And holiness leader Mary Boardman reminded her readers that Paul's words should never be read "as if what he said to a few dancing

Greek and Asiatic women, could be meant for all coming time, in all countries of the world."[21]

This relative ease in dismissing Saint Paul drew in part from past difficulties in reconciling Scripture with abolitionist and temperance arguments. Abolitionists dealt with the Bible's apparent support for slavery by thematizing it within a more general principle, the "law of love," and adopting a progressive interpretation that denied the apparent permissiveness of biblical writers a normative status. The temperance cause posed similar problems for evangelicals— Jesus himself turned water into wine. But here, as in issues concerning women's role, they adopted a historically relativist stance. As a Louisville clergyman related to the national meeting of the WCTU in 1882, "In those early days of my life there were two passages of Scripture . . . which I believed with all my heart. They were these: 'Take a little wine for thy stomach's sake,' and 'Let your women keep silence in the churches.' " Both, he believed, were never meant to be absolute, but were "provisional, prudential adjustment[s] to the times by a man who, where no fundamental principle was to be sacrificed, was all things to all men."[22]

Though not natural allies of feminists, evangelical women also shared some of their anticlerical sentiments. The 1880s and 1890s were frustrating years for churchwomen, for by then it seemed clear that their activities on behalf of foreign missions and temperance would not win them more general church leadership. In 1891 Methodist Mary Lathrap delivered a blistering attack on the "little male contingency" that had so long delayed women's entrance into the General Conference, reminding the brethren that they "would not have enough church to be buried in if it were not for the efforts of the women."[23] In 1880 a WCTU supporter exploded with indignation at a Yale chancellor's suggestion that the country needed less temperance "fanaticism" and more educated ministers: "Are we no longer to serve God and understand our Bibles by the light of our own intellects and consciences? Must we have theologically-educated *men* to interpret Scripture teachings . . . because we belong to an inferior order of creation?" "It would really be amusing if it were not provoking," Lillie Devereaux Blake wrote in 1883, "this calm way in which men undertake to dictate to women what they shall or shall not do. . . . These reverend doctors and other self-constituted critics look upon us, as it were, like so many vegetables, to be classified and arranged without the slightest regard to our wishes."[24]

Evangelical women also prized their lack of dogma as the truest expression of "woman's religion," and one powerful point of superiority to the masculine variety. "Dogmatic theology founded on masculine interpretation of the Bible is one thing," Blake argued, "what is true and lovely in Christianity is another and far different." "Men preach a dead letter of ecclesiasticism," Frances Willard charged, "women will declare a life. Men deal in formulas, women in facts." The masculine propensity toward multiplying dogmatic "creeds and sects," she believed, was one more reason why religious leadership should be taken from their hands.[25]

By the early twentieth century, the perception that men and women approached religion from opposite angles was widespread. Feminist Charlotte Perkins Gilman defined men's religion as an aggressive, competitive exercise. "Even the Christian, follower of the Prince of Peace," she sniffed, "is said to be 'fighting the good fight,' encouraged by "Onward Christian Soldiers, marching as to war." Writing "in defense of women," H. L. Mencken blamed men for the "sordid and literal" character of evangelical Protestant theology. "It was men, not women," he charged, who had reduced "the ineffable mystery of religion to a mere bawling of idiots."[26]

Fundamentalists defenders of the Bible seemed to share the assumption that their approach to religion was different, and essentially masculine. First, they refused to harmonize women's right to speak in churches with the biblical prooftexts against it, arguing that the position was "essentially infidel." One writer saw in the movement to ordain women individuals "laboring most strenuously to disparage the authority of Scripture," a list which included even A. J. Gordon.[27] G. F. Wilkin saw it as nothing less than a *subversion of Christian faith*. "The equality doctrine is dangerous," he warned, for it encouraged "a very decided tendency to scout and scoff at the only fundamental and authoritative law upon which the social fabric can securely rest, namely, the Word of God." He quoted Frances Willard as a case in point.[28]

Of course, even by the 1920s, the fundamentalists had no monolithic interpretation of biblical passages on women's role. Bible institutes remained heavily invested in preparing women for service and defended themselves for doing so even when attacked for biblical inconsistency.[29]

But as the fundamentalist defense grew increasingly embattled in the early twentieth century, it took on a more self-consciously masculine posture. And here conservative Presbyterians often took the lead. By 1930, for example, they were resisting women's ordination in the name of "masculine Calvinistic doctrines." The prohibition against "ecclesiastical fem-inarchy," one Calvinist intoned, "is an integral part of Princeton Calvinism." Likewise, another agreed that Presbyterianism was a "manly" faith, exhibiting "a certain robustness which . . . is essentially masculine."[30]

Though some thirty years apart, both Elizabeth Cady Stanton and the Presbyterian heirs of Hodge and Warfield suffered the same fate: ostracism by their more centrist colleagues. By the early twentieth century, both the feminist and fundamentalist battles for the Bible were losing their audi-ences as a succeeding generation looked less toward Scripture and more toward science and reason for authoritative answers. But neither were doomed to irrelevance. Modern fundamentalists and evangelicals have resumed the debate over Scripture and women's rights in nearly the same place where an earlier generation left off, with a nearly equal chance for resolution.

Dispensationalists and Gender

Though the battle for the Bible proved somewhat inconclusive in regard to the woman question, dispensational premillennialism, the theological system fundamentalists adhered to, offered an air-tight argument for fem-inine subordination. Taken in isolation, the numerous biblical texts on women's role could be a matter of endless debate; however, within the more rigid schema of dispensationalist interpretation all controversy ceased, for their meaning was clear. Although dispensationalism by no means set out to resolve the issue of woman's place, its clear, consistent logic played a powerful role in the rising debate. Dispensational premil-lennialism embedded the principle of masculine leadership and feminine subordination in salvation history itself and, perhaps more important, uplifted order as the highest principle of Christian life and thought.

Premillennialism is a theory about the end times, stressing the down-ward trend of human history. It is not necessarily unique to fundamen-talism. Since the time of Christ, believers had often held a cataclysmic view of the future, fueled by the hope that the end would occur suddenly, "like a thief in the night." But the temptation to set an exact time and date for Christ's return was often difficult to pass by—and brought disas-trous results. Late nineteenth-century dispensationalism was a system of premillennial interpretation designed to order and explain the intricacies of biblical prophecy and to eliminate the possibility of embarrassing errors in prediction. (In fundamentalism the two terms, dispensationalism and premillennialism, are basically synonymous.)

The rise of dispensationalism coincided with two trends in American Protestantism: the increasing frustration of hopes for instituting the kingdom of God on earth and a rising urgency to evangelize the world. Though the outcome of the Civil War confirmed rather than discouraged evangelical beliefs in national righteousness, postwar urbanization and industrialization soon undermined any cause for complacency. Gilded Age Protestantism shared the growing prosperity and optimism of its time but proved largely unable to penetrate urban culture, increasingly non-Protestant, and no longer northern European. Revivalists hoped to renew national righteousness by winning the urban business classes, but even they confronted rising secularism among men who bowed chiefly to material gods. As the discontent of the lower classes, spurred by the arrogance of capitalist robber barons, ignited violent labor strikes and urban riots, the churches seemed helpless to confront or to change this course of events.

Premillennialism offered an antidote to despair—if Christ was coming soon all was not lost—and a powerful rationale for evangelism. Revivalists adopted its language to argue for the necessity of immediate, personal conversion, warning that hard-hearted impenitents risked both the prospect of eternal torment and years of satanic tribulation after Christ came to reclaim his true followers. Missionary strategists pointed out that, according to biblical prophecy, Christ would not return until all the world had heard the gospel. Although Christians could not determine (or know) the exact date of the Second Coming, they could speed it along by aggressive proclamation to all the earth's peoples.

Another clear attraction of dispensationalist thought was its emphasis on order, in biblical interpretation and in society itself. C. I. Scofield, the leading progenitor of dispensationalist doctrine, argued that only his system could unlock the mysteries of biblical prophecy, for it offered the "same relation to the right understanding of the Scriptures that correct outline work has to map making." Non-dispensationalist readings faced "the inevitable penalty . . . of confusion everywhere."[31] The same principle held true for society. Left to themselves, human beings would descend into "chaos," warned James M. Gray, fueled by pride, the "root-sin" of Adam's race. William Evans, associate dean at the Bible Institute of Los

Angeles, defined sin as "a deliberate transgressing of the divinely marked boundary; an overstepping of the divine limits."[32] Alarmed at the rising disorder of the society around them, dispensationalists found comfort in the harmony and uniformity that were essential to God's divine nature. As G. B. M. Clouser put it, "God is the author of order; man of discord."[33]

Dispensational premillennialism was first introduced in the United States by British evangelist John Nelson Darby, and by the 1870s had found an audience within the ethos of urban revivalism. Popularized in Niagara Conferences, in Bible institutes, and through the untiring efforts of fundamentalist writers and spokesmen, it rapidly become a defining feature of the otherwise diverse movement.

Darby taught that not all the promises of God were meant for the present age; many were unique to earlier periods of biblical time, or dispensations. Because human beings repeatedly disobeyed God's will, each age ended with catastrophe and the divine program for salvation, which was never truly thwarted, began anew. Thus God first planned to bring about the future Messianic kingdom through the Israelite nation; after the Jews rejected Christ, God chose a new instrument, the Gentile church. Darby viewed the church as a spiritual rather than a social institution, with a mission to hold fast to truth as the cataclysmic end times approached. In dispensationalist theory, fundamentalist believers were a privileged and faithful remnant, watching the demise of their culture from a safe theological distance.[34]

This pessimistic logic put fundamentalists at odds with the majority of American evangelicals, who still held fast to their belief in human progress. What evangelicals took as proof of their cultural ascendancy, dispensationalists more often interpreted as signs of religious apostasy.

Thus, though most evangelicals applauded the rising social and religious prominence of women, dispensationalists saw such changes as a clear indication of approaching catastrophe. Although fundamentalist belief in the imminent Second Coming gave a new urgency to evangelism, and opened doors to women's participation there, it was essentially hostile to the ethic of social progress that energized women's work in missions and temperance. "The earth is a leprous house," Elizabeth Needham, a popular dispensationalist author, asserted. "May we keep ourselves unspotted from its contagion; living in wholesome loathing, and awaiting in eager hope the summons of the Royal High Priest."[35]

The Bible and Prophetic Conferences, which disseminated premillennialist doctrine within fundamentalism, appeared to share the larger movement's masculine ethos. Defenders of dispensational premillennialism often warned that their doctrines were not meant for the fainthearted. "There is an awful definiteness, a vivid realness, an intense literalness, about these truths," Gordon wrote, "that frightens a timid and sentimental faith."[36] Although some women, notably British suffragist Christabel Pankhurst and Elizabeth Knauss, were popular lecturers on the subject, the conferences themselves attracted a predominantly male audience of clergy and seminary professors.[37] Two lists of personal endorsements for premillennial doctrine, printed in 1886 and 1914, were entirely male, even though the names of "theologians, commentators, authors, educators, and pastors" also included numerous missionaries. After 1882 there is no record of separate women's meetings at the conferences.[38]

The immediate context of dispensationalist discussion on women's role was the rising popularity of female evangelists, especially in the holiness wing of evangelical Protestantism, characteristically the most open to women's public ministry. Indeed, from its inception, the holiness movement was nurtured and led by Phoebe Palmer and her host of female evangelists. In 1875 the Salvation Army, spurred by the outspoken leadership of evangelist Catharine Booth, explicitly opened all posts to women; by 1878 "Hallelujah Lassies" comprised nearly half its officers on the field.[39]

Female evangelists typically defended their role as a special gift from the Holy Spirit. They drew scriptural warrant from the Old Testament prophecy, repeated in the New Testament description of the first Pentecost, that "your daughters shall prophesy." While most, including Phoebe Palmer herself, stopped short of arguing for ordination, they clearly saw their calling as a sign of the spiritual outpouring the Old Testament prophets predicted for the latter days.[40]

Dispensationalist theology, however, emphasized the irreversible nature of Adam's—and especially Eve's—original sin. God had demanded obedience to his command not to eat from the Tree of the Knowledge of Good and Evil, and by the woman's rebellion humanity stood liable to the punishment of death. The time periods, or dispensations, which succeeded the first pair's fall from innocence all fell under the shadow of the curses recorded in Genesis 3:14–19. The Scofield Reference Bible, an annotated dispensationalist version of Scripture edited by C. I. Scofield, listed seven edicts of the new "Adamic dispensation": (1) a curse on the deceiving serpent, (2) the promise of Christ as the future redeemer of humanity, (3) a curse on the earth, (4) inevitable sorrow, (5) burdensome labor, (6) physical death, and (7) a "changed state of the woman" to include "multiplied conception," "motherhood linked with sorrow," and male headship, made necessary by the entrance of sin, "which is disorder."[41]

Although God's eternal plan shifted to accommodate the ground rules of each dispensation, these original curses could not be lifted within human time. The original divine decrees, as Crozer Seminary professor J. M. Stifler explained to a Niagara conference, could "no more be changed by man than he can change the course of the sun." Thus, feminine subordination was as inevitable as death itself.[42] George C. Needham's wife, Elizabeth, thus held that women would never lose the theological stigma of Eve's transgression, a "moral disability," whose "humiliation will abide even upon the last woman to the end of the age."[43]

Dispensationalism traced feminine subordination to the Fall rather than Creation, but even this did not end speculations about women's inherent inferiority. According to John F. Kendall, the nature of Eve's sin confirmed her original frailty and the wisdom of her subjection. "Woman never since occupied so responsible a position as that of Eve when Satan assailed and 'deceived' her," he wrote, "and by her failure then she showed that she had not the qualities which fitted her for a leader."[44]

Dispensationalist teaching on women's role thus clearly contrasted with Wesleyan perfectionism. Although both agreed that women were victims of the Fall, perfectionists emphatically denied the permanence of feminine subordination. They stressed Christ's example of respect for women during his lifetime, and the radical effects of his death and resurrection on sinful social institutions. As perfectionists denied the eternal weight of the Bible's apparent permission of slavery, and even of strong drink, they argued that women were full participants in the new age that began with the Resurrection of Christ and the outpouring of his Spirit on the church at Pentecost.[45]

During the late nineteenth century, some dispensationalists, apparently reluctant to accept the strict implications of their doctrine, adopted a version of this argument. Arthur T. Pierson, A. J. Gordon, and Frederik Franson argued from the prophecies in Joel 2 that women's gifts for evangelism were a positive sign of the approaching millennium. Although certainly not advocating women's ordination, they supported women's right to preach from the fulfillment of Joel 2 at Pentecost.[46] "It seems as if the Churches of God in this century need to have the scales taken from their eyes," Gordon wrote in 1887, "that they may see God wants women to prophesy in the power of the Holy Ghost." Yet he admitted too, that the entire prophecy calling for the Spirit to be "poured out on all flesh," was still unfulfilled. Women's speaking was a "miniature fulfillment" of a future, worldwide outpouring of the Holy Spirit.[47]

But James Brookes, founder of the Niagara movement, dismissed this argument contemptuously. "It is perfectly clear," he rejoined, "that the fulfillment of this prophecy will be witnessed only *after* the second coming of our Lord, and it has nothing to do with a woman preaching now." This position was wholly consistent with dispensationalist views on the Holy Spirit's outpouring at Pentecost. The spiritual gifts the apostles received then were unique and were discontinued until the final outpouring at the end of time.[48]

Other dispensationalists agreed that women's role was a secondary one. Moody associate D. W. Whittle did not object to women evangelists but was clear in his distaste for women in authority, an unmistakable sign of "failure and apostasy." Elizabeth Needham argued similarly from Galatians 3:28, a seminal verse for advocates of women's equality, which declared that "there is no male nor female" in Christ's spiritual kingdom. Even that classic statement of sexual equality, she contended, "*does not* obliterate the restriction of sex binding on womankind.*" In fact, she argued that the last line of the verse, that "all are one in Christ Jesus," indicated the future masculinity of God's creation. "It explains why throughout the New Testament... believers of both sexes are always addressed as SONS OF GOD."[49]

Dispensationalists referred to women preachers, especially those in pentecostal traditions, with deep scorn. "In this modern movement women seem to be very much in the foreground," Arno C. Gaebelein wrote in 1907, describing with evident distaste eyewitness accounts of hysterical feminine screeching that accompanied the gift of tongues. In his view, "the present day 'apostolic or pentecostal movement,' with its high pretensions and false doctrines, lack of true scriptural knowledge and wisdom, ... with its women leaders and teachers," had all the marks of a demonic counterfeit. The prevalence of female healers in pentecostal and holiness churches offered further proof to Gaebelein of the movement's theological bankruptcy. "*Who has authorized a woman to anoint the sick?*" he demanded. "Certainly not the Holy Spirit, who declares emphatically what a woman's place is to be in the Church (II Timothy 2:12–14)."[50]

Dispensationalists also looked with dismay and pity on attempts to reform women's social status. D. W. Whittle warned that "in the apostasy of the last days [women] will be tempted to take part in this or that social reform, to give their sex the ballot and place them on political equality with men." He urged them to resist; not only did such measures smack of worldliness, they were "unscriptural." Brookes agreed: "Something more than woman's vote is required to reform and regenerate mankind," he cautioned.[51]

Dispensationalists particularly opposed the rhetoric of the suffrage movement, which emphasized women's moral superiority. It was enough to point out that "unregenerate women are as mean as unregenerate men" and that "there are vicious and incompetent women as well as vicious and incompetent men."[52] Christabel Pankhurst, whose mother Emmeline was a militant British suffragist, once commented that she was glad women received the vote, "if for no other reason than to show that women are just as powerless as men to improve conditions in the world."[53] Indeed, negative portrayals of shallow society women and thoughtless mothers of wayward girls appeared more frequently in dispensationalist literature as the nineteenth century drew to a close.[54]

It was no great leap, therefore, to link emancipated women with the "apostasy of the last days." James Brookes's immoderate attack on "Infidelity among Women" in 1886 was the first of many diatribes against the New Woman. "The prominence assigned to women amid the evils of the last days, and in hastening the crash of the present dispensation, is well worthy of serious attention," Brookes warned. "When women lose conscience and faith, they surpass men not only in the indulgence of their grovelling appetites, but in the atrocity of their deeds."[55]

Not all depictions of women were negative, however, and it would be misleading to classify all fundamentalist men as shallow misogynists. This much is illustrated by the use of two prominent feminine images by dispensationalist commentators, the Virgin Mary and the "bride of Christ." These largely positive types were intensely attractive to fundamentalist men, who were at times capable of betraying a decidedly romantic streak. These images appeared frequently in dispensationalist literature and seemed to inspire powerful emotion in the men who spoke of them.

The fundamentalists' defense of the Virgin Birth as a primary article of faith nearly amounted to a passion. A statement of the doctrine by British theologian James Orr opened the first volume of "The Fundamentals" in 1910. The twelve-volume series, a statement of basic Christian doctrine, gave the fundamentalist movement a name as well as a "bottom line" on theological orthodoxy. In Orr's essay, and in subsequent defenses of fundamentalist doctrine, the Virgin Birth stood as a central proof for the divinity of Christ. Orr, who was not a dispensationalist, interpreted Mary's anointing as a partial sign of God's favor upon women, a step toward the final breaking of the curse at Christ's Second Coming. "It was through the woman through whom sin entered the race," he explained; "by the seed of woman would salvation come.... The promise to Abraham was that in *his* seed the families of the earth would be blessed; there the *male* is emphasized, but here it is the *woman*—the woman distinctively."[56]

Though the divine nod of favor on Mary honored womankind, it did not alter the essentially passive role of women in salvation history. Most arguments dealt more with Mary's "seed" than with her elevated character. "She, who was chosen by God's grace to be the blessed vessel," Arno C. Gaebelein wrote in 1907, "... was fallible and sinful like every other person." Explicitly rejecting Roman Catholic veneration of the Virgin, Gaebelein stressed that Mary could claim "absolutely no relation to the redemption work of the Son of God." Spirited defenses of the Virgin Birth perhaps mitigated the otherwise hopeless position of women in dispensationalist theology; in practical terms, however, their effect was slight.[57]

The "bride of Christ" typology was another major theme for dispensationalist commentators. Based on the passage in Ephesians 5 that compares the husband's devotion to his wife with Christ's love for his spiritual bride, the Church, the typology included all the brides of Scripture, beginning with Eve and continuing through Rebekah, Rachel, and Asenath (Joseph's wife) as figures of Christ's future church. Interpreters often added an element of romance to their discussion, depicting Christ's bride as a woman of mystery and attraction, and an object of intense yearning. As influential commentator William Blackstone described it, "the Church, as the Bride of Christ, is typified by the most intimate, tender, and sacred relationship known among the children of men."[58]

The bride of Christ was a feminine role that men could adopt without stigma—and a few described with genuine emotional verve. "Just 'a little while,' dear brethren, and 'the Lord shall descend from heaven with a shout,' " George F. Guille rhapsodized, "to say 'Arise, my love, my fair one, and come away.' " Baptist evangelist J. C. Massee compared the excitement of his own wedding day to Christ's longing for the Second Coming, casting himself in the role of the intended bride. "I can feel in my heart tonight," he confessed before a large audience, "my own joy in my bride of twenty-three years ago. The thrill of it lasts until this moment.... But my Christ's bride!" Massee was awestruck by the emotional power of the metaphor, that he himself could be the object of such love and longing.[59]

Still, the waiting bride was another essentially passive feminine type. The "intelligent submission" of Christ's consort, Elizabeth Needham wrote, was "the central force around which every gift and service of the Christian woman revolve in harmonious attraction." James Brookes actually used the typology as a reason for women's silence in church—"not because she is inferior to man, but because she is a type of the Church [and] has no right to teach anything, but only to be taught."[60]

Though powerfully attracted to these two feminine images, fundamentalists fervently backed away from any gross sentimentalization of women's nature. The equally powerful use of other female "typologies," or symbols, in dispensationalist hermeneutics revealed a growing bias, not simply against women in leadership, but against femininity itself. In dispensationalist commentaries, women appeared most often in connection with "leaven," a symbol of evil (referring to the woman in Christ's parable of Luke 15:20). "Whoever has eyes opened by the Word and the Spirit," wrote Gaebelein, "must see how well the *woman* has succeeded in putting the leaven of error and wickedness into the fine flour."[61] Of course Gaebelein was speaking figuratively. Typologies did not mechanically translate into social policy; however, consistent use of such negative association did reinforce the notion that women, once deceived by Satan, were forever untrustworthy as teachers of biblical doctrine.

Negative feminine types abounded in the prophecies of Revelation. The whore of Babylon, and her ominous associations with the beast and Anti-Christ, played a pivotal role in John's vision. Few commentators, however, used this as an occasion for editorial remarks on feminine sin; the whore of Babylon was most commonly identified as the apostate Roman Catholic Church. Dispensationalist interpretations normally avoided metaphorical speculation, insisting on the literal truth of prophetic images. Still, the language of interpretation betrayed a growing theological bias against women. In regard to the description of the 144,000 saints in Revelation 14:4 who were not "defiled with women," Gaebelein rejected the literal conclusion that all the saints were male. But he did use the occasion to remind his readers that "all Christless worldly systems of religion . . . in symbolical language are ever 'women.' . . . Beware, my fellow believers, of such 'women' today," he warned, "for there are many of them."[62]

Dispensationalism, though it purported to end fruitless speculation about the biblical intent for women's role, also revealed the complexities of fundamentalist attitudes toward femininity. For all its use of masculine language and insistence on feminine subordination, fundamentalism could still proffer images of women that were suffused with intense romantic yearning. Perhaps J. C. Massee put it best: "Oh woman!" he sighed, "How you bother us, how you puzzle us, how you exasperate us, yet how we love you!"[63]

Not surprisingly, fundamentalists were slow to adopt the full restrictive implications of dispensationalist and inerrantist teaching on the role of women. Even vocal spokesmen from within dispensationalist ranks, including Gordon and A. T. Pierson, chose to downplay the ramifications of their doctrine, emphasizing instead women's gifts for missions and evangelism. Representing another wing of fundamentalism, Jonathan Blanchard, a social reformer and influential president of Wheaton College, a leading fundamentalist school, heartily endorsed both the temperance movement and women's suffrage. His sympathy for fundamentalism did not prevent him from encouraging ties between his anti-Masonic crusade and the Woman's Christian Temperance Union, or from supporting Frances Townsley, a Wheaton graduate, in her ministerial career. Nor did his son Charles's conversion to dispensationalism dim the powerful role of Blanchard women in the early history of Wheaton College.[64]

George Marsden's depiction of early fundamentalism as a "mosaic of divergent and sometimes contradictory traditions and tendencies" is apt. His characterization rightly emphasizes the movement's complexities, as it attempted to meld the "authoritarian and ideological character of dispensationalism" with the "sentiment and activism" of the revivalist ethos.[65]

This is also an accurate depiction of fundamentalist approaches to women's role, during the movement's formative stage, before 1920. For though the balance of dispensationalist teaching and its inherent prejudices fell against women in leadership positions, most fundamentalists encouraged them to take an active role in spreading the gospel. Even as strict an interpreter of Scripture as Elizabeth Needham still encouraged most forms of "women's ministry." Her dispensationalist views prohibited only positions of leadership and authority; informal "prophesying" and evangelizing received her encouragement and approval.[66]

The implications of dispensationalist premillennialism were not fully realized until after the losses and disappointments in the decades following World War I, and then only slowly. But they were instituted. When the fundamentalist movement entered its militant, confrontational phase in the 1920s, the "woman question" took on a new immediacy. Women's increasing social freedom in the postwar era, symbolized by the passage of the suffrage amendment and typified by the rebellious "flapper," irrefutably proved the negative effects of unregulated feminine freedom and the necessity of imposing order. Dispensationalist warnings about feminine duplicity were vindicated in the theological encounters of the 1920s, when prominent laywomen appeared to throw in their lot with the liberal leaders of their denominations. Then the logic of dispensationalist teaching began to take root in reality.

Indeed, opposition to feminism remained a theme within fundamentalist literature. Women's social liberation during the twentieth century constantly fueled speculations that feminine "brazenness" was a sign of the last days.[67] "This world movement among women may not as yet be fully understood by [Christians]," one dispensationalist wrote in 1931, "but it has not taken them by surprise." Growing evidence of women's "rebellion," another commentator agreed, verified the apostle Paul's prediction that in the last days the gospel would be perverted by "silly women," chasing after every wind of doctrine.[68] "Is it a matter of no importance that just such emotional, unsubject [sic] women were the tools used by Satan for the starting and propagating of so many fads?" Harry Ironside wrote in 1947. "The spirit evinced among modern women is one of organized rebellion against God," a woman, writing in 1949, agreed. "As sin entered the world through the woman, in the beginning, so today she seems bent on finishing the destruction in these last days."[69]

Dispensationalism was far more than a theory for fundamentalists; they also used it to define reality. The relentless careers of many fundamentalist leaders suggest that they received the implications of dispensationalist teaching, especially God's curse on Adam, with utter seriousness. Once cursed, Clarence Larkin explained, man was condemned to a life of "hard labor" that would "wear out his system and end in physical death." And the lives of many fundamentalist leaders would testify to their obedience to this edict.[70] Many in fact found Jesus Christ a demanding taskmaster. Their hectic personal lives, which often left scant time for family relationships, amply filled the divine command to strive and toil. Though dispensationalism sharply critiqued the "evils of the present age," including economic selfishness and modern irreligion, it was not inherently opposed to the capitalist work ethic; indeed, it provided a clear theological rationale for endless toil.

To modern eyes, dispensationalism perhaps holds few attractions. Especially a way of life, it seems to raise more problems than it solves, for though it opened the Bible to plain reading by thoughtful Christians, it demanded unrealistic standards of obedience and separation, especially in regard to gender roles. Why then did it become so central to the fundamentalist mind-set?

Within the ethos of American culture a century ago, its meaning is clearer. Dispensationalist doctrine was not so much a refuge from change as a way of creating sense out of complexity. To women it offered an explanation for their social inferiority that, unlike feminism, required no unrealistic expectations of moral superiority. Dispensationalism allowed women the relief of being sinners, with full access to divine grace. It affirmed their desire to serve, and invested it with new meaning, for in premillennial thought, missionary service was more than a cultural imperative—it heralded the triumphant return of Christ himself. Men in turn found their masculinity both affirmed and challenged; even endless toil could be a form of spiritual obedience. And dispensationalism offered a more nuanced expression of manliness than the tireless virility demanded by the secular world. It opposed the feminizing forces in religion and society, yet allowed men a romantic, passionate outlet.

The roots of fundamentalist opposition to feminism lie deep within the culture of its origin. They grew from specific doctrinal points within fundamentalism that placed it squarely in opposition to the optimistic, ameliorative tradition of mainstream religion. But, to carry the metaphor a bit further, these ideals did not bear fruit as one might expect; the progress of antifeminist attitudes among fundamentalists was always hesitant and slow, normally held in check by the feminine substructure of a religious culture that fundamentalists could never entirely escape. Indeed, as the following chapters shall argue, antifeminism found its sharpest expression during periods of stress and transition, especially in the 1920s and late 1940s.

The role of women in fundamentalism was inherently problematic. Their very presence undermined the movement's masculine persona, and any drive for leadership directly undercut its commitment to biblical consistency. Thus, though fundamentalists imposed few blanket prohibitions against women in helping capacities, they prophesied severe consequences if they overstepped their bounds or "usurped authority." But this was bound to happen. With the institutional growth of fundamentalism after 1930 and the inevitable blurring of lines between the sexes in teaching and administrative roles, the difficulties, for women and men, would only increase.

Chapter Three

Fundamentalist Men and Liberal Women: Gender in the Fundamentalist-Modernist Controversy

Heed not the lying words of him
Who speaks his falsehoods through the men
That doubt God's Word, whose souls are dim,
Whose errors flow from lurid pen.
Why should you be another Eve
To question God? Why must you doubt,
And thus God's blessed spirit grieve,
While jeering demons raise a shout?

God spake! and what He spake is true,
And shall forever stand as such,
Though men deceive themselves and you
With flaunting errors overmuch.
Just be a child in humble guise,
And trust your Lord implicitly,
Then your own soul will hate, despise,
The Serpent's lie—and you'll be free!

—Eugene B. Kuntz, "The Serpent's Lie (To a Woman Modernist)," *MBIM* 30 (July 1930): 539.

During the 1920s, fundamentalism acquired the militancy it became famous for. In that overheated decade of stunning technological and social changes, face-to-face rivalries between modernists and conservatives split northern Presbyterians and Baptists into angry, competing factions. The confrontations were brief but left permanent rifts among evangelical Protestants. Fundamentalism fell into rapid decline after the Scopes Trial of

1925, descending unhappily into the cultural backwaters. As the mainline churches retreated to heal their scars, fundamentalists turned earnestly to fighting among themselves.

That decade was also a time of perceived changes in women's status, inaugurated by the passage of the suffrage amendment in 1920. Visible changes in dress reflected women's steadily enlarging social freedom, as short skirts and rolled-up stockings replaced whale-bone corsets and petticoats. Although the decade saw no revolution in women's social status, it brought into the open a shift in morals that had steadily been gaining ground since the turn of the century. The feminist movement progressed little during the 1920s, but young women enjoyed unprecedented amounts of freedom in a society reeling from the moral upset and economic prosperity of the postwar years.[1]

Although religious leaders of all stripes railed against flappers, they eagerly sought to retain the loyalty of this new woman, who no longer seemed unquestionably supportive of their goals. Churches now competed with secular society for women's energy and attention. "If the world outside is more hospitable to the claims of women, offers them larger opportunities of initiative, responsibility and self-expression," Baptist laywoman Helen Barrett Montgomery warned in 1923, "then the church must bear the consequent loss of power."[2]

The 1920s was a pivotal decade for fundamentalists and women. Although Protestant laywomen did not necessarily gain real power, their visible status changed considerably. Montgomery herself was named president of the Northern Baptist Convention in 1921. Other denominations, Northern Presbyterians most successfully, sought to end the pattern of gender-segregated missionary organizations by uniting women's groups with national bodies governed by men. According to one apt description, twentieth-century churchwomen were "friendly outsiders," at the same time "*of* the Protestant establishment and yet barred from its inner citadel." Fundamentalists, on the other hand, were rapidly becoming unwilling outsiders, often at the mercy of the same forces that brought women into the establishment. The mergers of women's missionary societies into denominational boards and token advances toward women's ordination coincided with the fundamentalists' loss of power and their unhappy exodus. Among Presbyterians disaffection with the women of their denomination paralleled their own sense of declining power.[3]

The movement of women into denominational bureaucracies and conservatives out of them proved significant for the social development of the fundamentalist movement. The apparent alliance between women and the liberal enemies of fundamentalism verified rising doubts about feminine morality. The events of the decade finally put to rest the old stereotype of women as the true guardians of religion, replacing it with a new one emphasizing their moral weakness and theological shallowness. In the new formulation, fundamentalist men forsook their previously passive role in religion and, in theory at least, assumed full responsibility for guarding orthodoxy.

Presbyterian Conservatives and Women

After World War I, liberal Presbyterian leaders seemed to be bending over backward to accommodate their female constituency. Twice, in 1919–20 and 1929–30, the denomination considered ordaining women as elders and, the second time, also as pastors. The measure failed in 1920 chiefly because of numerous abstentions. Despite the relative lack of interest among local congregations, denominational leaders pressed on, approving women deacons in 1922. In 1926 the General Assembly commissioned a searching study on "Causes of Unrest among Women of the Church," and in 1928 appointed a special committee of fifteen prominent laywomen to discuss their grievances with denominational officials, including Robert Speer and Lewis Mudge, clerk of the General Assembly. In 1929 a council of one hundred women ratified the demand for ordination, which passed through the General Assembly without debate or comment. Although the presbyteries rejected the overture for ministerial ordination in 1930, they voted to ordain women as elders by a wide majority.[4]

Those behind the 1929 overtures freely admitted their value in muting feminine anger over the loss of their independent mission boards. In 1922 the General Assembly had pushed through a merger of the women's foreign and home missionary agencies into two larger, denominationally sanctioned boards. The new boards represented women as one group among several, and in a proportion far below their numbers in Presbyterian churches. The stated purpose of the reorganization was to promote efficiency and cooperation; however, it left Presbyterian women fuming over their sudden loss of independence. "It comes as a distinct and disappointing shock," an Illinois woman confessed angrily, "that after so many years of faithful cooperation [the women's boards] should be 'swallowed whole' without even Fletcherizing"—referring to a popular stomach laxative.[5]

The push for women elders in 1929 was engineered chiefly by denominational officials who hoped that the promise of broader equality would compensate women for the loss of organizational independence. Clement MacAfee, moderator of the General Assembly, conceded that the 1929 overtures were neither "a yielding to the clamor of the women nor an acceptance of their demand," for there was "no such clamor, no such demand."[6] Most Presbyterian women gave the ordination issue scant attention, preferring the old pattern of separation to the new offer of equality. Even the 1929 demand for ordination by the council of one hundred women was halfhearted, according to participants. Katharine Bennett, speaking for the council, declared that "the women of the church as a whole have not been concerned with their ecclesiastical status; they have been anxious as to the future of... organizations which they have formed and fostered." Not surprisingly, the overtures failed to assuage feminine grievances or to alter their subordinate role in the denomination.[7]

Still, the implications of these events were not lost on Presbyterian conservatives. Their emotional opposition to the overtures in 1929–30 reflected a rising anger over their own loss of status. For although they objected to women elders on biblical grounds, their resistance actually ran much deeper.

Most conservatives had no fundamental objections to women in supportive church offices. Even Warfield himself had endorsed the office of deaconess in the 1880s. In 1920 the overtures for female elders occasioned a genteel debate in the *Presbyterian*, a leading conservative journal, over the fine points of Greek exegesis and hermeneutical principles, with most contributors guardedly in favor. When Warfield wrote an article strongly opposed to female leadership, more moderate contributors took him to task for ignoring the "time, conditions, and circumstances" of the Pauline proscriptions.[8] Nearly all endorsed the denomination's stance of the past half-century, that "women's work" in the church was impossible to restrict and too valuable to ignore.[9]

The next ten years brought a sudden and drastic change of status for Presbyterian conservatives. Their brief success in silencing liberal Harry Emerson Fosdick in 1923 was followed by a decisive defeat. The loss of control over Princeton Theological Seminary in 1925 was the beginning of the exodus of an exclusivist faction led by J. Gresham Machen. Ousted from Princeton, this group founded Westminster Seminary and, in 1936, the Orthodox Presbyterian Church.

Thus, when the debate over women's ordination resumed in the *Presbyterian* ten years later, the moderate voice that opposed Warfield in 1920 had all but disappeared. Most participants agreed that a liberal conspiracy was at work behind the overtures, sealing their plans by pushing women to the fore. Seattle pastor Mark Matthews saw the move to ordain women as the "well-laid plans, schemes and designs" of an elite few. Clarence Macartney regarded it simply as a "hankering and hungering after the fleshpots of this present world," the mad desire for "a new church and a new gospel."[10] College president Ethelbert Warfield agreed that it was "only one manifestation of a world-wide movement" in revolt against historical Christianity. As one layman saw it, if the overtures were to pass, the liberals would have won the day. "Will this not mean that in time many of our Presbyterian churches will be closed to me and others believing as I do?" he lamented. "Am I to be driven out of the church by— what shall I call them—Modernists!"[11]

The conspiracy seemed centered in the mission boards themselves, whose liberal drift was the focus of conservative discontent. The addition of female board members was largely superfluous and, they hinted broadly, only meant to pad the liberal majority. Finley Jenkins urged his denomination to "arouse itself, assert its own rights, and align members of the Home and Foreign and other Boards with the theological traditions and standards of the whole Church. The consecutive havoc which they and others have wrought with our ecclesiastical stability must be given the finishing stroke in the impending voting."[12] Robert Speer's prominent role on the mission board, and as a champion of equality for women, was not lost on his conservative critics. As a foreign missionary spokesman and devotee of Moody in early life, he had been a close ally of fundamentalists. But by 1927 he had adopted a more centrist position and, as moderator of the General Assembly, actively opposed Machen's demand for a separate mission board. This apparent betrayal earned him lasting disdain among Machen's defenders.[13]

The debate also unearthed a deeper pessimism about femininity itself. Conservative critics constantly warned that the overtures for women's ordination would open the floodgates to theological heresies of every variety. Clarence Macartney stated his belief that "many of the subtle and dangerous and seductive heresies and perversions and distortions of the gospel of Jesus Christ have sprung from the brain of woman. When the apostle speaks of false teachers leading off 'silly women,' " he reminded, "he has a very modern sound. From Eve down to Mrs. Eddy, women have played a sad part in the spread of anti-Christian doctrines, and that under the guise of Christian teachings."[14] "The adversary is clever enough in his dealings with men to inject in their theology many dangerous errors," agreed a fellow Calvinist, "but he got his masterpiece through a woman's brain."[15]

The widespread support for Pearl S. Buck, novelist and Presbyterian missionary to China, confirmed all these suspicions and more. When Mrs. Buck publicly supported the liberal conclusions of *Rethinking Missions*, an influential report published in 1933, conservatives rose to the attack. Her article, "Is There a Case for Foreign Missions?" brought on a direct confrontation with J. Gresham Machen which resulted in her resignation from the mission board, despite a spirited defense by Robert Speer.[16] Machen's temporary victory, however, was overshadowed by the outpouring of support for Mrs. Buck by the denomination's women. Mrs. Henry Gillmore, a leading Presbyterian laywoman, resigned from the national mission board in protest, as an "open and public declaration of [her] liberal principles."[17]

When Machen and his conservatives formed their own mission board, the Independent Board of Presbyterian Foreign Missions, it was dominated by men. Its executive board included eight men and one woman, a high school history instructor. Presbyterian women, long dominant in missionary work, were already bitterly complaining of their stingy representation on the denominational mission boards, where they held only fifteen out of forty seats.

Baptist Battles

Leading Baptist fundamentalists also worried about women's ability to withstand liberal enticements. In 1926 John Roach Straton denounced the Women's Missionary Society from his New York City pulpit. By accepting half a million dollars from John C. Rockefeller, he charged, this group of weak women "could not with any face at all resist the strength of the modernist."[18] Many fundamentalist Baptist leaders were particularly irked by the apparent naiveté of Helen Barrett Montgomery. In the early 1920s conservatives did not consider Montgomery a modernist; some even respected her biblical scholarship. Thus, her apparently partisan role in the Baptist controversy over its foreign mission boards came as a shock to fundamentalists. Overriding conservative complaints about heresy in Baptist seminaries and among missionary candidates, she publicly bestowed on both a "clean bill of health."[19] Moreover, in her convention address, as fundamentalist leader Chester Tulga later concluded, *she definitely weighted the scales against the fundamentalist proposal to adopt a confession of faith*," belittling it as a string of "petty accusations," "irresponsible statements," and "wild charges." "There is no doubt," Tulga wrote, "that this partisan address, delivered by a lady who for chivalrous reasons was difficult to criticize, prejudiced many delegates against the fundamentalists before they had a chance to be heard."[20]

Later events validated this concern. Tulga noted that women presided over the Northern Baptist Convention at two critical moments of defeat for conservatives, Montgomery in 1922 when the denomination adopted its "inclusive policy," and Anna Canada Swain in 1946 when the breakaway Conservative Baptist Missionary Society failed to receive denominational acceptance. Mrs. Swain, he noted, actively "used her influence and position to prejudice the delegates" against the new mission board. In her presidential address she chastised the fundamentalists and "reduced the controversy of the years over the great doctrines of the Christian faith to a disreputable level, [encouraging] thinking people to dismiss them as of no consequence."[21] (Mrs. Swain, for her part, treated her fundamentalist peers with cautious but bemused politeness. "The extreme conservatives are growing more and more difficult in their attempts to take over the convention," she confided to a friend in 1946. "They stoop to political connivings that make the Republicans and Democrats seem like angels of light.")[22]

Disagreements over the philosophy of foreign missions pitted women directly against fundamentalists. Most fundamentalists rejected the modernists' emphasis on social amelioration as a form of evangelism, a position that also placed them in conflict with most women's missionary organizations. Restricted from preaching the gospel, women's groups had learned to proclaim it primarily through education and health care. Maintaining a balance between these two concerns was difficult, however. In fact, a recent study of women's missionary groups seems to validate some of the fundamentalists' concerns. Patricia Hill has linked the decline of early twentieth-century women's missionary organizations to a secularization of their original mission. By the time fundamentalists raised objections to their role in foreign missions, women's groups had all but abandoned their initial emphasis on prayer and personal sacrifice and had adopted a more professionalized strategy of humanitarian outreach. In the early twentieth century they also began to embrace larger concerns of world peace and racial equality. But Baptist fundamentalists downplayed social service as a "popular vogue with the existing Mission Boards." The independent "faith" missions they went on to form emphasized verbal gospel proclamation to the near exclusion of wider social concerns.[23]

Women and Fundamentalist Doctrine

For their part, few women actively opposed the fundamentalist cause; leading Presbyterian and Baptist laywomen displayed a dismaying lack of interest in doctrinal controversy. Some observers suggested that squabbles between competing theologies simply did not interest women, who embraced more practical concerns. A female contributor to the *Presbyterian* belittled the debates over evolution and higher criticism as a waste of time, arguing that "a minister has a far more important mission, that of winning and saving souls. . . . If man's origin was in the mire and slime," she sighed, "many appear to be fast returning to it." From the liberal *Presbyterian Banner* came a similar lament from a female observer, calling for "less masculinity" and "more tolerance, spirituality and common sense."[24]

The lofty indifference exhibited by Montgomery and Swain typified the attitudes of many more Presbyterian and Baptist women. "The battle of Fundamentalism versus Liberalism might rage in the pulpits," Gladys Gilkey Calkins recalled in 1961, "and the Scopes trial make headlines in the newspapers, but these would not throw the women off course. There was too much that needed to be done."[25] Writing to Anna Canada Swain in 1943, a Wisconsin woman expressed frustration over the political naiveté of her local missionary group. Even though her organization included women with husbands "sympathetic with the Fundamentalist group," most women hoped to ignore what they saw as a remote constitutional issue. "They honestly believed that this would not divide our forces or hurt the work of the A.B.H.M.S.," she wrote. "I do not know how you can combat this belief that it is not divisive."[26] But even Baptist leaders seemed to share this apolitical attitude. In 1944 Alice Brimson, executive secretary of the Women's American Baptist Home Missionary Society, enraged fundamentalists with her offhand comment, widely reported, that "Baptist women are not interested in theology.... They want more real religion."[27]

Baptist fundamentalists could do little more than protest, however. In 1922 a critic of the Baptist Bible Union observed that not a single woman numbered among the 135 signers of its "Call and Manifesto." In 1924 the General Committee of Fundamentalists, a moderate group headed by J. C. Massee, listed 93 male members and only 7 women, 3 of whom were named with their husbands. The executive committee and all district chairmen were men.[28]

One possible exception to the drift of leading Baptist women away from fundamentalism was Lucy Waterbury Peabody, Montgomery's associate in the Woman's Baptist Foreign Missionary Society. In 1927 she led a group of conservative Baptists out of the denominational board to form the Association of Baptists for Evangelism in the Orient, an organization with clearly evangelistic goals.

But although Mrs. Peabody shared many of the fundamentalists' convictions on the inspiration of the Bible and the necessity of verbal evangelism, she did not join the rank and file of the fundamentalist movement. Her discontent with mainline Baptist missions grew primarily from her frustration with their enlarging bureaucracy. "Convictions are not popular nowadays," she wrote in 1928. "Our ideas are standardized."[29] Other sources suggest that some of the friction between Peabody and Baptist leaders was personal: one account describes her as "a wonderful mixture of the conservative churchwoman and the Bostonian grande dame."[30] But she also refused to accept higher criticism of the Bible because it undercut traditional arguments for women's role in foreign missions. "Women dare not let the Bible go," she warned, "nor any part of it. It makes the world safe for women and children."[31] Though Mrs. Peabody was willing to walk with fundamentalists in some enterprises, she was primarily concerned with maintaining women's role in world evangelization. "No one really yearns for a row, above all a denominational row," she confessed in 1926. "We are tired and busy; we are not convinced by the leadership of either side." Her sympathy for Baptist fundamentalists drew largely from her greater antipathy for an unresponsive liberal leadership.[32]

Guardians of Doctrine: Men and Fundamentalism

Leadership trends in independent fundamentalist organizations reflected the growing masculine dominance of fundamentalism. In 1930 the Independent Fundamental Churches in America explicitly eliminated women as voting members. The forerunner of the IFCA, the American Conference of Undenominational Churches, formed in 1924, had accepted female members, many of them as pastors or assistants to pastor-husbands. After 1930, however, according to one adherent, "they were almost a nonentity as far as formal activity was concerned."[33]

The World Christian Fundamentals Association (WCFA) had few women officers; even its committee on Sunday school literature was entirely male. The association also exhibited little interest in specifically feminine concerns. In 1931 the speakers for "women's day" were Daisy Wright, and two popular premillennial lecturers, Elizabeth Knauss speaking on "The Menace of Bolshevism" and Christabel Pankhurst on "The Lord's Return."[34]

Women assumed leadership in the WCFA by virtue of their philanthropic role. In 1928, Mrs. Carl Gray, wife of a Union Pacific president, ascended to the board of directors. A well-known Bible teacher, Mrs. Gray was later elected "Mother of the Year" by the Golden Rule Foundation.[35] In 1930 the WCFA formed a "woman's auxiliary," led by Mrs. Gray, Mrs. Wright, and Mrs. Lyman Stewart, wife of the wealthy oil magnate who had contributed thousands to the fundamentalist cause. In 1931 all three women ascended to the national board (of thirty-one men); in 1937, they were joined by Helen Gould Sheperd, the wealthy New York philanthropist.[36]

The controversies of the 1920s gradually discredited women in fundamentalist eyes. Many of the churchwomen fundamentalist men encountered seemed far too naive to recognize the damage they had caused or were too easily manipulated by unscrupulous liberals. Rising doubts about feminine nature appeared more frequently in fundamentalist literature after the 1920s, in accounts that emphasized their intellectual weakness and psychological vulnerability.

One example of this attitudinal shift is the changing treatment of women within a standard evangelical genre, books depicting their role in Bible history. No longer the pious examples of nineteenth-century hagiography, women emerged in two popularized accounts by Clarence Macartney and William Bell Riley as duplicitous and prone to evil. Macartney's women included only two types of females: passive and motherly, or shameless sinners. Riley's book, a collection of sermons preached during his years at First Baptist Church in Minneapolis, highlighted Eve, Jezebel ("A Woman of Supreme Wickedness"), Bathsheba ("The Woman Who Tempted a King"), and Job's wife ("The Woman Who Nagged a Noble Husband").[37]

Fundamentalists afforded women enormous moral influence yet doubted their morality. To the Victorian myth of feminine virtue they added an ominous corollary. "Since woman is the determining factor in social life," Massee warned, she "must of necessity be religious or destroy the very society she creates." "Woman is always greater or worse than man," Macartney agreed, "she lifts him to the higher places, or brings him down to the depths."[38] Such fears were not unique to male fundamentalists. Even one female observer agreed that the modern women had lost their spiritual power; short skirts and cigarettes were sad indicators of "a pitiful emptiness of heart and soul life." By the end of the twenties, most fundamentalists agreed that women had thoroughly abandoned their responsibilities as the natural allies of religion.[39]

The Masculine Ideal

The practical consequences of this shift for women's role will be discussed more fully in subsequent chapters; equally important, however, were its implications for men. For as women became identified with theological shallowness, men assumed a new role as the defenders of orthodoxy. In the 1920s fundamentalist attacks on liberals assumed a new, self-consciously masculine tone, a tactic that proved itself, again and again, a valuable offensive weapon.

Fundamentalist evangelists had always been fond of masculine imagery and language; indeed, the connection between Christianity and virility was well established by the turn of the century. In the increasingly militant ethos of the 1920s, however, masculine imagery took on a more combative edge and a new purpose. For one thing, the tactic prodded liberals at a vulnerable point: their own worry that modernism might become a thin, effeminate faith, devoid of honest emotion or strong conviction. "Conservative critics are telling us that our modern theology, though intellectually clear, is emotionally weak," the *Christian Century* admitted ruefully. "Modern religion needs stronger, sane feelings—the convictions, sentiments and loyalties which give dynamic to ideals." A writer in the *Atlantic Monthly* challenged modernists to "find a way to say the word 'God' in a voice of conviction and command." Even Harry Emerson Fosdick admitted freely that "a fundamentalist minister who... is centrally interested in the inward life... will do more good than a modernist who, in desperately trying to be modern, forgets what religion is all about."[40]

The masculine defense of Christian orthodoxy also served to protect a vulnerability fundamentalist leaders shared with their liberal peers: they were clergymen. As such they all fought the popular stereotype that men of the cloth were neither male nor female. As one layman put it, "Life is a football game, with the men fighting it out on the gridiron, while the minister is up in the grandstand, explaining the game to the ladies."[41] As if the unflattering image of Elmer Gantry was not bad enough, fundamentalist clergy found themselves portrayed by the media as Torquemadas and Cotton Mathers, moral killjoys of the worst sort. O. F. Bartholomew, a Methodist pastor, decried the "subtle propaganda" of liquor interests and socialists in the endless depictions of his colleagues as "high-hatted, sharp-nosed, inquisitorial" parsons.[42]

Individual fundamentalist leaders fervently resisted such stereotypes, projecting an assertive masculinity that gloried in controversy. William Bell Riley's biographers emphasized his fondness for outdoor sports and rowdy humor. Presbyterian Mark Matthews, whose long hair and willowy build sometimes prompted critics to label him "effeminate," prized his reputation as the "pistol-packing parson" of Seattle. John Roach Straton, fighting his reputation as a "dandy," regularly walked the streets of New York's red light district. An admiring friend reverently described him as "absolutely fearless. He never cringed; he never wavered; he never compromised."[43]

The fundamentalist defense of the faith passed beyond the rhetoric of "muscular" Christianity to a defense of the cause itself as essentially masculine. "It is manly to follow Christ," a writer for the Baptist *Bible Champion* insisted, arguing that "the Bible is virile literature" and Christ himself "the most manly of men." "Christianity has no place for pusillanimity or churlishness," Presbyterian David Kennedy agreed. "It makes bigger, stronger men in every way." Baptist fundamentalists defended their leaders as "manly, full-blooded," and "vigorous"— not a "soft, gushy and mushy group of men" to "shed briny tears" over heretics.[44]

The antithesis of true manhood was the pampered liberal scholar, or as Arno Gaebelein described them, "little infidel preacherettes." Riley, in a sermon on "She-Men, or How Some Become Sissies," recalled the soft, mincing tones of a radio commentator. "I feel absolutely sure," he confided to his Minneapolis congregation, "that that chap was not only a Ph.D., but he was also a full-fledged apostle of Charles Darwin. . . . I have seen their sort," he bragged; "[I] have even faced them in controversy, and felt half ashamed to pit my masculinity against their effeminacy."[45]

Fundamentalist men were supreme individualists who disdained religious bureaucracy. "The rationalist loves centralization of power," David S. Kennedy wrote, "the evangelical calls no man lord, nor master, nor father, nor teacher." The quest for orthodoxy could in fact be a lonely one. Reminiscing about the battles of the 1920s, a Baptist recalled that "some of us older boys have had to stand almost alone. . . . We were, humanly speaking, hopelessly out-numbered. We suffered for lack of fellowship and encouragement. Had it not been for our hope in God that he would see us through regardless of the overwhelming forces against us, we should have given up."[46]

This posture had a definite romantic appeal. Elizabeth Knauss's novel *The Conflict* presented an idealized portrait of fundamentalist manhood, pitting a young, questing fundamentalist minister against sleazy denominational bureaucrats and jaded laywomen. In the story, Paul Hadley's efforts to keep himself doctrinally pure are nearly thwarted by the machinations of Alice Jordan, a humanitarian do-gooder. She is clearly under the influence of the effeminate Dr. Frahm, a liberal preacher who has surrounded himself with a coterie of admiring females. Before their plans fully hatch, the novel provides Hadley with a pious young church secretary as well as a stalwart young companion, and together these three leave their apostate denomination and chart an independent path in small, rural fundamentalist churches. In the novel, women are clearly auxiliary to Hadley's lonely quest for an orthodox life, or they oppose it by their thoughtless conformity to bureaucratic power. The deepest friendship the story allows is between Hadley and his ministerial friend, a relationship based on their mutual yearning for doctrinal truth.[47]

Fundamentalist men prized their personal independence, and in their emerging organizations they shied away from top-heavy leadership. Supporters of the Baptist Bible Union, formed in 1922, insisted that it was "not an instrument of an organized ecclesiastical power to be used for the coercion of [dissidents]. . . . Refusing ourselves to be coerced, we have no intention of attempting the coercion of others."[48] Its successor, the General Association of Regular Baptists (GARB), took quasi-denominational form with a minimum of "machinery." A council of fourteen delegates, chosen for one- and two-year terms by representatives of each local church, formed the sole governing body. (The constitution explicitly required these officers to be male, and "pastors or laymen of Fellowshipping churches.") In 1938 the GARB eliminated the office of president, to avoid the appearance of a "one man operation."[49]

The romantic strain in fundamentalist masculinity often tempered its hardheaded rationalism. Fundamentalist leaders insisted that their core belief was not premillennialism or inerrancy but the supernatural reality behind their convictions. The will to faith despite the odds proved one's spiritual virility. As Curtis Lee Laws put it, "The rationalists would emasculate Christianity by cutting out supernaturalism."[50] Fundamentalist spokesmen of the 1920s insisted on the reality of the spiritual world and decried the "arid rationalism" of liberal scholarship. One writer described modernism as "the absence of that beautiful thing which we call reverence."[51] "There is something in the very atmosphere of the liberal group that chills the sensitive emotions of the soul," another agreed. And still another Presbyterian writer warned that "the soul that follows liberal modernism must perish from want of the water of life. It must dry up, scale off, and blow away."[52]

Fundamentalist men told of emotional encounters with the miraculous and insisted on the necessity of personal experience for true conversion. Laws described the power of the Christian life as simply "too deep for analysis," likening it to a "swelling vitality like that of the springtime when the tides of life run at the full." Frank Eastburg, a Wheaton College professor and Harvard Ph.D. who testified to a miraculous healing from polio, wrote that "the Christian religion is addressed not so much to the logical mind as it is to the deeper level of thought which is figuratively referred to as the heart." Even stalwart John Roach Straton wrote movingly of his twelve-year-old daughter's death from spinal meningitis in an article printed by the *Progressive Thinker*, a spiritualist periodical. At the moment of her death, Straton recalled, "her eyes, always blue-gray before, were wells of unfathomable amber light, into which I gazed fascinated. They were glowing like gold."[53]

Fundamentalist biblicism, however, prevailed against any slide into irrational religion. J. Gresham Machen in particular warned of using religious experience as a means of receiving theological truth. "If I could lead you...to turn away from Christian experience and back to God's word," he wrote to one seeker, "I should have performed for you a far greater service than if I attempted to do, in form, what you asked. There can be no true Christian experience that is not rooted in the facts about our Lord that are set forth in the Holy Scriptures." Fundamentalists clearly followed the evangelical Protestant tradition of employing self-evident "common sense" readings of Scripture to articulate propositional truths about the divine. Thus William Pettingill asserted that unbelief itself was irrational and "unscientific," and faith "above and beyond reason" but "not unreasonable."[54]

Fundamentalist manhood also emphatically rejected all forms of psychological coddling. "Wherever men and women are seeking pleasure and self-indulgence (euphemistically called 'self-development' and 'living one's own life')," Frank Gaebelein wrote scornfully, "Christ is being rejected." A Baptist writer ridiculed modern needs for "self-realization" as "a watchword for modernism. Man does not need 'creative life,' " he scoffed, "he needs 'eternal life.' "[55]

Fundamentalists and Femininity

Against this quest for personal self-control stood society's most potent symbol of unrestrained self-expression, the receding hemlines of the "French-heeled, kangaroo-shaped, fresco-faced, frizzle-headed flapper."[56] The social liberation of women posed immense difficulties for fundamentalist manhood. John Roach Straton complained that "for the sake of being considered 'smart,' " modern women gave men free reign to "surrender to their lower passions, and drift into sin." "We have heard much of the emancipation of the female part of the race," Arno Gaebelein noted dolefully in 1921, "it forebodes nothing but evil."[57]

One of the most visible symbols of moral decay in the 1920s was the female cigarette smoker. Fundamentalists shared the general dismay over the rising "cloud of feminine smoke" in the postwar years. Like many they saw it as a symbol of moral license and decay. "Feminine cigarette smoking is an unbeautiful aftermath of the World War," a Baptist fundamentalist complained, "invented by the devil, capitalized by the Tobacco Trust, and bill-boarded only by the theater." J. C. Massee agreed: "Smoking is symptomatic of the smoker's attitude to life. It is a definite claim to liberty that is often interpreted, and frequently accepted as license."[58]

For fundamentalists, however, it was also a telltale sign of modernist theology. One article on British churchwoman Maude Royden described her triumphantly as both a "cigarette smoker and theological liberal."[59] J. C. Massee further warned that cigarettes themselves weakened moral resolve, as "impure blood is carried by the veins and arteries into the heart, [and] goes into the brain, debases the judgment, inflames the imagination, [and] arouses unholy desires. . . . Somehow I cannot visualize American society in which women promiscuously smoke, with all that it implies."[60] Smoking, like bobbed hair, lipstick, and short skirts, were fads that true Christian women should avoid. "Does the Word of God call Christian women to a sedate and sober life," a Colorado Baptist demanded, "or to a career of worldliness? Does God desire His followers to be a horde of tomboys?"[61]

Women's dress was another source of alarm. Here fundamentalists charged even well-meaning Christian women with sexual weakness and alarming naiveté. "If the professing Christian women in the churches had done their full duty and had not surrendered to Satan," wrote one scandalized critic, "there would have been firms manufacturing the kinds of dresses, etc., that they needed." As one minister charged, "Many men are made to commit sin in their hearts by the unclothed bodies of women who may be professed Christians and ignorant of the evil they are doing in causing a brother to stumble and become weak."[62] "The young man who is trying his utmost to keep himself clean," another commentator complained, ". . . has trouble enough without his sisters throwing a monkey wrench into his moral machinery." The warning was clear: "Every man has a quantity of dynamite, or its equivalent, in him. The matches have, as a rule, been in the hands of the world's womanhood."[63]

Sensitive to such concerns, schools like Moody Bible Institute issued careful measures to insure modesty among female students. Before they even set foot on Moody's campus, young women received a detailed description of dress codes from the superintendent of women, followed by regular warnings and discussions. Initial failure to comply with the rules rendered students liable to discipline and continued failure to dismissal. Follow-up measures were still necessary, however; well into the 1940s Moody Bible Institute students ate in separate dining rooms and studied in sex-segregated classrooms.[64]

In the end, however, fundamentalists emphasized masculine self-control as the only reliable way to avoid evil. Thus work itself became, for some fundamentalist leaders, a nearly monastic endeavor. While the average American work week declined and leisure time increased, fundamentalists rarely rested. Boston preacher A. Z. Conrad assured the pulpit committee at Park Street Church that his physical problems were of no consequence: "If I had been content to do two mens [sic] work instead of three or four I would have probably have stood it ten years longer before having to rest," he wrote, with more than a hint of bravado.[65] Riley worked sixteen-hour days until bronchitis forced him to cut back to eight. Mark Matthews worked twelve to sixteen hours a day, seven days a week. Straton, according to one eulogist, never took vacations and "worked incessantly." J. C. Massee could not be induced to take up any recreation until late in life.[66]

Fundamentalist leaders appeared to take the divine curse that doomed men to toil and sweat with utter seriousness. Moody Bible Institute president Will H. Houghton, who suffered from recurrent migraines and literally died from a headache in 1945, urged an audience at Toccoa Falls Bible Institute to "work, work, work!" His own six-day work week stretched from six in the morning till midnight. William Ward Ayer, Straton's successor at New York's Calvary Baptist Church, boasted of a schedule that included four Sunday messages, staff and committee meetings, a radio ministry, and voluminous correspondence. Even on Saturdays he toiled alone in his office until nearly midnight.[67]

Marriage distracted men from higher things, Presbyterian bachelor Clarence Macartney declared. "Far better to take the journey solitary and alone than to take it with one who would lead you from the path. . . . In the heat of ardent and mutual affection, there is always the risk that moral principles and convictions be melted and dissolved." Evangelist R. A. Torrey's son also recalled the "tender but matter of fact love" his parents shared. The two agreed that Torrey's work would always take preeminence and "home life must be strictly limited."[68]

Here fundamentalist ideals clashed openly with changing cultural ideals of marriage as secular advice columnists urged young wives to be their husbands' romantic friends and intellectual companions. Marriage should in some way duplicate the free and easy comradery of the co-ed college campus, they believed, not any artificial set of rules. Such advice reflected the early-twentieth-century reorientation of masculine roles, deemphasis on masculine individualism, and accent on "easy virility, domestic comfort, and constantly expanding consumption" as true indicators of manliness.[69]

Fundamentalists, however, preferred to keep women at a distance. They did not simply rail against the excesses of their age; their lives exemplified an approach to love and marriage that departed decisively from the popular standard. Fundamentalist men sought to sustain their masculinity through the individualistic, solitary pursuit of truth; cooperation with women necessarily entailed dangerous compromise.

Yet avoiding women entirely was certainly impossible. Women still performed valuable services in evangelism, foreign missions, and ministerial support. They contributed financially to fundamentalist causes, and, especially during times of war, were the majority of Bible school students. While Presbyterian conservatives could openly risk offending the women of their denomination, independent fundamentalists depended upon their willing support.

Fundamentalist attitudes toward women thus combined a measure of scorn with a distinct sense of longing and regret—a view that parallels fundamentalist opinion on the Jewish role in salvation history. Premillennialists believed that the nation of Israel, as God's first chosen people, occupied a special place in his program of salvation. Indeed, their reading of biblical prophecy necessitated a Jewish return to Palestine and conversion to Christianity before Christ could return. Yet premillennialists knew that the Bible also recorded the continued disobedience of Israel and its ultimate rebellion against God's plan, bleakly symbolized in the crucifixion of Christ. Thus, although many fundamentalists actively proselytized Jewish converts and were ardent Zionists, the movement also demonstrated a clear anti-Semitic strain. William Bell Riley's fervent denunciations of Jewish apostasy, even during Hitler's persecution of Jews in World War II, is perhaps the most ringing example of the persistent doubts fundamentalists entertained about God's chosen people.[70]

Fundamentalist ambivalence about women also mirrored their stance toward American culture itself. The movement was willing to deny the world only to a point; though fundamentalists believed that the world was inherently evil and urged separation, they still regretted their loss of cultural ascendancy. As George Marsden has argued, American society represented both apostate Babylon and the heavenly Jerusalem. And, as he explains, the movement's "fortress mentality" of the 1930s and 1940s was one way to deal with the pain of separation and to develop a new "basis for solidarity" in a hostile world.[71] The masculine image of a fortress is an appropriate one. In the new institutions fundamentalists created, women might be supporters, but they could never be rivals. Their support for fundamentalism always imposed a cost that, in time, the movement's leaders would find impossible to bear.

Chapter Four

Gender and Vocation in Fundamentalist Institutions

Although the fundamentalist movement disappeared from the public eye after 1930, its adherents were busier than ever. In the air of millennial expectancy that grew under the approaching shadow of World War II, they embraced any and all modern technologies that aided their evangelistic outreach. Thus, while mainstream denominations complained of a religious "depression" after 1930, fundamentalists were hard at work constructing a complex infrastructure of independent churches, publishing companies, and electronic communications.[1]

Fundamentalism had always demanded a lifelong commitment to work from all believers, male and female. "God has no place in His plan for Christians who are looking for an easy job," the *Pilot* reminded its readers in 1921, "any more than an employer has for a man looking for a snap." A young woman agreed: "Are we to sit back and relax and say, 'Thanks, Lord, for salvation. Now I'll just take it easy[?]' God forbid! We are to serve to the uttermost of our ability . . . as long as life shall last."[2]

Work, of course, was synonymous with verbal evangelism. "It is God's will," a Moody Bible Institute instructor declared, "that every Christian should assume the obligation to evangelize the whole world." Some fundamentalists in fact denied that secular vocations had any intrinsic merit. "The real business of Christians is to win people to God," Bob Jones declared in 1940. "Practicing law is what you do to get something to eat while you work with God."[3]

Behind the institutional expansion of the 1930s and 1940s a delicate process was taking place: fundamentalists were slowly sorting out the practical implications of their views on gender. This meant assigning gender categories to the new religious vocations their entrepreneurial vision was constantly creating, a process that raised new and difficult questions. How might women contribute but still retain their submissive role? How would men exercise their newly achieved religious leadership? The answers did not always come easily.

Women's role was a knotty question, but in fact fundamentalist attitudes toward vocation posed equally if not more difficult problems for men. As one female commentator noted in 1930, parents who gladly gave their daughters for Christian service still hoped to reserve their sons for careers in medicine and law. It was still harder to convince promising young men that lower-paying, less prestigious occupations in missions and evangelism were worth their higher sacrifice, she complained. When all else failed, appealing to masculine pride was still a useful tactic. "Anybody with brains can be a professional man," she argued. "But one must have brains, brawn, heart, and sand to be a servant of God. He must be a real man, a God-directed man."[4]

But such appeals masked a real problem. In a sense, fundamentalist culture actually narrowed the range of career possibilities for young men. The evangelistic ministry remained the highest masculine calling, even though that career had clearly declined in social status since the days of Dwight L. Moody. Fundamentalists endorsed other areas of masculine achievement, especially the work of the "Christian businessman," but encountered difficulties here as well. The evangelist's role, by its very nature, demanded a much higher degree of cultural separatism than that of the businessman. Competition between the two was nearly unavoidable.

As they developed in the 1930s, feminine vocations encompassed a far broader range of possibilities. Institutional Protestantism already offered a variety of female occupations, from religious education to various forms of social work; the evangelistic ethos of fundamentalism expanded these still further. In 1948, an article in *HIS* magazine, directed to female college students, filled half a page describing the "crying need for trained stenographers, typists, bookkeepers, accountants, receptionists, and file clerks." Christian publishers needed artists, writers, proofreaders, and editors; Christian camps needed teachers, directors, counselors, and cooks; churches needed pastoral assistants, secretaries, youth directors, and music directors. This was above and beyond the constant call for missionaries and field workers in specialized organizations, such as Inter-Varsity, Young Life, Pioneer Girls, and Child Evangelism. "And notice," the author enthused, "that it is not the dull, routine jobs that so often go unfilled, but the interesting administrative positions that call for initiative, resourcefulness, and keenness of judgment." Thus through the 1940s, fundamentalist women shared, and even surpassed, the national trend toward female employment after World War I. Though economic depression and war brought millions of American women into the work force in the mid-twentieth century, the perception persisted that women worked for "pin money," and not out of economic necessity.[5]

The expansion of women's roles in fundamentalism also contrasted with their increasingly marginalized position in other Protestant institutions. As "subordinated insiders" in the major denominations, women filled a variety of supportive posts, often as deaconesses or religious educators. But female church employees were too often underpaid, inadequately trained, and denied professional recognition; churches were hard-pressed to retain their women workers when secular opportunities beckoned.[6]

Fundamentalists, however, assured young women that their work was deeply necessary. A book describing "God's Ideal Woman," written in 1941, declared that "every girl should . . . be self-supporting." The author, president of a Kansas City Bible college, discouraged young women from marrying too soon, especially if it meant choosing a non-Christian. The worst thing, he warned, was to be a "silly girl," frivolous, selfish, and "without worthy ambitions."[7] Even John R. Rice, one of the most conservative expositors of women's role, discouraged his daughter Grace Jean from marrying a banker, since, as he said, she had been educated for "full-time Christian service," not to be a banker's wife. Grace had a bachelor's degree from Wheaton College and a graduate degree in music from Bob Jones University, and worked alongside her evangelist father. Fortunately for the young couple, Grace's suitor subsequently discovered a call to the ministry, and they married soon after he completed his studies at Bob Jones University.[8]

The highest female career, that of Bible teacher, reflected the fundamentalist emphasis on public speaking as a sign of leadership and seemed, at least initially, not to contradict rules against women teachers. This role offered women a very different voice than the one it demanded of men. It was nonauthoritative and private, for the female teacher derived her authority from the book she expounded and spoke to the inner circle of fundamentalist believers, not to the skeptical public. Her words were nonjudgmental and often couched in intimate terms. Through this means, women maintained a voice in fundamentalism. Though often difficult to discern, it provided a necessary counterpoint to its public masculine language of confrontation and command.

But problems remained. By the end of the 1940s, the growing visibility and popularity of female Bible teachers, missionaries, and educators had passed beyond acceptable levels—women seemed again poised to feminize fundamentalism, as they had dominated evangelical Protestantism fifty years before. Many of these vocations, therefore, did not survive the sharply conservative swing of fundamentalist teaching during the postwar era.

Defining the Masculine Vocation

In the early twentieth century, ministerial vocations suffered under a general declining status, due in part to their connection with a predominantly female constituency. In their study of "Middletown," Robert and Helen Lynd observed ministers "eagerly lingering about the fringes of things trying to get a chance to talk to the men of the city who are in turn diffident about talking frankly to them."[9]

Fundamentalist clergy suffered acutely under this disability in addition to the social ostracism they experienced in the 1920s. "Ministers in some circles are looked upon as a group of weaklings," one clergyman complained in 1937. "In the mind of some unjust critics they think a minister could not succeed in any other line of work."[10]

In the decades after 1930, fundamentalism did not so much actively limit women's role as it tried to propel men forward. The movement took pains to emphasize the special masculine challenges of the pastor's job and denied that Christianity was in any way "womanish." "The very fact that preaching the gospel is tough, trying work . . . ought to challenge us to tackle it," a writer in *Moody Monthly* challenged. "Since when are we such panty-waists that we must run from a responsibility because it is hard?"[11] A Baptist minister, who as a college football player had scorned the campus seminary students with their "black, shiny suits and shell rim glasses," finally became converted when he met "genuine Christians" who spoke to him in "an aggressive, masculine manner." "The need for fearless, powerful, well-spined Christians," he declared in 1945, "is greater today than at any other period in the history of the Church." "A sissy cannot be much good as a preacher," John R. Rice agreed. "It does not take muscle, but it surely takes courage."[12]

The ideal fundamentalist minister was vigorous and energetic, following the masculine model of the evangelist rather than the feminized one of the church pastor. Evangelists were to exhibit gifts both spiritual and physical. A Baptist periodical described evangelist Harry Ketcham as one who "packs a punch" for the Lord. "From the moment he starts till the end of the message, there isn't a moment's let up; he hits the devil with both fists, then jumps on him with both feet."[13] John R. Rice often credited his football career at Decatur Baptist Junior College as essential to his ministerial preparation. "Some preachers are such sissies," he declared, "that I wish they could have played a few years of football so they would not be so afraid of hurting somebody's feelings."[14] In a similar vein, Presbyterian Mark Matthews called for "preachers who spurn pink teas and seek the fields where sin-sick men are dying." The "supreme need of the church," he declared, was to ordain "preachers who are too busy seeking lost souls to chase elusive golf balls." M. E. Dodd likewise excoriated "lolling, lounging couch lizard" preachers and praised men who would "work early and late, long and hard," willing to "put out their last ounce of physical, intellectual and spiritual strength for the sake of their church and the cause of Christ."[15]

The highest calling, therefore, was that of an evangelist. "One can be a modernist and be a pastor," Rice commented. "But one cannot be a modernist and be a real evangelist. For that reason there is an antipathy between modernists and evangelism, a fight to the very death." A pastor content to "teach" his congregation was a "backslider at ease in Zion, lukewarm, not willing to pay the awful price that it takes to be a real soulwinner."[16]

Within the masculine realm of evangelistic preaching, women were clearly subordinate. As William Bell Riley advised his fellow clergy, the image of the busy, engaged pastor could be further elevated by a female pastor's assistant, sometimes even referred to as "assistant pastors." The position had evolved from the work of deaconesses in the early twentieth century, who often aided pastors in urban evangelism while remaining under the authority of their denominational deaconess boards. Although pastoral assistants followed a similar line of tasks from visitation and Sunday school leadership to church administration, they were clearly subordinate to the senior pastor. "Effective men often have anywhere from two to twenty secretaries," Riley reasoned, "and in a big business even more. We know rather prominent pastors who are still compelled either to write their sermons and all their letters... with their own hand or on a typewriter. It is a species of white slavery for a pastor," his appeal concluded, "and prosperous laymen ought to be ashamed to impose this manuel [*sic*] work upon him."[17]

Pastors' wives also supplemented their husbands' careers, most often as informal leaders of women's groups. Theirs was a position with many responsibilities, but little power. As one woman reminded her sisters: "You will do well to set a good example in attendance, in promptness, and in reverence at God's house." Beyond that, however, the requirements were less clear. One sympathetic observer commented that the pastor's wife "must be capable of filling positions of leadership in the church, but woe be to her if she is too executive! She should be present at all the meetings of the church, lest she be thought indifferent. She must beware of interests outside the church, or run the risk of being considered worldly."[18]

Leading fundamentalist ministers avoided any image of public rivalry from their wives. Harold Ockenga, pastor of Boston's Park Street Church and leader in the neo-evangelical revival, housed his family in a suburban neighborhood, so that his wife could "occupy herself more with her family and less with the work of the church." He did "not look with favor on a pastor's wife holding office in any of the church organizations." William Bell Riley, whose first wife was a model of quiet feminine deportment, counseled young seminarians to "suppress your wife's ambition and quiet her tongue." "If you will take my advice," he enjoined, "you will seek the girl who would gladly serve Christ without official distinction."[19]

Fundamentalist ministers drew their spiritual authority from their pulpits. Fighting modern trends that made pastors little more than administrators or community organizers, fundamentalist churches emphasized the power of preaching. "Unless we chain ourselves to our pulpits," a Winona Bible Conference speaker advised his fellow clergy, "we will discover at the end of the way that we have spent our lives on things of secondary importance."[20]

Fundamentalist ministers allied themselves with lay businessmen. As a writer in the *King's Business* declared in 1923, the hope of revival centered in the "*men of the church*. They pay the bills; they have the controlling power; they have the right to *demand* that the old Gospel shall be given" and make "the ecclesiastical politicians . . . bow the knee."[21] The formal relationship dated back to Billy Sunday's crusades when businessmen's clubs formed in major cities to apply "business methods to their religious and evangelistic work." In the 1930s, Christian Business Men's Committees worked to mobilize lay support essential for revival. The movement propelled some prominent businessmen, including Robert LeTourneau, to leadership in the fundamentalist movement.[22] Laymen also formed the backbone of organization for Billy Graham's evangelistic crusades in the 1950s.[23]

Businessmen injected the language of capitalism into fundamentalist piety, as unsaved individuals were urged to "do business with God." In 1939 C. B. Hedstrom, a shoe salesman from Chicago and chair of the Christian Businessmen's Committee there, described God as a "partner who never knew of failure." "God's appointments dovetail, work together," Arnold Grunigen, a San Francisco businessman explained. "Keeping them is effective, big business, His business."[24] Lay leaders also urged ministers to present the gospel in terms that these men of the world could understand. "Preach the Word, convict of sin, present the Saviour," Grunigen urged, "and red-blooded men who read the papers and know the world is bruised, battered, and bewildered will accept Christ, one by one. If you don't, the laymen will run the life boats and you can run the hulk."[25]

Fundamentalism was pro-businessman more than pro-business. Premillennial denunciations of wealth and materialism were relatively common, especially during the Depression. But these were largely apolitical complaints, and fundamentalism never approved of New Deal "socialism" or the politics of Franklin Roosevelt, the man who had ended Prohibition in 1933. By the 1940s the movement more openly supported conservative politics, but backed off from any secular agenda that undercut its primarily spiritual concerns for the national welfare. Fundamentalist support of Christian businessmen endeavoring to live morally in an immoral, cutthroat world sometimes served as critiques of capitalist excess.[26]

But the role of the businessman in midcentury fundamentalism required far less personal and cultural strain than that of the evangelist. Inevitably, the more world-affirming goals and values of fundamentalist businessmen challenged the lonely masculine ethic of fundamentalist pastors. "I am having a good time serving the Lord," LeTourneau claimed in 1945. "I know I ought to be a better man and I am asking God to help me be better. But . . . I think many people get just enough religion to make them miserable and not enough to make them happy." Such benign self-confidence stood in marked contrast to the dour workaholism of the old-time evangelist. "Don't be content to go through a normal service like an old Russian priest," as one layman advised the clergy in 1937. "Go out and sell the Gospel as a salesman goes out to sell insurance, automobiles, or vacuum cleaners."[27]

Not surprisingly, fundamentalist preachers and evangelists met this advice with some defensiveness, as well as a measure of scorn for its "worldly" assumptions. Noting that "Jesus was crucified, not crowned," John R. Rice declared that "to be a Fundamentalist is to have the reproach of this old wicked world." Similarly, William Bell Riley excoriated the materialistic drive for success that kept able men from considering ministerial careers. "If the ministry is presented as a *profession* to be gauged by what it will pay a man in dollars and cents, of course men will not respond," Riley huffed, "and we are glad of it. . . . It was not money that made Peter and John preachers of the Gospel," he reminded. "It was real Christian manhood."[28]

The conflict between these two masculine types, minister and businessman, suggests some of the inherent difficulties fundamentalists encountered as they negotiated the thickets of twentieth-century secularism. The gregarious, manly ease of the Christian businessman blended far better with the more world-affirming goals of neo-evangelicalism than it did with strict fundamentalist separatism; indeed, the inherent conflict between these two types of masculinity is one manifestation of a growing fault line within fundamentalism that produced the neo-evangelical movement in the 1940s.

Despite the rising prestige of the Christian businessman, the role of evangelist and preacher still maintained its power throughout the World War II era. Fundamentalists always valued the spoken word. Their heroes were evangelists and pulpiteers, not humanitarians, speakers more than doers. Fundamentalists endorsed an ethic of service but reserved their greatest rewards for eloquent men, equating masculinity and power with a spellbinding platform presence and confrontational preaching style.[29]

The Search for Woman's Role

Women, however, were to avoid verbal confrontation. J. C. Massee, for example, found a contemporary lesson for all women in the story of Eve's conversation with the serpent. "The safe course," he believed, "is not to answer at all. The Devil may . . . present himself as a gentleman of culture, but whenever he speaks, raising the question of God's integrity or faithfulness or wisdom, . . . the wise woman will refrain from answering and straightway depart from his presence."[30]

While fundamentalist men were urged to be uncompromising, women were to retain the more "passive virtues" of sensitivity and tact. Men could denounce evil, but a Christian woman "must know of a heart-breaking hypocrisy, and never breathe it to a soul. She must see the frailties and failings of others," a young "Christian worker among women" explained, "without a word passing her lips." While male evangelists denounced sin, a female soul-winner was to "be careful to act modestly, not to call undue attention to herself, and not to offend good taste or get herself talked about."[31]

Still, fundamentalism never imposed a blanket silence on the women in its ranks; to do so would have been nearly impossible. The institutional growth of fundamentalism constantly blurred the lines around Pauline proscriptions which knew nothing of religious education curriculum or radio ministry. Most authorities agreed that as long as women remained submissive, their sphere was virtually unlimited. "Woman's field for labor is an extensive one," the *Pilot* declared, though "in no case must she fail to recognize and evince her subordination."[32]

When fundamentalist magazines fielded occasional inquiries about women's proper place they usually appealed to I Timothy 2:11–15. In this passage the apostle Paul barred women from teaching doctrine because they were by nature unreliable. Harking back to Eve's transgression, he declared that "it was the woman who was deceived and became a sinner."

But even the Bible left ample room for honest confusion; Paul himself had kind words for the women who assisted in his missionary travels. Perplexity over this biblical ambiguity was particularly evident in Bible institutes, which had already trained a generation of female evangelists. In 1923 *Moody Bible Institute Monthly* responded to charges of inconsistency for the school's laxity in allowing women to teach, despite its allegiance to biblical authority. In response, the editor admitted that "we take Paul's words literally, but we are not clear as to the application of them under all conditions and in every case." Perhaps William Bell Riley was closest to honesty when he simply shrugged and concluded that, as far as female pastors were concerned, "it will be forever a debatable question as to whether this choice of a profession by women can be Biblically defended."[33]

Most fundamentalists seemed to agree, however, that they would know a rebellious woman when they came across one. The profile nearly always included some form of public display. Arno C. Gaebelein registered open scorn for the "nauseating forwardness and audacity" of Aimee Semple McPherson, described by an even less charitable critic as a "pulchritudinous pinnacle of pseudo-Pentecostalism."[34] Their objections were based less on scriptural grounds than on their obvious distaste for her pentecostal doctrine and Hollywood demeanor. Mary Baker Eddy was another case in point. "Christian Science exists because a woman did not keep silence," I. M. Haldeman charged, warning that just as "the Devil fooled the world through the first woman, he is now trying to fool the world through another woman." "Whenever a woman has headed an authoritative preaching movement," Harold Ockenga agreed, "heresy has crept in."[35]

Of course, the fundamentalist movement had always had its female evangelists, and their defenders. Although most of these women were less visible after 1930, they did not disappear. In 1942 the membership list of the Interdenominational Association of Evangelists included forty-two women, roughly 25 percent of the total, and listed Helen Sunday on its board of directors.[36]

Still, their voice was not authoritative. During the 1920s, the most widely known female evangelist in fundamentalist circles was a preadolescent girl, Uldine Utley. In 1926 John Roach Straton published a lengthy defense for her ministry based in part on her "modest and humble" demeanor. "For myself," Straton argued, "I will say that I do not think there is a man upon this planet who abhors more deeply than I do the brazen, pushing, unspiritual, self-assertive type of so-called 'modern woman.'" Uldine was clearly an exception. Straton not only publicly sponsored Utley's career but regarded "this precious little child" with fatherly affection. Not surprisingly, Utley's career halted soon after she passed adolescence.[37]

The real limit of women's role was their status as the weaker vessel. "Women preachers have given the world the impression that Christians are emotionally unstable, that preaching is a racket," John R. Rice complained in 1941. "You can be sure that the kind of Christianity that produces Aimee Semple McPherson does not at the same time produce Spurgeons, Finneys, Moodys, Torreys and Chapmans."[38] Though women's activity in foreign missions and religious education constantly belied that weakness, the fundamentalists' experience of feminine disloyalty in the 1920s would not allow the conviction to fade.

Finding a voice was difficult for fundamentalist women, but not impossible. Many women on evangelistic platforms were vocal soloists, following the popular tradition set by hymn-writer and vocalist Ira Sankey in the Moody crusades. In Billy Sunday's entourage, six of his fifteen female associates were musicians, some, like Virginia Asher, nationally known for their musical ability. Women also traveled with their evangelist husbands, supplementing the preached word with a "message in song."

Female novelists and biographers also enjoyed wide popularity in fundamentalist and neo-evangelical circles. Grace Livingston Hill's sentimental novels of "love and faith" earned her a loyal female following. At her death the Bible Institute of Pennsylvania instituted a memorial fund for a Grace Livingston Hill Memorial Library. Women authors also predominated as narrators of conversion epics. Writers like Catharine Marshall, Elisabeth Elliot and Eugenia Price acquired celebrity status for their moving accounts of personal crisis. The popularity of female authors in this genre is not accidental. In conversion narratives, "women use *God's* language, not their own," Virginia Brereton writes. "To the degree that the traditional rhetoric is somehow uniquely 'feminine' in its orientation—in its frequent allusion to submission, surrender, yielding, self-sacrifice, and to converts as brides of Christ—it protects evangelical women narrators from the inroads of male sports and business language. Conversion rhetoric . . . helps women insofar as it retains a beauty, a rhythm, and perhaps most important, a safe distance from humdrum reality."[39]

For women, to speak authoritatively meant deriving power from an unimpeachable source. In 1927 a Christian and Missionary Alliance female evangelist recounted her wrenching encounter with I Timothy 2:11–15. After tears and soul-searching, she finally "knew a strong selfwill and a reluctance to die to public speaking . . . were being assailed by these words. I at last yielded the dearest thing in life, the only channel of communication to a lost world and the bride of Christ—a voice to speak his message." On the other side of silence, however, she found a new, more powerful language as "God's mouthpiece." Once she had "died to self," the Holy Spirit spoke more clearly through her nonrational mind. "The closer you live to God the more you will be used to give pure prophecy," she observed, "unmixed with your own conclusions."[40]

More often, however, the Bible was the true source of authority. Ironically, the book that silenced fundamentalist women also provided the basis of their quasi-public role as Bible teachers. Many women's occupations in fundamentalist institutions, especially those associated with leadership, involved some form of biblical exposition. Though extemporaneous speaking, lecturing, and public preaching remained a closely guarded male preserve, women could assume the softer tones of instruction and guidance.

Activities loosely described as "personal work" and Bible study formed the basis of a large, informal network of fundamentalist women. The Bible Institute of Los Angeles (BIOLA) owed its existence and continued vitality to the women who organized and led young women's "Euodia Clubs" in the Los Angeles area. The clubs originated in the work of Isabel Horton, a popular Bible teacher, who in 1910 led a canvass of the city with eight female volunteers. Each women was assigned a district where she conducted visitation and led Bible classes. By 1930 Horton had helped establish forty-three Euodia clubs, taught by eight full-time "Bible women" and ten volunteers.[41] Under the leadership of Mrs. Lyman Stewart, women at BIOLA remained highly visible. In March 1937 BIOLA's Bible women reported 458 classes held, with a total attendance of 9,945, despite a week's holiday for the Easter season. The results were equally impressive: 100 conversions, 19 backsliders returned to the fold, and 38 lives "surrendered to the Lord."[42]

Networks developed in churches as well as Bible schools. The female members of First Presbyterian Church of Hollywood, California, were divided into twelve "parishes," each under the care of a woman Bible teacher. Classes met weekly, attended by over 200 students, as teachers conducted a "verse by verse" study of a book of the Bible. Carrie Roper, a Moody graduate and pastor's wife at the Scofield Memorial Church in Dallas, began holding Bible classes in 1928 which were so successful that the church eventually added Roberta Townsend to its permanent staff, just to run the expanding neighborhood program. Mrs. Roper continued to train the teaching staff, composed of both men and women, even as the outreach grew to more than 150 local classes by the mid-1950s.[43]

Another Bible teacher, Virginia Asher, created a formal organization for women, the Virginia Asher Businesswomen's Council, in 1922 in Winona Lake, Indiana. Mrs. Asher led the women's meetings in Billy Sunday's crusades and gained a national reputation as a powerful and emotional Bible teacher, with a special appeal to young women. One observer recalled with evident pleasure a meeting in Atlanta where "there wasn't a man in sight, except the janitor." Women ushers passed the offering plates, as Florence Kinney and Grace Saxe, also Sunday associates and Bible teachers, addressed the crowd of over 500.[44] Mrs. Asher also hosted hundreds of young women at meetings of the Winona Lake Bible Conferences, and her conviction grew that "businesswomen," largely shop girls and clerical workers, needed her motherly attention.[45]

The Virginia Asher Businesswomen's Councils addressed the emotional needs of working women; they were not by any means professional organizations. Emphasizing "friendliness, helpfulness, and responsibility," the organization's main purpose was to promote Bible study and "personal loyalty to Jesus Christ." Mrs. Asher discouraged "the study of other literature or planned programs of a different type."[46]

Besides the nationally based Virginia Asher Businesswomen's Councils, local organizations also drew together lonely single women in the business world. In Boston, Alice Theobald began a Business Women's Council in the wake of Billy Sunday's highly successful crusade in 1916. The group met monthly for prayer and fellowship, featuring inspirational speakers such as Robert Glover, director of the China Inland Mission, and Donald Grey Barnhouse. Like the Virginia Asher groups, the council's aim was social and evangelistic, rather than professional. In 1949, the council sponsored a citywide meeting, addressed by Helen Duff Baugh, chair of the National Christian Business and Professional Women of America, who promoted the "dinner meeting ministry" as a means of reaching unsaved friends.[47]

One testimony to the power of these female networks was their relative immunity, at least through the early 1940s, to charges of "usurping authority." In 1939 the American Bible Society honored Inez Johnson Woodall for fifty-seven years of Bible teaching, thirteen of them leading the adult Bible class of the Jackson Heights Community Church in Long Island. A report in the *Pilot* praised the class, with 150 members of both sexes, as a "tower of strength to the church" and a "marked influence in the community." Mrs. Carl Gray, who sat on the national board of the World

Christian Fundamentals Association, taught a Bible class of 300 students at the First Baptist Church in Omaha, as well as a class of more than 3,000 in Kansas City. Another woman, Mrs. W. F. Barnum, led a nationally popular Sunday school class over the radio, as well as several weekly classes in local churches. Chosen for her "singularly clear voice," Mrs. Barnum also taught fundamentalist doctrine. Her listeners could read the weekly installment of International Uniform Sunday-school lesson, and tune in to her commentary "as a safeguard against... unsound literature."[48]

The growing popularity of "inductive Bible study" among conservative Protestants also owed much to female Bible teachers. The method, which originated in the Biblical Seminary of New York under Wilbert W. White, drew from the educational philosophy of John Dewey and William Rainey Harper, White's teacher. In this method students and teacher analyzed a text without notes or commentaries. Together they examined a biblical passage, asked questions of it, and applied it to a practical problem. Rebecca Price, a Biblical Seminary graduate, brought the method to Wheaton College in the 1930s.[49] Jane Hollingsworth, a graduate of both Wheaton and Biblical Seminary, established inductive Bible studies in the work of Inter-Varsity Christian Fellowship, a national evangelistic organization for college students, during the 1940s.[50] Many observers agreed that this pupil-oriented method allowed women to lead Bible studies without undue exercise of intellectual authority.

Bible teaching formed the basis for feminine networks and leadership as well as careers for women in fundamentalist circles. The clustering of fundamentalist women in religious education is not surprising, given women's longstanding leadership in that field. Since the late nineteenth century, prominent women wrote and edited curricula for children as well as adults and organized training institutes and teachers' organizations. By the turn of the century, religious education was a lynchpin in the expanding network of "women's work." Indeed, many of the women who became leaders in foreign missions and temperance, including Frances Willard herself, began their careers with training in a Sunday school "normal institute." Throughout the twentieth century religious education remained one area that women in all the major denominations could safely dominate.[51]

The fundamentalist movement's emphasis on religious education allowed some women to ascend to top leadership positions. The most famous religious educator, and perhaps the best-known woman, in fundamentalist and evangelical circles, was Henrietta Mears. A graduate of the University of Minnesota in 1913, she began her career in religious education teaching an overwhelmingly popular girls' Sunday school class in William Bell Riley's First Baptist Church in Minneapolis. Mears taught briefly at Northwestern in 1921 but was far too energetic to fall easily within Riley's shadow. In 1928 she and her sister Margaret left for California, where Henrietta became the director of education in Hollywood's First Presbyterian Church. Within two and a half years the Sunday school grew from 450 students to 4,200. In 1933 she began Gospel Light Publications to distribute the Sunday school curriculum she herself authored. The enterprise grew so rapidly that by the mid-1950s it had become one of the largest distributors of Sunday school literature among conservative churches.[52]

Two other single women, Lois and Mary LeBar, also contributed to the "renaissance" in conservative Christian education during the 1930s. At Wheaton College in Illinois, they maintained a Christian education program that attracted nearly 1,000 students during their thirty-year tenure. As students of Rebecca Price, who was hired in 1936 as Wheaton's first professor of Christian education, the sisters also pioneered in educational theory, arguing for a more "child-centered" curriculum. Rather than present biblical facts from a podium, they emphasized the necessity of shaping the lesson plan to the needs and interests of the individual student. The sisters published widely in Scripture Press, another conservative publishing enterprise, and led in the formation of the National Sunday School Association.[53]

Even married women pursued active careers. The personal histories recorded in a 1983 reunion of Northwestern Bible College's class of 1933 include many accounts of marital partnerships. Burchard Ham, for example, included his late wife Eva in his resume "because we were a team" and added a special page of tribute to her work as "one of the pioneers of Daily Vacation Bible School in northern Minnesota." Eleanor Hansen Burgess, the first woman to earn a Th.B. from Northwestern Seminary, which Riley formed in 1935, married in 1939 and together with her husband earned a B.A. and M.A. from Hardin-Simmons University in Abilene, Texas. While he pastored, both went on to teach at Hardin-Simmons and to lead extension Bible classes for Black pastors and their wives. In 1947 both also earned M.R.E. degrees at Southwestern Baptist Seminary in Fort Worth, and she continued to teach high school English for the next nineteen years, while raising three children. Burgess reflected with pride that God had given her "a husband with life-goals similar to my own."[54]

Fundamentalism also offered numerous opportunities for entrepreneurial single women. Many of them used existing institutional networks, or created their own, to support their emerging careers. In the 1930s Elizabeth Evans, a 1922 graduate of Wheaton College, helped found the New England Fellowship (NEF), a renewal organization committed to filling rural pulpits with "Bible-believing" ministers. Under J. Elwin Wright the NEF became the nucleus of the National Association of Evangelicals, whose formation in 1942 marked the emergence of the neo-evangelical movement.

Evans began her work with NEF opening churches in rural Vermont, where she and her mother conducted preaching services. In 1937 she began to sponsor vacation Bible schools and release time classes for rural schoolchildren. Under her leadership, teams of young women traversed the muddy backroads of Vermont and New Hampshire, often filling local pulpits. From a beginning group of twelve volunteers, the ministry grew to seventy-seven workers. Evans also wrote "Bible-based" curriculum, which she taught at all the major fundamentalist schools in New England—Gordon College, Providence Bible Institute, and the New England School of Theology. When asked, in later life, if she found her sex a hindrance, Evans simply laughed. "I didn't see that it did," she told her interviewer. "They needed every one, you know."[55]

Vacation Bible schools were a natural outlet for women with relatively minimal training. The program was developed for unchurched children, often from rural areas without a strong church presence. Alumni notes from Bible institutes show a preponderance of women graduates in vacation Bible school work, often as part of a team effort with young men, who concentrated on pulpit work.[56]

Single women also dominated on the foreign mission field. While the 1920s brought the demise of many independent women's groups in the mainline denominations, in fundamentalist-oriented "faith" missions feminine energy continued unabated. At the meeting of the World's Christian Fundamentals Association in 1930, a ceremony honoring missionaries brought thirty-two women to the platform (twenty-six of them single), visually overshadowing the ten men alongside them (only five of them unmarried). When the China Inland Mission called for two hundred volunteers in 1929, 70 percent of those who left for China the following year were women, and all but four were single. By the late 1940s, the General Association of Regular Baptists, easily the most conservative of all Baptist groups, listed more women missionaries than ordained clergymen. In 1948 the denomination reported 297 ministers and 393 women missionaries, 245 of whom were single.[57]

But women's dominance on the mission field did not extend to the sending organizations. Men staffed the home office of nearly all the new faith missions.[58] When women formed separate societies, they filled a limited, clearly auxiliary role. In fundamentalist churches, pastors discouraged women's missionary societies from exercising too much independence. William Bell Riley found them both "potent and problematical" and urged younger pastors to woo them carefully.[59] At Toronto's Jarvis Street Baptist Church, T. T. Shields attempted to forcibly merge the women's missionary society with the Union of Regular Baptist Churches. When the president, Mrs. J. C. Holman, objected, Shields accused her of "petticoat rule" and expelled her from the church.[60]

The Response to Feminization

Women's overrepresentation on the mission field inspired some jealousies and rising frustration among fundamentalist men, for that career perhaps came closest to usurping masculine prerogatives for verbal proclamation. Zoe Anne Alford, a missionary teacher at the Union Bible Seminary in India, recalled that the school's principal refused to let her lead a course in Christian apologetics—and then used her notes to teach the class himself.[61] Primarily, however, men themselves were the object of frustration, and the object of repeated appeals to accept their responsibility for world evangelization. "Missions is primarily and peculiarly a man's job," George Brown declared in 1935, reminding his readers that the Great Commission to evangelize the world was given first to twelve *men*, Christ's apostles.[62] In 1933 Brown formed a Men's Missionary League, and wrote a popular booklet on "An Adventure in Masculine Missions" to dispute the claim that missions was "women's work."[63]

The opening of new missionary fronts after World War II brought redoubled efforts to move men off the sidelines. Evangelist Merv Rosell challenged his masculine audience to help the "sweet suffering servants" on the mission field. "Young men," he barked, "it is our solemn duty to carry this converting challenge to every war-sodden corner and crevice of this shrinking globe." Donald Nelson took an equally confrontational tone. "Well, young men," he wrote in 1949, "as we sit and read these combat reports for the young women in the Lord's Army who are facing Satan's fiercest onslaughts, what are we going to do? [Will we] finish school, receive a call to our pastorate on the crossroads and then . . . remember them in prayer?"[64]

When sense of duty failed, spokesmen appealed to masculine pride. "What's the matter with the young men who say: 'Yes, God, here I am, send my sister?' " Harold Ockenga demanded of students at Fuller Seminary, citing statistics that for every male recruit, six women volunteered for the mission field. Nelson agreed sarcastically that "we do have some men in this country. Fine young men, and well-trained too. Well trained to take care of the nurseries, warm the bottles, make the beds, and even change diapers daily. . . . Buddy, if you want to be a soldier, then pack your miserable barrack-bags, and shove off where the soldiers are . . . in the battle!"[65]

The most telling criticisms of this sort, however, came from women themselves. Speaking to a Wheaton College audience in 1958, Zoe Anne Alford summed up her career with the conclusion that "far too much of the work I've done on the field has been a man's work." A Baptist woman agreed. "Men—you pride yourselves on being the stronger sex. What are you doing with your strength? Women are doing your work out here—hard, health-blasting work. They must go out and do it or it never will be done."[66]

Nagging worries about "feminization," muted in the 1930s, resurfaced in the fundamentalist movement's doldrums of the late 1940s. By then the overrepresentation of women in the movement's rank and file visibly contradicted the claim that orthodoxy was a masculine preserve, setting off fears of feminization that had been part of the fundamentalist ethos since its earliest stages. As a Baptist pastor chastised, "We men stand by the book all right, and subscribe to Baptist Doctrine and . . . then say, *Go ahead girls . . . do your best!*" Even the more culture-affirming ideals of neo-evangelicalism did not substantially alter this competitive dynamic.[67]

Consequently, enthusiasm for fundamentalist career women gradually diminished. Even the relatively positive image of the Christian businesswoman, inspired by Virginia Asher, met negative qualification. In 1935, an article on Lydia and Priscilla, two New Testament models of working women, emphasized their attitude of submission. Priscilla, the author wrote, "never forgot her place as a wife and did not attempt to usurp authority (I Tim. 2.12). Nor did she undertake any venture apart from her husband." In 1950 the Bible Presbyterian *Christian Beacon* announced, with evident satisfaction, that "Career Women's Number Will Never Be Legion."[68]

Moreover, both fundamentalist and neo-evangelical leaders chose not to admit women into the movement's professionalizing ethos, one that elevated preaching careers as paramount. Female Bible teachers, despite their popularity, were not a professional class. Many were apparently self-taught, and few were highly theologically trained, except for perhaps a Bible school education. In fact, the inductive approach, with its emphasis on the student instead of the teacher, was highly adaptable to minimally trained leaders, especially in college campus settings.

In the 1930s some fundamentalist Bible schools actively began to restrict the enrollment of women students. The quotas generally reflected a desire in some quarters of fundamentalism, those more closely identified with neo-evangelical currents, to eliminate "amateurism" among its leadership. As Wheaton College president J. Oliver Buswell, Jr., announced in 1932, "Now is the time for us to emphasize theological learning and careful preparation and training."[69]

Here, of course, these institutions were no different from many medical and law schools, which either barred women or kept quotas drastically low. Nor were they any less restrictive in their policy than mainline seminaries, also dominated by men. But quotas and restrictions in fundamentalist schools were not normative; they were a clear reversal of open policies which had, in the past, allowed disproportionate numbers of women into Bible schools and colleges. The significance of these policies is compounded by the fact that, in the absence of much ecclesiastical structure, Bible schools served as "denominational surrogates." As Ernest Sandeen commented, and subsequent studies have amply borne out, educational institutions, not church hierarchies, served as centers of "primary allegiance" in the expanding social structure of fundamentalism and neo-evangelicalism.[70]

In 1930 president Nathan Wood instituted a quota for women students at Gordon College of Theology and Missions in Boston, reducing the proportion of female students to one-third of the total. The quota immediately reduced the disproportionate number of women applicants to half the male enrollment, even though, as his wife, the school's academic dean, admitted, "this has meant turning away many splendid girls."[71]

The move reflected President Wood's desire to build an academically respectable seminary out of a coeducational Bible school. He apparently hoped the limitation on women students would heighten the institution's professional aura and create space for the growing numbers of male applicants. In 1934 Wood rescinded one woman's promised teaching position because, as he said, "it would mar the image of the school." Wood himself had no scriptural bias against women in ministry; he proudly assisted in the ordination of numerous female graduates well into the 1930s. Still, this development suggests that the neo-evangelical revival, in which Wood and his school would play a prominent role, would offer fewer opportunities for women than fundamentalism did.[72]

The quota effectively dried up the supply of women applicants. By 1944 the Gordon Divinity School, as a separate entity from the college, reported seventy-two incoming male students, and only three women. That year the trustees lifted the quota on female students, responding to the absence of male candidates during World War II; however, by the mid-1950s, the Gordon campus was entirely male.[73]

William Bell Riley's Northwestern Bible Institute followed a different path to the same destination. As an old-school fundamentalist, Riley emphasized evangelistic vocations more than academic excellence, a position that, for a time, kept the door open for women students. Riley began a seminary program in 1935 with the stated understanding that it was "not primarily intended for women students, as we hold that the primary product of the seminary is *the pastor*, and find no women pastors mentioned in the New Testament." Nevertheless, the school announced its intention to continue admitting female students, by virtue of their role as missionaries and "wives of pastor-husbands."[74] Despite this open policy, however, relatively few women entered the program, at least compared to their far greater numbers in the Bible school. Most women seminarians received specially designed Th.G. degrees, for students without a high school education, or masters in religious education. By 1946 the ratio of men to women was 19 to 3; by 1955 the Northwestern student body, like Gordon Divinity, was entirely male.[75]

These numbers accurately reflect president Riley's goal of filling Minnesota pulpits with his "boys," a project in which women's contribution was clearly limited. In the 1930s and 1940s, the aggressive fundamentalist preachers trained in his school effected a virtual takeover of Minnesota Baptist pulpits. In 1944 "Riley's boys" succeeded in electing Riley president of the Minnesota Baptist Convention.[76]

There is little evidence that the founders of neo-evangelical Fuller Seminary ever envisioned training women workers, in spite of its enlarged vision for engaging secular society. In 1947, when the school opened, the faculty voted to exclude women from classes and to discourage auditors. In 1949 Fuller reluctantly admitted Wellesley graduate Helen Clark, who received a degree in sacred theology, substituting courses in Christian education for homiletics. Although a few other women took classes at Fuller, Clark was its sole female graduate in its first ten years of operation, and something of an oddity to its student body and faculty. Careful admonition against flirting with male divinity students was one condition of her attendance at Fuller.[77]

Schools also attempted to direct men and women students into separate vocations. In 1947 Gordon's faculty adopted a recommendation to channel all female students into a B.R.E. degree, designating the A.B. in theology for male students only. The faculty envisioned its women scholars as destined largely for careers as "church workers, pastors' wives, [and] missionaries" with no need for a broader liberal arts education. Only the continual demands of women students for special transfers to the A.B. persuaded the faculty to lift the requirement in 1949.[78] Northwestern began a secretarial program in 1928, which attracted an entirely female clientele. After the seminary was formed, the Bible college continued to offer courses in homiletics, but in 1938 restricted them to male students only. The catalog records a simultaneous new course offering for women in "Ethics and Ideals," taught by the second Mrs. Riley, Marie Acomb, dean of women students. Required for women in all degree programs, the course promised practical help with "a girl's problems, emphasizing her relationship to the home, with suggestions for the development of Christian womanhood."[79]

Thus, despite the career possibilities fundamentalist and neo-evangelical institutions offered to women, they acted on a tacit assumption that feminine work was clearly secondary. Henrietta Mears, a gifted public speaker who always refused opportunities to fill a pulpit, was only tangentially interested in her female students. Her goal, as one admirer described it, was to train young men to be "spiritual leaders." "I always try to win leaders first," Mears explained; "then I know the followers will come. And I know that if I can win the young men, the girls will come too!" Men were the prime movers in the "building of spiritual empires" and had to be actively recruited. After that, she reasoned, "there will always be enough work for the women to do as we follow in their steps." Mears gathered around her a remarkable group of young men, many of whom would become leaders in the rising generation of fundamentalists and neo-evangelicals. Billy Graham, who called her "one of the greatest Christians I have ever known," credited Mears with the deepest influence on his life, next to his wife and mother.[80]

The LeBar sisters, who attracted mainly female students, also encountered rising prejudices against women's work. When Wheaton College sought to strengthen its academic reputation during the 1940s and 1950s, adding new faculty and pursuing an aggressive building program, the Christian education program indirectly suffered. Perceived as a "scissors and paste" operation by the rest of the faculty, the department grew marginalized and intellectually isolated. Christian education itself was a career without much upward mobility. Directors of Christian education in local churches occupied a role clearly subordinate to that of the senior pastor.[81]

Elizabeth Evans also apparently understood that neo-evangelicalism was a "man's world." Although she parlayed her credentials as a religious educator into a role in the National Association of Evangelicals (NAE), her position was relatively minor. She served as secretary (and sole female member) of its Commission on Education, the group which determined standards of membership in the National Association of Christian Schools. Though not an official delegate to the original meeting of the NAE in 1942, Evans recalled that she took minutes of the proceedings. Even in that capacity, she was one of the few women represented in what was predominantly a masculine cause. "You see," she explained, "NAE was for the men, . . . and some of us single girls were there to help them out."[82]

When a women's auxiliary to the NAE was formed in 1946, Evans served as secretary. The auxiliary, which was firmly subordinated to the leadership and goals of the NAE, provided fellowship for wives of its members and the opportunity to work for "enterprises of the parent organization in which women may effectively engage."[83] Leaders of the NAE took pains to warn the women about the dangers of "decentralization" and exercised tight control over the women's fellowship. They often assumed that the women knew little about parliamentary procedure and reserved the right to oversee even the smallest changes in the auxiliary body's constitution.[84]

Fundamentalist piety, with its emphasis on self-abnegation, also militated against any outward show of forwardness or ambition, especially by young women. In 1934, an aspiring medical student wrote to popular advice columnist "Mother Ruth," confessing her fear that she was not called by God to such a lofty career. "Should I continue along the way I have planned," she asked, ". . . or shall I cast it all aside, and see what the Lord may have planned for me in a more humble field of service?" Mother Ruth urged the young woman to "take your eyes off self! Don't miss the 'high road' because you are being blinded by your Adversary, who waits to lead you to make the wrong choice." Similarly the *Sunday-School Times* applauded the example of "Mother Green," a former business executive and fashion designer who left her "worldly and selfish" life to run the Christ Faith Mission in Los Angeles. "She is not a preacher or public speaker," an admirer explained, "and never appears in the pulpit of her own assembly room. All she does in public life is to tell the story of her conversion out of a full heart." After her husband's death, Edith Norton, a dynamic public speaker, refused to take leadership of the Belgian Gospel Mission, even though she had previously shared that role with her husband. She told her friends that she preferred to be "not so much the Director as the Mother of the Mission," to visit recent converts and " 'mother' them in every way."[85]

Women's vocations in fundamentalism were limited by far more than the apostle Paul's prohibitions against female teachers. A lingering sense of divine calling by default discouraged women from entering more visible, professional roles. "Man is in God's image in a sense that women are not," Rice wrote in 1947, arguing that God simply expected more of his masculine disciples. "Preachers, are you willing for your church to be run by a handful of godless old hens who want to tell you where to head in? . . . If God is going to win this country, He must do it through men."[86]

Fundamentalists understood that while war and the economic hardships of the Depression kept men temporarily out of Christian ministry, women could meet the emergency. Once the crises had passed, however, the women were expected to step aside. Moreover, the voice women assumed—interior, private, and nonjudgmental—often ran counter to the public voices of confrontation more common among fundamentalist men.

Though perhaps this feminine voice more closely typified the grassroots culture of twentieth-century fundamentalism, it was not one the outside world normally heard. And its tones were becoming softer.

After World War II a new emphasis on women's role in the home, evident in both fundamentalist and neo-evangelical periodicals, further undercut the old fundamentalist ethic of Christian service. "A true Christian woman," *Eternity* declared in 1956, "has her first duty under God to her husband; her second duty is to her children. Only in the third place does she have any duty to Christian work." Inter-Varsity staff worker Jane Hollingsworth recalled poignantly that "when I married Peter Haile [in 1954], it was as if I had died. I was never asked to do another thing for students." In 1949, a speaker at a meeting of fundamentalist Baptist women outlined Christian service for women entirely in terms of home-based activities: she omitted any mention of missions or Bible teaching and emphasized the apparently endless possibilities of "telephone ministry," writing letters to missionaries, "using the car for the glory of the Lord," the "smiling ministry," and being sociable in church, "but not while the preacher is preaching."[87]

The demand for feminine submission, as it was formulated in the 1950s, necessarily curtailed activities outside the home, and often seemed to be directed specifically against female Bible teachers. "The woman is allowed to teach the Bible with the authority of the Word of God as her credentials," Moody Bible Institute's Kenneth Wuest wrote in 1956. But he added to that permission a hazy set of negative conditions that could conceivably apply to nearly any teaching situation. "The instant her teaching is in a sphere where she exercises authority over the man in defining church doctrine or administering church discipline," he declared, "she has stepped outside of the realm of her legitimate teaching of the word."[88] The doctrine of submission, with its heavy emphasis on marriage, assumed that the proper sphere of the Christian woman was the home; outside activities were clearly secondary.

Women's new career was marriage. Although fundamentalists and neo-evangelicals cast this role as a valuable form of "ministry," the change was radical; home became an alternative to active service. In that increasingly privatized realm, women would struggle to reformulate their duty to God, with increasing difficulty, and diminishing success.

Chapter
Five

The Fundamentalist Family

A symbolic moment occurred in May 1950 when the fervently premillennial magazine *Our Hope* published an article on "The Ministry of Women." As the piece itself testifies, by the end of World War II even the most world-denying fundamentalists were shifting their vision from eschatological pursuits to smaller, more practical concerns. Indeed, the scene of battle was shifting from the heavenly realms to the social institution most basic to morality and most threatened by secularism: the Christian home.[1]

For decades the editors of *Our Hope* had tracked the rise and fall of European kingdoms, noting every human catastrophe that pointed to Christ's second advent. But the end of World War II brought no clear outcome, and the attention of the magazine's readership appeared to waver. Letters to the editor called for less apocalyptic speculation and more answers to practical issues of moral conduct. Editor Arno C. Gaebelein found himself particularly besieged with knotty questions about the role of women that he was reluctant to address, though for months he promised his readers a reply. Finally, in 1950, the article appeared.

The author was H. A. Ironside, former pastor of the church established by Dwight L. Moody in Chicago. Ironside, then approaching the end of his career, had been an authoritative voice for an earlier generation of fundamentalists, as Gaebelein had been. No doubt Gaebelein hoped Ironside's answer would quickly end the growing confusion.

Ironside began by admitting that the issue "is one that occupies rather a prominent place in the minds of many at the present time," much of it due to the rising numbers of women with a "marked gift and ability in opening up the Scriptures." Ironside answered the question with an orthodox dispensationalist line of interpretation, stressing the dangers of women usurping male prerogative. He conceded that, in times of human failure, God could "transcend his own rules." But this did not necessarily mean, Ironside warned, "that He endorses the manner in which it is given out."[2]

In one sense, the article contained nothing new. Ironside's response conceded little in terms of strict biblical interpretation and exhibited the typical fundamentalist reluctance to endorse women in positions God ideally intended men to fill. Yet the very fact of its appearance in *Our Hope*, in answer to the evident confusion of Gaebelein's readership, also reflects a desire within fundamentalism for more uniform standards of feminine conduct and a movement toward greater structure in gender relationships.

Ironside's article was one of the more striking moments of change within a larger shift among fundamentalists and neo-evangelicals. As the previous chapter has described, attitudes toward female vocations, especially Bible teaching, grew steadily more restrictive after World War II; women's primary energy was to be spent in the home. During the postwar era, fundamentalists, and neo-evangelicals as well, added to this proscription the understanding that women's domestic role was to be an entirely submissive one, subordinated within an external structure of obedience to masculine "headship."

The new emphasis was in one sense hardly surprising, for fundamentalists had long abhorred modern tendencies to blur distinctions between the sexes. Masculine and feminine were never mere social categories, they had consistently argued, for gender differences reflected the very nature and purpose of God. Neither sexless nor androgynous, the fundamentalist God was the sum of all male and female qualities, modelling feminine giving and grace as well as masculine power and authority. To conflate these categories would diminish the divine nature, as well as confuse the social order.[3]

Under the stresses of rapid social change during and after World War II, emphasis on gender differences shifted toward an insistence on hierarchy and masculine control. The change reflected a widening gulf between male and female experience in fundamentalist and neo-evangelical institutions. It was an estrangement that ordered, but also deeply complicated, the rhythms of family life.

The Family and Secularism

Fundamentalism had always placed a high priority on the family. It attacked twentieth-century individualism—and perhaps tempered its own penchant toward that direction—by exalting an essentially Victorian ideal of the Christian family as the foundation of social morality. In 1931 J. C. Massee lauded the "old-fashioned home" as "God's institution for the preservation of order, the creation of integrity, [and] the maintenance of truth and purity in human relationships." "I believe we would all be happier," radio preacher Carl Sweazy concluded in 1945, "if we should pattern our home life today, as nearly as possible after the old-fashioned home."[4]

Homes were also a psychological bulwark for embattled fundamentalists, who often laced their descriptions with military imagery. "When things were difficult," a Presbyterian conservative reminisced in 1940, "it was in the home that the joy was found that eased the burden of the battle." Similarly, Bob Jones urged that "home should be a retreat in time of battle. . . . If we cannot preserve one place to go to, to get a rest from the battles of life, I don't know what is going to happen."[5]

But, as fundamentalist spokesmen warned, even this righteous retreat stood in mortal danger. Clarence Darrow's stated belief that "every child ought to be more intelligent than his parents" touched the deepest fears of fundamentalist parents. Modern immorality, or as Massee termed it, "the seepage of the cesspool of human lust," threatened the preservation of all religious values and could only be avoided if children followed carefully in the ways their parents taught. Fundamentalists warned that the ungodly drive for personal "self-expression" had infiltrated every aspect of modern living; young people were particularly vulnerable to its dangers. Robertson McQuilkin's partial list of hazards included everything from "movies, dancing, drink, [and] cards," to "amateur theatricals, uncontrolled automobiles, unregulated radios, [and] excessive attention to sports and music."[6]

Not a few fundamentalist spokesmen of the 1930s pointed to Russian communism as both symbol and source of American family decline. Pre-millennialism, as its students have pointed out, easily lends itself to conspiracy theories, finding satanic infiltration in nearly every human endeavor. The public atheism of Russian Communists and their collective ideals betrayed the Christian family on every level. William Biederwolf thus described Soviet Russia as "the most gigantic orgy of licensed sensuality that any country professing civilization has ever known." "This modern belittlement of the home," Dan Gilbert warned in 1939, "is part of the communistic program for breaking down resistance to the 'new order' which revolutionary radicals wish to establish. If youth can be led to believe that the abolition of family life will benefit humanity, they will not only cease to oppose, but will be predisposed in favor of the communist order which promises to do away with the home."[7]

Fundamentalist Motherhood

Through the 1930s, most fundamentalists afforded women a central role in maintaining the Christian household. Despite their well-publicized suspicions of feminine morality, the movement's leaders never went so far as to disparage domesticity. The home was a man's "fortress in the warring world," as evangelist Robert G. Lee explained, "where a woman buckles on his armor in the morning as he goes forth to the battles of the day and soothes his wounds when he comes home at night."[8]

Biographies of fundamentalist leaders also offer strong testimony to powerful maternal influence and example. In many accounts, fathers were either absent or emotionally distant authority figures. William Ward Ayer, for example, was left at age five in the care of his abusive father after his mother died. Yet he considered his adult conversion "living proof of the validity and power of the influence of a godly mother."[9] A friend of Clarence Macartney observed that his mother "by the unanimous testimony of the children, was the dominant person in the home." Her tender, sensitive nature stood in stark contrast to the elder Macartney's frosty Scottish reserve. The testimony of sons to their mother's desire that they enter the ministry was nearly a staple of fundamentalist biography.[10]

Women assumed their domestic responsibilities with alacrity. Despite periodic pleas for more involvement from fathers, fundamentalist mothers embraced the family as their common prerogative. Although these women seemed largely unaware of the negative assessments of feminine character coming from the movement's leadership, they did conceive their role in far more limited terms than their Victorian predecessors. Unlike an earlier generation of evangelical women, they did not use the home as a base, or model, for social reform. Fundamentalist homes were thoroughly insulated from secular influences; they were arenas where women could do indirect battle with modernism, from the safety of their private, domestic sphere.

Common concern for the home did provide occasions for women to engage in semipublic dialogue. Beginning in the 1930s, fundamentalist magazines became popular forums for feminine admonition and encouragement in a running conversation that added warmer emotional tones to the relatively limited, strident range of fundamentalist discourse. Women's concerns were practical and immediate; they rarely invoked larger issues of familial order and structure, a theme much more prevalent in male discussions of the home. Maternal figures, such as "Mother Ruth" Paxson and "Aunt Mary," offered a constant stream of advice for mothers and young girls (and a substantial number of young men who also sent in letters), couched in firm yet intimate language. Mrs. Carl Gray, the "American Mother of 1937," regularly offered the wisdom borne of her many years of experience to readers of the popular *Sunday-School Times*. The Christian home is a "God-ruled factory," she enthused, sending out "each day a fresh supply of joy, hope, trust, confidence, obedience, loyalty, and love."[11]

Fundamentalist mothers worried deeply for their offspring. "So many parents thoughtlessly permit their children to go into the world, schools, and even churches," Mrs. Gray admonished, "with no knowledge of the sin, temptations, and false teachings that will surround them." "Even a slight compromise is deadly danger," a "Farm Mother" agreed. "Both sacred history and common experience present tragic instances of children from homes outstandingly Christian who have become so flagrantly sinful as to cast a serious blight upon the parents' testimony."[12]

Thus mothers advised each other to begin a child's religious instruction as early as possible. Never coercive or didactic, their techniques were indirect and often gently manipulative. Lucretia Hanson began praying for her infants even before birth and recited Scripture while dressing and bathing them. She urged other mothers to choose hymns and scriptural verses "to implant on their subconscious minds, and . . . repeat and sing these over and over in their presence." "I think the secret of success is to start very early," another woman offered. "Correct them while they are still babies, and they will not forget the punishments received and will retain the habit of obedience required."[13]

The value of such training emerged as children confronted the world's evils in later life. "Before the teachers ever begin the teaching of evolution," one mother advised, "we can prepare the children's armor by telling of these teachings which they will meet, and explaining that they are Satan's attacks against God's plan of redemption."[14]

But even so, parents were to remain vigilant in protecting their children against secular dangers they were too young to resist. And in daily encounters with secular influences, mothers formed the first line of defense. "I did not allow my children to spend the night with other children," one successful Christian mother explained. "They were not allowed to go to school until it was time and came home immediately when school was out. Their playmates were welcome in my home, and I knew what they were doing when there."[15] "Aunt Mary" advised one mother to plan ahead with other entertainment so that her children would not ask for a trip to the circus when it came to town. On the question of skating rinks, however, she was less certain. In her view, a conscientious parent should first pay a visit there, checking for negative "influences," such as "smoking, drinking, dance music, [or] sex stimulation." But the best solution, she advised, was for a group of Christian parents to rent the rink some evening themselves "so that your children can skate for hours in company that your Lord would approve."[16]

Ultimately, however, much Christian motherhood relied on various forms of manipulation, rather than direct confrontation. One mother related that she would allow her teenage son to attend a movie, but only after telling him, "Darling, I am *letting* you go, but *you know* how I feel about it." "Perhaps this had a psychological effect," she wondered, adding that she found the remedy completely effective.[17]

Fundamentalist motherhood in fact was a role with great responsibilities and limited moral authority, a fact that many women seemed to realize—and agonize over. For not even the most conscientious mother could ensure her child's salvation. She could but entreat and stand alongside a rebellious youngster, much as the Holy Spirit waited patiently for the Christian believer to submit her restless heart. Motherhood was a "school of suffering" which one pastor's wife likened to Christ's redemptive work on behalf of humanity. "Tremendous possibilities for good [God] wrapped up in that helpless babe," she admonished a new mother, "and chiefly on you rests the responsibility for the making or marring of that God-given life."[18] One particularly earnest "Christian Mother" related that success came only after "I fell on my face before God and begged his forgiveness for my presumption." God answered her prayers for her family "when I acknowledged my utter inability to do the task and laid the entire burden on him."[19]

Fundamentalist spokesmen, already prone to doubt women's moral superiority, confirmed all these doubts and more. Mother's Day celebrations often occasioned outbursts of irritation against the "sentimental nonsense" of cards and flowers. Frank Gaebelein, Arno Gaebelein's son, declared that "contrary to much present-day sentimentality the fact that a woman is a mother does not in itself make her good." The *Christian Beacon* agreed: "The exaltation in the Church of Mother's Day just because a woman has given birth to a child and become a mother is nothing short of paganism."[20]

Fundamentalist Fathers

In fact, other voices in fundamentalism, most clearly articulated by evangelist and editor John R. Rice and coming to prominence in the late 1930s and 1940s, decried the prevalence of "bossy wives" and placed a far greater emphasis on masculine leadership in the home. In a popular tract on "Rebellious Wives and Slacker Husbands," written in 1937, Rice argued that the man "is to be like a god in his home, verily a high priest and prophet of God." Joe Henry Hankins, a Southern Baptist evangelist agreed: fathers should exercise "absolute authority" over their wives and children. He likened their relationship to their children as "God to his saints."[21]

Indeed, most of Rice's teaching on family life was directed to masculine "slackers" in the home, not to women. Rice's teaching seemed designed as a corrective to the clearly dominant role fundamentalist mothers played in their children's lives, and to their implied failure to fulfill that responsibility. "The wife is to come to her husband and find God's will," he declared, warning that God would hold men personally accountable for the disorder of their homes. "God intended every husband and father to know more Bible than his wife and children. Any man who does not has slacked; he has shirked; he has quit on God."[22]

In contrast to the gently manipulative mother, the fundamentalist father Rice described was quick to confront and punish childish rebellion. Although often remembered with affection, his kindness was equated with mercy, never indulgence. Rice recalled that his own father whipped him until he cried and continued until the crying stopped. "I will never forget the first time I whipped one of my children until blue marks appeared on her fat little body," the evangelist once confessed to his readers. Although both he and his wife wept over the punishment inflicted, they did not relent. "She must learn to mind," he had argued to himself. "She must submit to orders."[23]

Fundamentalists attached deep theological significance to the father's role, for it modelled the absolute sovereignty of God over creation. "The core-principle of all civilization and society is respect for authority," Joe Hankins wrote, "and if that isn't taught to the children in the home there never will be respect for authority and the children will grow up anarchists and rebels." "All the trouble in the world," Rice agreed, "can be traced to rebellion against authority." A wise parent therefore broke his child's will early and decisively. "There is something terribly evil and wicked in the nature of every human being," he reasoned, "that will only be . . . driven out by punishment."[24]

In theory, the swift surety of parental punishment also taught children the benefits of obedience to the divine will. "There can be no real Spiritual wisdom," Rice wrote, "until a child learns the self control, reverence and obedience to authority and the anxiety to do right which comes by the punishment for wrong doing."[25] And it served as a safeguard against the evils and temptations of the world. Parents should never be afraid to punish, Rice counseled, for "the child will get far tougher treatment at the hands of the world." His brother, Bill Rice, agreed: "It is a great deal easier to lead a disciplined child to Christ than it is to win a spoiled brat."[26]

Though often physically absent from the home, the fundamentalist father expressed his love through discipline and sacrifice. Like God the Father, he exercised daily care for his children only indirectly, by the threat of punishment and the presence of material provision. Although men may not be able to raise their children day by day as mothers do, Hankins explained, the father's work in the world was equally if not more important. "He is out in the battle of life, in the struggle to support his home."[27]

The Postwar Search for Order

Yet despite their ambivalence about the mother's moral leadership, fundamentalist men and women enthusiastically participated in postwar celebrations of motherhood and nuclear family life. Never wholeheartedly behind the trend toward working mothers during the war years, they uniformly encouraged young women to embrace marriage and motherhood as the most satisfying career possible. "Many a modern woman has found that the petty annoyances and the feelings of frustration that arise from modern emancipated living are dissipated by the tremendous satisfaction that comes from going back to her right places as wife, as homemaker, and as mother," *Moody Monthly* noted with satisfaction. "Give me a man who will work twice as hard to keep his little wife and mother in the home," Carl Sweazy enthused, "and give me the woman who will be content with half as much in order to be permitted to remain in the home with the babies, where she is certainly more needed than anywhere else in the world."[28]

This new emphasis on women's domestic role occurred just as conservative religion poised for rapid growth. In the 1950s, Billy Graham found an eager public audience searching for "peace with God" in the terror and uncertainty of the nuclear age. Church steeples appeared in every new suburban neighborhood, beckoning freshly scrubbed families to an array of activities both religious and social. Fundamentalism even took on an air of social and intellectual respectability with the rise of the neo-evangelical movement in the mid-1940s. Neo-evangelical scholars and clergymen, led by Carl F. H. Henry and Harold Ockenga, sought to update the fundamentalist message by engaging liberal academia with conservative critiques. And popular evangelists, spearheaded by Billy Graham and the Youth for Christ movement, received national attention in their efforts to bring about spiritual revival.

Ironically, the neo-evangelical movement, for all its relative openness to secular thought, carried into its "renaissance" an extremely conservative approach to gender roles. Despite its willingness to engage religious liberals in intellectual dialogue, the movement rarely, if ever, examined its fundamentalist legacy of attitudes toward masculinity and femininity.

The new interest in religion during the postwar decades reflected in part a deepening anxiety over the growing lack of stability in American homes and was founded on the dimming hope that families that "prayed together" might "stay together." The new mobility of the population after World War II and the seeming rootlessness of suburban culture attracted the worried attention of both religious commentators and secular social scientists. The new family appeared to one scholar as "a country which, having operated under an authoritarian form of government, has suddenly switched to a democratic form."[29]

Most noted pessimistically that husbands and wives fulfilled neither roles nor responsibilities. "It is hard to see that we assign obviously distinctive roles to men and women," Rhoda Bacmeister wrote in 1951. "Our ideals of what is 'manly' and what is 'womanly' seem confused." Some pointed to increasing employment among married women; others simply decried the growing absence of commuting fathers from the home. Nearly all wondered about the future of the nuclear family, described by one observer as "an aggregate of persons with little reason or motivation to stay together."[30]

Even popular culture and the images of the family in Hollywood cinema reinforced the notion that the American family was in deep trouble. The growing youth rebellion was the most painful, visible symptom of domestic decline. James Dean, the young "rebel without a cause," fell into his career as a juvenile delinquent when his parents, especially his weak-willed, henpecked father, failed to provide moral guidance or sympathy. "What can you do when you have to be a man?" he asked his father, a sorry figure without the slightest idea of an answer.

Indeed, the comfortable image of the suburban father seemed to have little basis in reality. The flight of women from the "feminine mystique" of postwar suburban life paralleled rising discontent among men. The masculine heroes of the 1950s were loners and individualists, like John Wayne and Marlon Brando, Jack Kerouac, and Allen Ginsburg. The rising popularity of Hugh Hefner's "playboy philosophy," as well as a soaring divorce rate, belied the contentment of the "organization man." Masculinity itself seemed problematic for men who had traded the glories of the battlefield for the stable, domestic comforts of the suburban neighborhood.[31]

Most mainline churches responded readily to the new challenge on the domestic front. In 1954, for example, Methodists sponsored a National Conference on Family Life endorsing "The Christian Family—the Hope of the World." In 1958 John Charles Wynn, chairman of the National Council of Churches Committee on Family Life, reviewed the literature on church and home and estimated that "it would not be difficult to list well over five hundred current titles on such subjects from our denominational presses."[32] "It might not be difficult," Wynn concluded, "but it would be tedious." He found the literature "depressingly platitudinous," for it merely insisted *"ad nauseam* that that family that prays together stays together, without a glimmer of criticism to that claim." Most failed to address the rising incidence of sexual misconduct, alcoholism, and family violence that threatened even the most saintly of homes. Rapidly losing the attention of their increasingly secularized constituents, mainstream churches struggled to move beyond timid discussions of table graces and family recreation. "If family life could be made Christian by resolutions and convention statements," Wynn noted caustically, "the City of God would already have become situated on the earth."[33]

Fundamentalists readily adopted a more confrontational approach to the problem of family decline. The new crusade in fact brought them back to familiar ground, though in the 1950s the home, rather than the church, emerged as a primary field of battle with liberals and secularists. And in this crusade, women occupied a weaker, clearly secondary role. Masculine leadership was paramount.

Feminine Careers and "Christian Homemaking"

The new emphasis on women's role in the home paralleled the decline of feminine vocations elsewhere in fundamentalism and neo-evangelicalism. Motherhood became a valuable form of "ministry" but was in fact an alternative to "full-time Christian service." In 1948 *HIS* magazine, a relatively progressive periodical for college students, promoted "Homemaking for Christ," featuring the enthusiastic testimony of a young woman who had given up a calling to the mission field for a sheltered, domestic life. "It is obvious," she concluded, "that the Scriptures portray the normal Christian woman as a homemaker."[34]

Homemaking, in the postwar years, emerged as a thoroughly privatized alternative to full-time church work. Making a happy home "is every bit as important in God's scheme of things as are the more obvious forms of Christian service," Luci Deck Shaw wrote in 1955. Although domestic duties left little time for church work, they offered ample occasions for supplementing the work of others. "Have you checked on Bobby to see if he has his Sunday school lesson prepared?" a Baptist woman urged. "Have you drilled little Esther on her Bible verses for next Sunday? Have you impressed upon Dick the importance of having his five minute message for Junior Fellowship well prepared?" Evangelical periodicals also advised Christian mothers to tap into wider ministries, such as home Bible classes, child evangelism, and neighborhood visitation.[35]

Christian homemaking also freed men for higher service. Luetta Kiel, a freelance writer, told of her decision to give up all outside ambitions and activities, even church work, to pursue a greater good. Following the example of a friend she admired, "I made up my mind to try to do a better job of making a home and not to think so much about outside service." Though the change was difficult, she "realized more clearly how much a husband's success and also his Christian service and leadership depends upon his home life—the cheerfulness, the restful atmosphere, punctuality, good food, and little attentions meant for him alone."[36]

Ruth Graham's willing commitment to her husband Billy's evangelistic career provided a strong public model of Christian womanhood. At the time of their courtship, she was planning a missionary career in Tibet, having grown up on the mission field. Her ambitions soon gave way to the greater demands of marriage and motherhood. The Grahams divided their household according to "territory," as she explained to one interviewer in 1955. Ruth took responsibility for domestic duties, while Billy tended to his pastoral work and later to an evangelistic career that took him away from home for months at a time.[37]

The Order of God's Household

In their elevation of home and mother, fundamentalists and neo-evangelicals scarcely differed from most middle-class Americans. But they insisted that their homes were different. Pastor Mac, a popular columnist in the *Pilot*, complained that even church people scoffed at him as an "old fogy" when he aired his views on women's role. "They assure me that if women want to be out working in the world it is *their* business," he added indignantly. "We are being told that we must not curb our children," Carl Armerding protested. "Instead of training a child in the way he should go, we must let him go where he pleases. And the results speak for themselves."[38]

The key difference between a conservative evangelical household and the average American home, spokesmen explained, was the presence of an ordered hierarchy. "The normal Christian home consists of husband, wife, and children," Charles Ryrie wrote in 1952, "each with his or her own particular place and responsibility." In this scheme, women were to be "obedient in *all things*. . . . This is not a popular doctrine in these days, when the cry is for liberation and equality; and although Christianity as no other religion gives freedom to women, in the Christian home this freedom is distinctly regulated."[39]

This new emphasis on order was in part a response to a perceived decline and rising disorder within postwar fundamentalism. In a 1947 address to the Winona Lake Bible Conference, William Ward Ayer admitted his disillusionment with the growing acrimony among fundamentalist leaders. Their infighting and competition made them worse than modernists, he noted with discouragement.[40] Moreover, the repeated failure of premillennial prophets to correctly interpret the eschatological meaning of Hitler, Stalin, and Mussolini brought growing restlessness to the ranks. And the rise of neo-evangelicalism in the mid-1940s put more conservative fundamentalist brethren into a fighting mode. The battles surrounding biblical inerrancy that dogged the faculty of newly established Fuller Seminary seemed to surpass even the struggles with modernists two decades earlier.[41]

The search for order was also integral to dispensationalist theology. During the epoch-shaking years of the 1930s, fundamentalists took up this theme with renewed vehemence. "We find chaos and disorder in society, in politics, in the home, in the church," Herbert Bieber wrote presciently in 1937, "but in the life of a born-again-one there is order."[42]

Dispensationalists took comfort in the unshakable nature of God's "plan" for humanity. Despite the ominous events in Europe, Presbyterian Donald Grey Barnhouse declared in 1934, peace lay ahead. "All this will be because God's own benevolent Dictator, the Lord Jesus Christ, will come to govern with all wisdom and all power." "The world is not like a helpless iceberg drifting as the changing currents and contrary minds determine," W. H. Rogers wrote reassuringly in 1942. "It is more like a majestic ship with chart, compass, and rudder, with the great Captain on the bridge, and taking its determined course by His providence."[43]

This conviction had both a social and a personal application. The root of sin, Lewis Sperry Chafer, the dean of dispensationalist theologians, wrote in 1935, is "the restless unwillingness on the part of the creature to abide in the sphere and limitations in which the Creator, guided by infinite wisdom, had placed him." Sin is not mere "maladjustment," Wheaton College's J. Oliver Buswell agreed, but "disorder."[44]

More specifically, Louis Bauman pointed out that the Greek translation of "dispensation" was "oikonomia," referring to "the divine management of a household," and denoting the *order, or arrangement of the divine household.*" It was no great leap, therefore, to transfer this understanding to Christian family life, and especially to the role of women.[45]

The rebellious woman, who already loomed large in fundamentalist demonology, assumed center stage again during World War II and the postwar era. The pin-up girls who decorated countless army bunk beds symbolized "the licentiousness, lust and immorality of a people," Harold Ockenga declared, "a depraved element perennially present in mankind." And modern movie sirens, with their countless love affairs and scandalous divorces, signalled an even worse desecration of modern womanhood.[46]

Rebellious women loomed everywhere. After World War II, women's ordination became a pressing matter for mainline denominations. In 1948 the World Council of Churches issued a study on "the life and work of women in the church," reflecting the ecclesiastical situation in wartime Europe, where women often filled pulpit vacancies in the absence of men. In response, the National Council of Churches instituted a survey on the status of women in 1953. Pressure for ordination, a recurring issue for Methodists and Presbyterians since the turn of the century, mounted steadily. In 1956 both denominations gave full ordination rights to women.[47]

The rising popularity of John R. Rice also influenced conservative evangelical opinion. In 1940 the erstwhile Southern Baptist preacher moved his entourage and magazine, the *Sword of the Lord*, from Dallas to Wheaton, Illinois, a center of fundamentalist and evangelical activity. During the 1940s, the circulation of his periodical doubled every two years; by 1950 it had reached nearly 75,000.[48] With him Rice brought an assortment of conservative Southern social attitudes and a deep-rooted sense of masculine prerogative. The showcase of his Dallas church was a Sunday morning Bible class that catered to a masculine clientele. "Most Sunday Schools are run by the women-folks and appeal primarily to women and children," one advertisement ran. "We seek to care for the needs of children and give woman her rightful place, but New Testament teaching and preaching was usually directed first of all to men, and we seek to have it so here."[49]

During his self-imposed northern exile, Rice gained national fame for his no-nonsense approach to the ethics of sex and family life. While conducting evangelistic crusades in the Chicago area, Rice began introducing a series on "Bobbed Hair, Bossy Wives, and Women Preachers" into afternoon services. The size of the crowds attending these messages convinced him to issue a book on the subject; not surprisingly it was well-received by the fundamentalist public, at least according to Rice, and widely endorsed by its leadership.[50]

The late 1940s and 1950s brought forth a spate of books and articles calling for a reinspection of biblical material on "women's role." The new teaching came from the undisputed centers of fundamentalist culture, primarily Moody Bible Institute and Dallas Theological Seminary. Though the books varied in emphases, and sometimes in conclusions, they shared a common air of exasperated authority at the confused state of gender relationships in postwar society.

P. B. Fitzwater's book *Woman: Her Mission, Position, and Ministry*, published in 1950, built off an essentially Victorian approach to sex roles. Fitzwater, a popular teacher of theology at Moody Bible Institute, argued that "men and women are differently organized, both physically and psychically." Thus, "man is organized to operate in the affairs of science, commerce, and the state. The woman is organized to regulate the home and family." Fitzwater emphasized the complementary nature of the sexes, though he stressed their differences over their mutuality. "Differences of sex are not to be toned down and obliterated," he argued, "but to be accentuated and brought into moral harmony. . . . A masculine woman and a feminine man are monstrosities to be abhorred."[51]

Accentuating differences, however, did not afford women a "separate space" for exercising leadership. "Woman's constitution determines her mission," Fitzwater believed. "She is physically constituted to bear children and mentally and spiritually fitted to develop and mold their lives." The husband played an extremely limited role in the home because his greater responsibility to "affairs of the state" made it "impossible for him to nurture the children." Still, he was more than adequate to handle all manner of public duties without feminine assistance. "Had not sin entered the race and dislocated society," Fitzwater concluded, "there would have been no need for woman's ministry outside of her home."[52]

Charles Ryrie, a dean at Dallas Theological Seminary, followed a strict dispensationalist line of reasoning to a similar conclusion. In a lengthy analysis of relevant biblical texts and materials from early church history, he concluded that though the sexes shared equal "spiritual privileges," women were to remain subordinate to men. This, he argued, was by virtue of "the Christian doctrine of order in creation," which could never be abrogated. "As long as the race continues and men are men and women are women, then women are to be subject to their husbands as unto the head."[53]

Ryrie agreed that women's work inside the home was primary, although in cases of emergency they might find themselves filling a masculine role elsewhere. Still, he cautioned, "any woman who finds herself doing a man's work should so aim her own work that a man can assume it as quickly as possible. The acid test any woman can apply to such situations is simply this: Would I be willing to give over all my work to a trained man if he should appear today? To know the Scriptural pattern is absolutely essential."[54]

After World War II discussion of gender issues by both fundamentalists and neo-evangelicals revolved around concepts of order and place. A woman in leadership was "out of order," as one Baptist periodical put it. Although this understanding owed much to dispensationalist theology, it was not exclusive to it. Neo-evangelical thought, centered more in conservative Calvinism, also emphasized God's "order of creation" as a way of negotiating sex roles. Thus, though theologically distinct, the two traditions shared a common emphasis on order. Although the literature of the 1940s and 1950s is more clearly dispensationalist than Calvinist, with the rise of the more Calvinist-oriented neo-evangelical movement, the order of creation terminology would enter and dominate the discussion more fully, especially after 1960.[55]

By all accounts the new emphasis on order in gender relations was greeted with enthusiasm. Fundamentalist and evangelical periodicals reviewed books on the subject with unrestrained praise, and their readers purchased them with equal zeal. Their appeal was based on much more than a masculine drive for supremacy; women also received the new guidelines with visible relief. A *Moody Monthly* writer argued that a truly biblical "pattern of authority" would provide women with "the security and protection" they unconsciously longed for, as well as "the perfect safeguard against arbitrary, harsh, or self-assertive authority on the part of the husband." Feminine endorsements of Rice's *Bobbed Hair, Bossy Wives, and Women Preachers* often noted the salutary effects of its teaching on non-Christian husbands. A St. Louis woman reported that after reading the book she "cried and cried, for I knew I had failed my husband, but most of all, my God." But, she continued, "I believe my husband will be saved now. I'm letting my hair grow long."[56]

Indeed, women showed few signs of rebellion; the arrangement appeared to promise them a modicum of power. In a sense, by submitting to their husbands they actually gained moral and psychological leverage. "What can I do to get my husband to let me stop working and stay home so I can be the wife I want to be?" a woman wrote to the *Pilot*'s advice columnist Pastor Mac in 1954. Pastor Mac responded sympathetically, though with some irritation. He advised the couple to read Ephesians 5: 21–33 and seek immediate marriage counseling, preferably from him. "What did he marry you for—a meal ticket?" Pastor Mac growled. "I am not trying to be smart, but I have seen so much of this in my counseling that it makes me sick."[57]

To a degree, much of the postwar literature reintroduced the sentimental picture of motherhood earlier fundamentalists had rejected. In 1948 John R. Rice's "tremendously popular" book, *The Home: Courtship, Marriage and Children*, offered purchasers a marriage certificate, family record, and a "madonnalike picture of [the] author's wife and baby."[58]

Fundamentalists and Sex

The new literature on family life and sex roles both reflected and perpetuated the "homosocial" nature of fundamentalist culture. One dimension of fundamentalist separatism was its careful monitoring of interaction between the sexes; the ideal was to keep their worlds as distinct and separate as possible. Although fundamentalists have often been accused of being terrified of sex, they were in fact primarily concerned about the possibility of disorder, which they believed was the inevitable result of unrestrained human lust. And the best means of maintaining order, they reasoned, was to avoid any undue mingling of the sexes.[59]

Fundamentalists had never shied from frank discussions of sexual ethics. Billy Sunday, for example, often warned young women of the dangers of venereal disease and abortion in vivid, statistical detail. Homes for unwed mothers and reclaimed prostitutes were a staple of rescue missions, and gloriously specific denunciations of sex sins a common feature of evangelistic oratory.[60]

Fundamentalism in the 1950s was no less frank. By then strict standards on physical intimacy and courtship behavior were carefully imposed at Bible institutes and colleges. Students at Bob Jones University, for example, wooed each other in the "date room," a large parlor staffed by vigilant chaperons. Never far from their sight was a large portrait of Christ with his arms encircling a young man and woman on either side, Bibles in their grasp and "the glory of Heaven on their faces."[61]

"Sex sins are special sins against the body as no other sins are," John R. Rice warned. Even the most casual physical contact therefore invited danger, a temptation few could easily resist. Rice singled out dancing as the root of much evil. "If the finest Christian girl and a most upright and earnest Christian young man dance together, bodies against each other or arms about each other," he warned, "the bodily desires will be aroused just as with unconverted people."[62]

Although Rice believed sexual attraction was natural, he also argued that with a little willpower it could be avoided. Adam and Eve were indeed naked in the Garden of Eden, he admitted, but "it is very likely that sex matters were not then a constant temptation as they are now" and hinted that coitus was simply infrequent before the Fall.[63] Thus, he counseled, "some of the happiest couples I have known never even kissed each other until after marriage." Engaged couples might enjoy some intimacies, Rice advised, but they should be "so modest that it does not unduly arouse passions, but only expresses affection in a way that would not grieve the blessed Holy Spirit of God."[64] Mother Ruth agreed: "Things like holding hands and kissing good night are unwise, for they lead to dangerous things, which often mean sorrow. . . . The right kind of boy—the pure, clean Christian boy—will think more instead of less of a girl who would not cheapen herself with exchanging kisses and caresses as is done so much today by the ungodly."[65]

Rice, the father of six daughters, was particularly outspoken in his warnings to young women about the male sex drive. Somewhat paradoxically, however, most commentators agreed that women were primarily responsible for maintaining the "high spiritual tone" of a godly relationship by restraining their own desires. Modesty in dress was paramount. "A Christian woman may be absolutely *fundamental in her doctrine*," Kenneth Wuest argued, "yet defeat the power of the Word by the *modernism of her appearance.*" "Since the coming of sin into the world," C. Stacey Woods wrote in 1948, "woman has been so constituted that her desire is toward man in the direction of pleasing and attracting him.... It should therefore be quite obvious why counsel concerning modesty and balanced attire is addressed particularly to woman." "There are more girls seducing boys in America," Bob Jones agreed, "than there are boys seducing girls. ... Oh, the grip of a woman's power over a man."[66]

But perhaps they need not have worried. Standards of fundamentalist manhood, with their strict ethic of individualism and manly achievement, allowed scant room for feminine companionship. Romantic entanglements often brought a "loss of spiritual power." Many men seemed to find far greater comfort and comradery with their peers. In 1959 a young man declared that although relationships with women could be profitable, "it is the friendship of other Christian men for which I owe my Lord greatest thanks." Women simply demanded too much intimacy. "Danger comes," he warned, "when we (as men) turn to women for long introspective talks where souls are laid bare and dreams are toyed with." Even the most casual "brother-sister" relationship could end in a premature commitment to marriage.[67]

Women, on the other hand, freely shared their exasperation with masculine faults. A college woman complained of their "conceit" and shallowness, and the propensity of Christian men to choose wives who were "younger and dumber than they." All this explained her decision to remain "happily unmarried" and to pursue "full-time Christian work."[68]

Marriage was often a demographic challenge for devout fundamentalist and evangelical women. Finding a mate who was spiritually equal or superior was difficult, especially with such a woefully small pool of applicants. As "Mother Ruth's" column amply testified, many young women faced the choice of an "unequal yoke"—marrying an unbeliever— or remaining single. And, as her correspondence also suggested, not a few fell into the former trap. It was a situation doubly complicated by the fact that even the most godless husband could demand a submissive wife; indeed, as a few commentators argued, the need for submission was actually greatest in these situations, as it might lead to their eventual salvation.[69]

Thus many women also turned to each other for primary friendships, though these feminine relationships found far less approval than mas-

culine ones. And while Christian periodicals often advised that certain
forms of "sublimation" could be helpful for single women, they also warned
them to avoid "exclusive and intense" relationships. "An unhealthy sign
is an undue physical demonstration of affection," one woman advised in
1958. "One meets a good many examples of this, even in Christian circles,
usually with a sad loss of spiritual power in both parties concerned."[70]

In the long run, the new emphasis on order and the psychic distance
it created between the sexes was costly. Although conservative evangelical
and fundamentalist literature was silent on the subject of domestic violence, the model of family life it endorsed was a risky one. Modern studies
have found the highest incidences of spousal and child abuse in families
that are socially isolated and characterized by rigid sex-role stereotypes,
poor communication, and extreme inequities in the distribution of power
between family members.[71]

Although this is not to say that fundamentalist families were by nature
abusive, John R. Rice himself argued that "nowhere in the Bible is a wife's
duty conditioned on [a husband's] character . . . or the way he treats her."
A firm advocate of corporal punishment, he also declared that "God wants
children to obey their parents even if their parents are wicked." Other
fundamentalist spokesmen counselled women to stay with non-Christian,
even alcoholic, husbands, holding out the possibility (as expressed in I
Peter 3:1–6) that they might convert their unsympathetic spouses.[72]

Ironically, though fundamentalists and evangelicals believed they had
successfully opposed the modern tide against family dissolution, their solution opened them to significant difficulties. Their model of family life
provided women and children little protection from an abusive husband
or father, whose domestic power was theoretically unlimited. And it left
them entirely unprepared to answer the feminist critique of the nuclear
family and the rising aspirations of middle-class women it fostered.

The hierarchical model of fundamentalist and evangelical family life
involved far more than a retreat from social disorder, although this clearly
played an important role. The wish to impose order was central to dispensationalist as well as Calvinist theology. During the twentieth century,
social forces shaped its piecemeal yet steady application to gender relationships in fundamentalist institutions. Pragmatic desires to employ the
gifts and energy of a largely female constituency weighed most heavily
during periods of growth and expansion, during the late-nineteenth century, and in the 1930s. But deeper concerns about masculine status, ex-

pressed most clearly by the fundamentalist ministers who spoke for the majority, rose more powerfully during times of doubt and retrenchment, in the 1920s and late 1940s.

The neo-evangelical resurgence of the postwar era came at a time when conservative Christians believed they had finally eliminated the specter of competition between the sexes. Although this new voice advocated more careful, measured response to secular ideologies, it ignored or dismissed the feminist appeal. Operating largely outside of ecclesiastical structures, centered in personalities and the print media, neo-evangelicalism had neither the will nor the power to give voice to women's aspirations or, in fact, to silence them.

Epilogue: The Meaning of
Evangelical Feminism

Long before it showed any sign of winding down, the neo-evangelical debate over feminism seemed to grow stale. Though it generated immense energy, it resolved little, and despite its intensity barely budged the male monopoly on evangelical leadership. To a great degree, in fact, the evangelical-feminist controversy virtually replayed arguments thoroughly explored nearly a century before.

But few modern participants recalled that first encounter between turn-of-the-century fundamentalists and advocates of women's right to preach. With little memory of the past, evangelicals seemed doomed to repeat it. A remarkably similar confrontation took place in the late 1960s, when the secular feminist movement shattered the relative peace of the neo-evangelical revival.

Both times conservatives approached the prospect of change dubiously. In the first encounter, dispensational teaching on Eve's subordination, buttressed by an inerrant reading of the Bible, offered a theological rationale for dismissing feminism. Indeed, early fundamentalists took the lead against "women's religion" in the churches, arguing persuasively for a more masculine expression of the faith. Nearly a century later, the struggle, if not the result, was much the same. In the 1960s and 1970s, evangelical feminists pressed for change and set off a new round of complicated, high-stakes theological debate. And in response, conservatives once again pitted biblical inerrancy against feminism and reopened old disagreements between Wesleyans and Calvinists over the social implications of Eve's original sin.

But the second round of controversy had much more ground to cover than the first, for neo-evangelicals had inherited a set of proscriptions on women's role far more restrictive than any previous fundamentalist practice. The context for neo-evangelical understanding of women's place was the sharply conservative attitudes of the post–World War II era. During the 1960s, the continuities between that period of fundamentalism and neo-evangelicalism grew painfully obvious in light of the entrenched conservatism that met even the mildest forms of feminist protest.[1]

Of course, the theological controversy is not the entire story, for like many earlier generations of fundamentalists, neo-evangelicals did not always align practice with ideology. Some observers suggest that despite their public resistance to feminist ideals, evangelicals have unconsciously internalized feminist attitudes. As David Harrington Watt has pointed out, even the most antifeminist polemics in recent evangelical literature accept feminist norms of self-realization and personal autonomy. Modern evangelicals, it would seem, are not nearly as conservative as they, and others, would like to think they are.[2]

Still, the tenacity of each side in pursuing the conflict, for nearly thirty years now, belies a picture of slow infiltration. Evangelicals remain keenly aware of the progress, or lack of progress, of feminist ideals in their schools and churches. As the history of fundamentalism itself makes clear, the energy behind the continuing debate over feminism is not entirely theological; it lies in that murky area where sincerely held doctrinal beliefs meet unexamined cultural attitudes toward gender.

In the second round of controversy, neo-evangelical men had far less cultural permission, as it were, to assert masculine ownership of the faith. Modern feminism's indictment of male chauvinism was so comprehensive and vigorous that it was virtually impossible for male evangelicals to construct the masculine language and comradery that had proved so important before. Talk of "virility" and "manliness" was labeled hopelessly "macho," and masculine homosociality, in modern eyes, had unavoidably homosexual connotations. Indeed, in the cultural climate of the 1970s, it was difficult to speak of masculinity at all.

Thus, neo-evangelical debate shifted onto other, far less productive ground. Disagreements over the proper interpretation of Scripture, always an energetic topic of discussion within fundamentalism, resumed anew.

And when neo-evangelicals took up issues of gender, they did so gingerly. Most retreated to well-traveled ground, discussing the age-old topic of women's role in terms already familiar to generations of fundamentalists. Few had anything to say about the meaning of masculinity.

Neo-Evangelicals and Feminism

The "new evangelicals" encountered the feminist movement unwillingly, for very little in their collective past had prepared them for the encounter. Their fundamentalist heritage had provided no strong, public feminine voice or rhetoric of sexual equality. For decades, fundamentalists had elevated masculine leadership, depicting women as theologically and morally untrustworthy. As a result, feminist ideals penetrated its leadership slowly. (As late as 1973, one prominent scholar dismissed women's liberation as the intellectual equivalent of "sensitivity training and other fads of the New Left."[3]) The "gender gap" in conservative circles was pervasive and purposeful—and proved nearly impossible to breach.

But the feminist movement was equally difficult to avoid. Strict fundamentalists might insulate themselves from its secular message, but neo-evangelicals had purposefully opened themselves to dialogue with the intellectual culture of their society. And feminism soon became one of the most powerful currents of modern thought, especially in theological schools and mainline churches where women possessed superior numbers and traditions of leadership. Moreover, the movement's attraction for neo-evangelical women is not hard to gauge: the strict hierarchical teaching gaining vogue in fundamentalist and neo-evangelical circles in the 1950s undoubtedly persuaded many women in those traditions to demand a public voice.

The loose structure of neo-evangelical institutions hampered progress from the start. The National Association of Evangelicals, formed in 1942, was for years an unstable coalition of conservative denominations with relatively little in common theologically; as a body devoted to interchurch unity it possessed little power to alter ecclesiastical polity on women's issues, and even less desire to do so. With no single church body or institution to channel and order discussion, neo-evangelical magazines provided a forum for argument. But even in that relatively open setting, women's voices emerged with difficulty. Editors wielded considerable power in shaping opinion, a situation intensified by the fact that by 1970 only 10 percent of the member periodicals in the Evangelical Press Association had female editors, and few in consulting or contributing roles.[4]

Undoubtedly many evangelicals first encountered feminism while browsing unwarily through Christian periodicals. Few seemed prepared for an article which appeared in *Eternity* in February 1966, on "Woman's Place: Silence or Service." The author, Letha Dawson Scanzoni, was at the time an Inter-Varsity staff worker at the University of Indiana, studying for a graduate degree in sociology. The article, generally a well-mannered plea for more serious attention to feminine vocations in the church, called attention to the growing inconsistencies in practice that prevented Scanzoni from teaching a mixed Sunday school class but allowed her to lead an evangelistic service for an all-male group of penitentiary inmates.[5]

The tone of reader response two months later, mostly one of offended disbelief, testified to the vast psychic distance between feminist consciousness and neo-evangelical thought. A Texas pastor found Scanzoni's article "a perfect example of why a woman is admonished to be silent in the church," concluding that "most women seem to be incapable of consistent logic when their emotions are involved." Another contributor wondered why the apostle Paul's "simple rules" against "over-ambitious" women dominating Bible studies were so difficult for Scanzoni to understand. "The Bible study leader should invite the ladies to share any ideas they might have as long as the men retain the leadership and control of the group. The women should always be subjective [*sic*] enough to wait until they are invited to participate." Still another letter writer, a Baptist pastor from New England, admitted that women were "filling a gap in many areas of the ministry today where there ought to be men." Still, he cautioned, the New Testament passages against women teaching must be observed; in his view a more appropriate title for the article would be "Women's Place: Silence *in* Service."[6]

But the air of finality in these responses was far from prophetic; feminism was not an issue that neo-evangelicals were destined to deal with gracefully. *Eternity* published another article by Scanzoni in July 1968, this time advocating a biblical basis for marital "partnership." Actually, as the story goes, the article slipped past editorial scrutiny; thus before its final publication the editors requested an accompanying photograph of

Scanzoni alongside her husband, with a description of their mutual hobbies and interests, apparently to tone down the potentially "radical" impact.[7]

Even by the early 1970s, feminist consciousness had not penetrated far into neo-evangelical social concern. At a Thanksgiving workshop held in Chicago in 1973, a distinguished group of fifty-three evangelicals met to draw up a progressive social agenda—with only three female delegates. A feminist plank was inserted when one of the women, Nancy Hardesty, then an editor for *Eternity*, responded to a whispered invitation from one of the male delegates. Through this route the 1973 Chicago Declaration acknowledged feminism, but with the relatively mild admission that "we have encouraged men to prideful domination and women to irresponsible passivity," calling both sexes to "mutual submission and active discipleship."[8]

That simple statement, far from radical by secular standards, was strong stuff for most neo-evangelicals. Although many were more than willing to admit that inequities existed, especially at top leadership levels, they balked at endorsing an explicitly feminist agenda. The editors of *Christianity Today* reluctantly concluded in 1973 that though it might be time for evangelical women to organize and "fulfill themselves as human beings with God-given abilities, . . . we wish it were unnecessary."[9]

And, to be sure, the Evangelical Women's Caucus, one of the several "workshops" to emerge from the 1973 meeting, generated its share of controversy. At the second meeting of Evangelicals for Social Action in 1974 a hastily submitted proposal by Evangelical Women's Caucus leaders to endorse both the equal rights amendment and women's ordination provoked intense controversy. The latter proposal, according to one report, was a "source of anguish" that left the assembly angrily divided and the women quickly heading into a separate organization.[10] The rift was growing on both sides. As Rufus Jones, a Conservative Baptist member of the planning committee, confided to an irate constituent, "we will not let this happen again. . . . The problem is we did not want to create an organization. It was merely a discussion group which had no proper organization and . . . got out of hand when three or four extremists took advantage of the situation."[11]

Despite this reluctance among evangelical leaders, feminism was finding adherents among the ranks, particularly in the wake of enthusiasm surrounding the Chicago Declaration. Left-wing evangelicals, most of whom subscribed to the *Other Side* and the *Post-American* (later *Sojourners*), embraced it with enthusiasm. Evangelicals for Social Action became a firm advocate of feminist goals. Even mainstream evangelical periodicals published cautious endorsements of women's rights, at least partly in response to a growing curiosity, though not necessarily full support, from their readers. In 1975, the evangelical feminist handbook, *All We're Meant to Be*, by Letha Scanzoni and Nancy Hardesty, was voted the "most influential" book of the year by subscribers to *Eternity*; Fuller professor Paul Jewett's controversial book on *Man as Male and Female* won fourth place.[12]

But suspicions remained that feminism itself, with its emphasis on self-realization and personal autonomy, was basically antithetical to evangelical religion. It not only clashed with historic attitudes toward feminine submission but rejected the self-abnegating tone of much evangelical piety, which had not drifted far from its fundamentalist moorings. Evangelical feminism forsook the passive feminine voice for the masculine one of social critique, and with it the largely feminine piety of self-denial and service. The strident tones of feminists clashed uneasily with the quiet, intimate voice women normally assumed in fundamentalist discourse. Moreover, to neo-evangelical ears, the feminist critique of male chauvinism was laden with negative implications; demands for more women leaders only served to underline the socially vulnerable position of evangelical men in a largely female-dominated constituency.

Biblical Battles

But these underlying concerns were soon subordinated to an intense debate over the proper interpretation of Scripture. The controversy in one sense defused some of the more difficult issues feminism raised for evangelical men and women; combatants could exhaust themselves over the precise meaning of Greek verbs and pronouns without confronting far more problematic issues raised by feminist social critique. But the debate largely failed to convince the evangelical public one way or the other, or to create a common ground for dialogue between the two extremes.

The lines did seem to be clearly drawn, although the heat of controversy soon blurred the finer points of most hermeneutical arguments. In the tradition of Elizabeth Cady Stanton and the female scholars who assembled the *Woman's Bible* in the 1890s, evangelical feminists sought to reinterpret the words of Scripture into more egalitarian language. Actually, despite the common charge that evangelical feminists, in emphasizing the role of experience and the example of Christ, verged on dangerously "neo-orthodox" hermeneutics, the tradition they embraced was more Wesleyan than anything else. More properly their arguments harked back to the feminist tradition within the holiness movement, which fundamentalists had emphatically rejected decades before. Evangelical feminists discarded both Calvinist and dispensational systems of interpretation and adopted largely perfectionist arguments for the equality of the sexes. Small wonder, perhaps, that the biblical debates over modern evangelical feminism have a curiously antique ring to them; they are a nearly complete restatement of an unsuccessful dialogue that began nearly a century ago.[13]

Only this time the debate pitted perfectionists against a more formidable opponent. Most neo-evangelicals were conservative Calvinists rather than dispensationalists, standing in direct line with J. Gresham Machen rather than Bob Jones or John R. Rice. They abandoned the separatist stance of classic fundamentalism for a more world-affirming Calvinist position that true Christianity could gradually transform secular society into a more godly mold. Although this understanding allowed them to speak to social issues of race and economic inequality, it actually increased their conservatism on the woman question.

Calvinists rooted sexual inequality in the original created order, in contrast to dispensationalists who traced it to the curse of Eve. At the turn of the century, this latter stance proved adequate to refute arguments against women's ordination. Since few women, aside from radical feminists, argued for full social equality of the sexes, dispensationalists were even free to speculate about the original equality of the first pair. In more recent years, however, sexual equality has been a central point of disagreement between feminists and conservatives. Theirs is a wider debate about feminine submission both in the church and in the family.

Latter-day Calvinists found a pattern of hierarchy and rule embedded in God's original intent for humanity. "In the created, natural order," Elton Eenigenberg wrote, "... the principle of subjection is permanent, even with Christians." He argued that equality between the sexes belonged to a future state; on earth "the principle of subjection is with us on every hand: wife to husband, children to parents, citizens to the state, and congregations to elders or bishops. This is not our arrangement but God's."[14]

Buttressed by this certainty, neo-evangelical opponents of feminism pressed their case still further. Critics of evangelical feminist hermeneutics warned that its errors would inevitably lead to apostasy. "Whether these individuals have a proper right to the term *evangelical* is a difference of opinion," H. Wayne House conceded, "but that they have weakened the walls is undeniable." Harold Lindsell warned that feminists argued for equality "by directly and deliberately denying that the Bible is the infallible rule of faith and practice. Once they do this, they have ceased to be evangelical; Scripture is no longer normative."[15]

In fact many feminists did reject neo-evangelical orthodoxy. In 1974 John Alexander, editor of the *Other Side*, admitted that he found no way of getting around the passages of Scripture that demanded women's silence and submission. The only possible solution, he wrote, was to "fudge on the Bible's authority." In 1975 he conceded in an interview with evangelical feminist Virginia Ramey Mollenkott that Paul might have been simply mistaken in his apparently sexist views.[16] Paul K. Jewett's book, on *Man as Male and Female*, arrived at much the same conclusion and provoked a new round of controversy among Fuller Seminary's already conflicted faculty. Jewett retained his faculty position only after delicate negotiating.[17]

Redefining Gender

Leading feminists and neo-evangelicals parted ways in the 1970s over biblical matters, leaving behind a constituency increasingly confused about the practical implications of either position. In the wake of widening controversy, both sides had left scant room for productive dialogue.

Many evangelical feminists responded to the order of creation argument by denying the spiritual reality of gender distinctions. Virginia Mollenkott, for example, denounced hierarchical thinking as "unbiblical and anti-Christian." "Women in society ought to be viewed and treated not as women *per se*," another apologist agreed, "but as spiritual beings no different from men."[18]

Such views were much easier to state than to practice. Critics easily took feminists to task for oversimplification, arguing that the idea of "non-differentiated, unisexual, neutered personhood" stripped even biological sex differences of meaning or purpose. Elisabeth Elliot Leitch, reporting on the 1975 convention of the Evangelical Women's Caucus, decried what she saw as a "faceless, colorless, sexless wasteland where rule and submission are regarded as a curse" and replaced by a "selfish and egocentric insistence on 'rights.' " She noted with dismay that "womanliness was not mentioned at the Caucus" and no workshops were offered on "what it means to be a woman."[19]

Actually, practical questions of this type were attracting growing interest among evangelicals in the 1970s, especially in more conservative quarters. Bill Gothard, a teacher clearly in the mold of John R. Rice, gained an enormous following for his seminars on "Basic Youth Conflicts." Fully aware of the growing evangelical perplexity over sex roles, Gothard emphasized a domestic "chain of command," a progression of authority that began with God and husbands and descended to wives and children. Though hardly democratic, Gothard's teachings did do away with painful ambiguity. As one male enthusiast claimed, "it erased all shades of gray. I'm convinced that God did not make gray. When it comes to moral issues, things are black and white."[20]

By the mid-1970s most evangelical feminists found the conservative mind-set seemed everywhere triumphant. In 1980 Patricia Gundry, a feminist commentator, noted sadly that chain of command thinking "is so widely accepted among believers that it is seldom questioned at all," a statement that still describes many conservative evangelicals today.[21]

But difficult questions remained. Though conservative evangelicals devoted an inordinate amount of attention to the precise dimensions of "women's role," they rarely addressed the men in their audience with equal clarity. The result was a genuine confusion over what true Christian manliness entailed. In sociologist Judith Stacey's recent description of an evangelical marriage, the husband rarely invoked his god-given authority for he appeared to have little understanding of his masculine prerogatives or any will to enforce them. His wife deferred in submission, but often as a less than subtle means of compelling him out of religious passivity.[22]

Such instances are hardly evidence of feminist success; rather, they indicate a huge void in evangelical discussion of sex roles. One need not search far to find detailed, sometimes exhaustive, teaching on the role of women in evangelical literature; only recently have evangelicals returned to what should be a historically familiar topic, the masculine dimensions of their evangelical faith.

And they have done so with zeal. A recent issue of *Focus on the Family*, highlighting the "Christian men's movement," listed numerous organizations and resources for evangelical men in search of spiritual peers. The Promise Keepers, a group founded by Bill McCartney, a University of Colorado football coach, vowed to "revolutionize this continent by teaching and encouraging men to embrace the balanced concepts of biblical manhood."[23]

From this point in time, however, it appears that the evangelical men's movement will only widen the existing standoff between feminists and conservatives. In his book *Straight Talk*, Focus on the Family president James Dobson reminded men that their new-found emotional sensitivity did not allow them to abdicate the "time-honored relationship of husband as loving protector and wife as recipient of that protection." Gordon Dalbey, author of *Healing the Masculine Soul*, pinned equal blame for the masculine crisis on "a woman's movement that requires they abdicate masculinity to gain sensitivity and a deluge of Rambo-like media portrayals."[24]

All of this suggests that the real work for evangelicals still remains. It is rare to encounter neo-evangelical men who are aware of the issues feminism raises for their own sex, at least in categories that are not merely antifeminist. Equally rare is any critique of the pervasively masculine orientation of much evangelical practice and historical expression. Authentic masculinity is an elusive matter in the late-twentieth century, but it should not be ignored. It is perhaps the place where fresh social dialogue among evangelicals might begin. Indeed, if healing is to occur, this is where it must happen.

Abbreviations

ABHS	American Baptist Historical Society
BC	*Bible Champion*
BST	*Bible Student and Teacher*
KB	*King's Business*
MBIM	*Moody Bible Institute Monthly*
MM	*Moody Monthly*
OH	*Our Hope*
SL	*Sword of the Lord*
SST	*Sunday-School Times*
Truth	*Truth; or Testimony for Christ*
WE	*Winona Echoes*

Notes

Introduction

1. The Danvers Statement first appeared as a paid advertisement in the January 13, 1989, issue of *Christianity Today*. See also R. K. McGregor Wright, "A Response to the Danvers Statement," paper presented at the Christians for Biblical Equality Conference, June 1989, St. Paul, Minn. See also Nancy Ammerman's depiction of sex roles in a contemporary fundamentalist congregation in *Bible Believers*, 134–46; on Dobson, see Stacey, *Brave New Families*, 6–63; for a feminist critique, see Spretnak, "Christian Right's 'Holy War,' " 470–96.

2. Hunter, *Evangelicalism*; see also Quebedeaux, *Young Evangelicals*.

3. Stacey, *Brave New Families*, 41–174.

4. See Hunter, *Culture Wars*, esp. 176–96.

5. See, e.g., A. Duane Litfin, "Evangelical Feminism: Why Traditionalists Reject It," *Bibliotheca Sacra* 136 (July–September 1979): 267; and Alexander, "Are Women People?" 31, 33.

6. John R. Rice, "Father, Mother, Home, and Heaven," *SL* 9 (August 1946): 4.

7. Two foundational studies are Marsden, *Fundamentalism and American Culture*, and Sandeen, *Roots of Fundamentalism*. For a succinct sorting of fundamentalism's role in contemporary evangelicalism, see George Marsden, "Fundamentalism and American Evangelicalism," in *Variety of American Evangelicalism*, ed. Dayton and Johnston, 22–35.

8. In 1936, e.g., John R. Rice rejected the label Holy Roller from his fellow Texas fundamentalist, J. Frank Norris, with the defense that he did not believe in tongues, sinless perfection, or women preachers. On the issue of miraculous healing, which Rice tended to support, the line was less clearly drawn; both

groups retained ample room for the possibility of supernatural events. See "Pastors Refute Attack on Rice," *SL* 7 (February 1936): 1.

9. See Hunter, *American Evangelicalism*. On neo-evangelicals, see Marsden, *Reforming Fundamentalism*. In its popular usage, "evangelical" also includes an array of conservative Protestants, including charismatics and neo-pentecostals.

10. Wills, *Under God*, 21. See also Frances Fitzgerald's depiction of Jerry Falwell's empire in *Cities on a Hill*, 121–201.

11. Moore, *Religious Outsiders*, 163–72.

12. See Hofstadter, *Anti-Intellectualism*, 117–29.

13. Caroline Walker Bynum, ". . . And Woman His Humanity," in *Gender and Religion*, ed. Bynum et al., 269.

14. Macartney, *Ancient Wives and Modern Husbands*, 103, 154.

Chapter One

1. Hatch, *Democratization*; Smith, *Revivalism*.

2. Simpson quoted in Andrews, "Restricted Freedom," 220.

3. Palmer, *Promise of the Father*; Smith, *Revivalism*, 143–45; Melder, *Beginnings of Sisterhood*; Ryan, *Cradle of the Middle Class*.

4. Frances Willard, "Woman and Philanthropy," *Woman's Magazine* 10 (August 1887): 604; Ehrenreich and English, *For Her Own Good*, 33–98.

5. "Female Usefulness in the Church," *Christian Advocate and Journal* 17 February 1859, 28. See also Smith, *Revivalism*, 114–34; Loveland, "Domesticity and Religion"; Andrews, *Sisters of the Spirit*.

6. Donald W. Dayton, "Introduction" to *Holiness Tracts*, viii–x

7. Palmer, *Promise of the Father*, 345, 328.

8. Ginzberg, *Women and the Work of Benevolence*; Hill, *The World Their Household*.

9. Eaton, *Heroine of the Cross*, 28.

10. Sewall, speaking at 1895 meeting, quoted in *History and Minutes of the National Council of Women*, 215; Willard, *Woman in the Pulpit*, 21.

11. Myers, *Why Men Do Not Go to Church*, vii.

12. Brinkerhoff quoted in Jenny Bland Beauchamp, "Apostasy in the Churches," *Christian Alliance and Foreign Missions Weekly* 21 February 1896, 179. See also DeBerg, *Ungodly Women*. The national censuses for 1906, 1916, 1926, and 1936 reported denominational membership and sex ratios, the 1936 census in greatest detail. Although it is not possible to calculate changes in relative numbers of male and female church members with high accuracy because of inconsistent data, the disproportionate number of women was clearly significant. In the major denominations

two-thirds of members reported by sex were female; only some of the smaller sects and immigrant churches reported anywhere near even numbers. See also Fry, *United States Looks at Its Churches*, 14, 24.

In terms of actual church attendance, an even more difficult figure to report accurately, estimates ranged from three-fourths to nine-tenths female. See, e.g., Lynd and Lynd, *Middletown*, 359.

It did appear, however, that campaigns to recruit laymen had a positive, though not dramatic, effect on membership in some denominations. Northern Presbyterians in particular reported gradual growth in male membership in the twentieth century. Still, throughout the entire period, females remained in the majority, even in male-dominated sects like the Plymouth Brethren.

13. Filene, *Him/Her/Self*, 69–70. See also Wiebe, *Search for Order*; Sennett, *Families against the City*; Clyde Griffen, "Reconstructing Masculinity from the Evangelical Revival to the Waning of Progressivism: A Speculative Synthesis," in *Meanings for Manhood*, ed. Carnes and Griffen, 183–204. See also E. Anthony Rotundo, "Body and Soul: Changing Ideals of American Middle-Class Manhood, 1770–1920," *Journal of Social History* 16 (1983): 23–35.

14. Helen Campbell, "Certain Forms of Woman's Work for Woman," *Century Magazine* 38 (June 1889): 219.

15. Holland quoted in Victor, *Women's War*, 5–6; "The Women and the Temperance Question," *Nation* 26 February 1874, 136.

16. Pierson, *Modern Mission Century*, 162.

17. James Buckley, "Because They Are Women," in *Debate in the Methodist Episcopal Church*, 8. See also Mary T. Lathrap, "Women in the Methodist Church," in *Transactions of the National Council of Women in the United States*, ed. Avery, 109.

18. Rev. Willis H. Butler, "What Men Like: Three Things That Stir Enthusiasm," *Congregationalist and Christian World* 23 September 1911, 411.

19. *Presbyterian Brotherhood: Report of the First Convention*, 67; *Presbyterian Brotherhood: Report of the Second Convention*, 26.

20. Walter Rauschenbusch, "The Gospel for the Men of Today," *Congregationalist and Christian World* 23 September 1911.

21. Susan Curtis, "The Son of Man and God the Father: The Social Gospel and Victorian Masculinity," in *Meanings for Manhood*, ed. Carnes and Griffen, 67–78; Fishburn, *Fatherhood of God*.

22. Butler, "What Men Like," 411. According to Susan Curtis, the Social Gospel failed in part because its redefinition of masculinity melded too easily with the businessman ideal of twentieth-century capitalism; see her "The Son of Man and God the Father."

23. "Busy Week for Dr. Riley. Evangelist to Conduct Meetings in Men and Religion Movement," *Duluth Herald* 19 February 1912, William Bell Riley Papers; Gray, *Bible Problems Explained*, 40 (the "Bible problem" under discussion was "Why do not men go to church?"); Myers, *Why Men Do Not Go to Church*, 31.

24. "Wheaton's 300 Per Cent Growth in Ten Years," *SST* 26 February 1938, 151. For striking portraits of these and other leaders see Russell, *Voices of American Fundamentalism*. For a more detailed discussion of fundamentalist constructions of masculinity, see chapter 3.

25. Smith, *Revivalism*, chapter 4; Bell, *Crusade in the City*, 196–97.

26. Sizer, *Gospel Hymns and Social Religion*, 138–39.

27. Willard F. Mallalieu, "Mr. Moody's Ministry to Men," in *Dwight L. Moody: His Life and Labors*, ed. Davenport, 124–34.

28. "Sermon to Fallen Women," in *Moody: His Words, Works, and Workers*, ed. Daniels, 433–42.

29. "Editorials," *Record of Christian Work* 11 (September 1892): 262.

30. William Biederwolf, "The Office of an Evangelist," *WE* (1904): 131–49; A. J. Gordon, "Plain English on Church Rackets. No. 2," *Watchword* 14 (December 1894): 312–15. See also Henry Varley, "Evangelists," *Watchword* 1 (December 1878): 35.

31. Moody, "Address to Young Men," in *Great Joy*, 308, 316.

32. A. J. Gordon, "Editorial," *Watchword* 2 (May 1880): 141.

33. George Marsden has described the American Keswick movement as "male-dominated." See Marsden, *Fundamentalism and American Culture*, 78–80.

34. "Manliness in Religion," *New York Observer* 7 April 1870, 109.

35. Brereton, *From Sin to Salvation*, 39–41. See also Epstein, *Politics of Domesticity*, 47–63.

36. A. J. Gordon, "Editorial," *Watchword* 3 (February 1881): 81.

37. Marsden, *Fundamentalism and American Culture*, 72–80.

38. *Victorious Christ*, 13. Keswick teaching also had a feminist dimension, as Jessie Penn-Lewis argued in *The Magna Charta of Women* (1919; reprint, Minneapolis, Minn.: Bethany Fellowship, 1975).

39. *Victorious Life*, 330–31, 338–39.

40. A. J. Gordon, "To Ministers," *Watchword* 1 (March 1879): 108; A. J. Gordon, "The Inner Life," *Watchword* 6 (December 1883): 52–53.

41. John Balcom Shaw, "The Good and Bad in Modern Evangelism," *WE* (1909): 40.

42. Wacker, "Holy Spirit," 45–62. During this period, Wacker finds more disparity between Wesleyan and Reformed views of holiness than between the "new theology" of so-called liberals and the higher life teaching.

43. *Victory in Christ*, 36.

44. Billy Sunday, "Positive vs. Negative Religion," Box 9, Folder 79, William A. Sunday Papers, Billy Graham Center Archives, Wheaton, Ill. See also Dorsett, *Billy Sunday*; William Ward Ayer's description of his conversion during Sunday's famous "baseball sermon" in Mel Larson, *God's Man in Manhattan: The Biography of Wil-*

liam Ward Ayer (Grand Rapids, Mich.: Zondervan, 1950), reprinted in Joel Carpenter, ed., *Enterprising Fundamentalism.*

45. Mencken, *In Defense of Women*, 177.

46. Dixon and Smith referred to in "Men and Religion," *Christian Workers Magazine* 11 (May 1911): 759.

47. *Winona*, 7–9; Kane, *All About Winona*, 6–7. Originally acquired by the local body of the Presbyterian Church as a meeting ground, Winona was soon sold to Christian entrepreneurs who self-consciously described their business careers as inherently godly undertakings. The Chautauqua and Bible conferences used the same meeting grounds but met separately.

48. Fred B. Smith, "Evangelistic Work for Men," *Addresses Delivered at the Winona Bible Conference, . . . 1902* (Winona Lake, Ind., 1902), 50. Smith was also a well-known leader in the Men and Religion Forward Movement.

49. Edwin Hughes, "The Layman," *WE* (1916): 96. Note that the precise gender definition of "layman" was not always uniform and was a matter of dispute in the Methodist Episcopal Church when women argued for full laity rights. See Alpha J. Kynett, "Our Laity: And Their Rights without Distinction of Sex in the Methodist Episcopal Church," in *Debate in the Methodist Episcopal Church*, ed. DeSwart Gifford. Women never used the term *laymen* to refer to themselves, however.

50. George R. Stuart, "Who Is My Brother?" *WE* (1912): 110. Blanchard's audience included numerous temperance women, but appeared to be predominantly male. See list of signers (where 2 out of 331 were female) in "Call for a Conference of Christians on the Secret Lodge System," *Christian Cynosure* 27 February 1890, 7, 13. The secret societies themselves, like fundamentalism, represented a masculine alternative to "feminized" evangelical religion in the nineteenth century. See Carnes, *Secret Ritual.*

51. Simpson quoted in Andrews, "Restricted Freedom," 237.

52. Elizabeth Needham wrote a conservative treatment of women's role in a book entitled *Women's Ministry* (1895); Maria Gordon, who retained a leadership role in her husband's Clarendon Street Baptist Church in Boston for years after his death, wrote a famous article on "Women as Evangelists" in *Northfield Echoes* (see, e.g., Mrs. A. J. Gordon, "Women as Evangelists," *Northfield Echoes*, vol. 1 [E. Northfield, Mass., 1894], 147–51); and Helen Sunday was a sought-after speaker both during and after her husband's lifetime. Billy once praised her as "not the best looker in the world, but she's got more horse sense in her old pate than any woman I've ever met." See Parker, *Billy Sunday Meetings*, 41. Of Sunday's 50 various assistants, 15 were female. See "The Papers of William and Helen Sunday: A Guide to the Microfilm Edition," ed. Robert Shuster (Billy Graham Center, 1978), 26–27; G. P. Pardington, *Twenty-Five Wonderful Years, 1889–1914: A Popular Sketch of the Christian and Missionary Alliance* (Christian Alliance Publishing, 1914; reprint, New York: Garland Publishing, 1984), 205. Asher's work will be discussed more fully in chapter 4.

53. On Moody and Dryer, see Hassey, *No Time For Silence*, 34–36; Mrs. A. T. Gaylord, "Students' Aid Society of the Women's Department," *Institute Tie* 1 (December 1900): 114; Robinson, *A Reporter at Moody's*, 95. Moody was initially reluc-

tant to begin training men for the ministry because he believed this would bring his school into direct competition with denominational seminaries.

54. Robinson, *A Reporter at Moody's*, 33, 65. Surveys of enrollment figures for Northwestern Bible Institute, Gordon College of Theology and Missions, and Moody Bible Institute reveal consistently high proportions of female students. Moody was the only school I encountered in my survey of enrollment statistics where men ever outnumbered women in a given year. On Bible schools, see Brereton, *Training God's Army*.

55. "Northwestern News," *Pilot* 6 (April 1921): 54; "The World's Lighting System," *Christian Fundamentals in School and Church* 3 (April–June 1921): 36–39.

56. "Our Girl Evangelists," *School and Church* 1 (October 1916): 4; Trollinger, *God's Empire*, 105–7. See Appendices 7 and 8 in Hassey, *No Time for Silence*, 169–82, for lists of women preachers, evangelists, and Bible teachers of Moody Bible Institute.

57. Getz, *MBI: The Story of Moody Bible Institute*, 37, 62–65. Moody's address is found in *Record of Christian Work* 5 (February 1886): 5–6.

58. Brereton, *Training God's Army*, 129. For further discussion of restricted programs and quotas, see chapter 4.

59. Jessie Van Booskirk, "Studies in the Book of Judges," *School and Church* 2 (January 1918): 11; Simpson quoted in Andrews, "Restricted Freedom," 226–27.

60. "Evangelistic Work," *Union Signal* 13 March 1890, 8; "Chautauqua Training School for Temperance Workers, Under the N.W.C.T.U.," *Our Union* 8 (February 1882): 10.

61. *Minutes of the 3rd Convention of the National Woman's Christian Temperance Union, Held in Newark, NJ . . . 1876* (Chicago, 1889), 107; "Shall Women Preach?" *Union Signal* 7 March 1889, 8.

62. The tactic sometimes brought controversy: see Boyd, "Shall Women Speak?"; and Willard, *Women and Temperance*, 183–84.

63. A. J. Gordon, "The Ministry of Women," *Missionary Review of the World* 17 (1894): 910–21; see, e.g., "Editorial," *Friends' Missionary Advocate* 3 (February 1887): 24; W. L. Parsons, "May a Woman Speak?" *Advance* 21 September 1876, 43; "Womanly Propriety," *Advance* 5 October 1876, 72–73.

64. Merriam, *A History of American Baptist Missions*, 99; Horton, *The Builders*; "The Women's Building Dedicated," *Christian Workers' Magazine* (July 1911): 979–80; Brereton, *Training God's Army*, 55–63.

65. Willard, *Glimpses of Fifty Years*, 359–61; Daniels, ed., *Moody: His Words, Work, and Workers*, 508–10. Suffragists reported Willard's exit from the Moody campaign with some glee, decrying the denominational bigotry of the "vain and fanatical Evangelical revivalist," even though her role in the Boston controversy was a matter of some dispute. See "An Awkward Situation," *Ballot Box* 2 (August 1877): 5; "Miss Willard, Her Position as Regards the 'Liberals'—An Explanation," *Ballot Box* 2 (November 1877): 2.

66. E. P. Marvin, "Separation," *Watchword* 14 (September–October 1894): 232–33.

67. "Gentle Womanhood," *Christian Workers Magazine* 11 (April 1911): 673.

68. "The Church and Men: Its Hold on Them Considered by Evangelist W. B. Riley in Revival Discourse Last Evening," 3 March 1910, unid. clipping, William Bell Riley Papers.

Chapter Two

1. See DeBerg, *Ungodly Women.*

2. Note the observation by Mila Frances Tupper that churches with centralized governments were slowest to ordain women and that more congregational ones allowed for the greatest diversity, as well as influence by local preferences. See "Present Status of Women in the Churches," *Transactions of the National Council of Women*, 98–107.

3. On women in mainline denominations, see Virginia Lieson Brereton, "United and Slighted: Women as Subordinated Insiders," in *Between the Times*, ed. Hutchison, 143–67; Chafe, *The American Woman*, 25–47.

4. See Marsden, *Fundamentalism and American Culture*, 109–18; Noll, *Between Faith and Criticism.*

5. Charles Hodge, "The Bible Argument on Slavery," in *Cotton Is King* (Augusta, Ga., 1860), 861, 863, 848. Hodge was less willing to defend Southern slavery in practice, however.

6. Hogeland, "Charles Hodge," 251–52.

7. "Dr. Burr's Appeal 'To Laymen,' " *BST* 1 (March 1904): 194. The article subsequently appeared as a "Bible League Tract No. 1" entitled "To Christian Laymen concerning the Higher Criticism." "League Notes and Points," *BST* 1 (August 1904): 512.

8. Niebuhr and Williams, eds., *Ministry in Historical Perspective*, 250–88.

9. Francis Patton, "The Present Assault on the Bible," *BST* 1 (May 1904): 267; Rev. Dr. Worden, "The American Bible League and the Sabbath School," *BST* 1 (June 1904): 382; W. E. Scofield, "The Pastor's Opportunity as a Bible Teacher," *BST* 4 (March 1906): 211. Like any new enterprise, the League also recognized the practical benefits of male support. "Christian men control . . . almost one-half of the wealth of the globe," one supporter reasoned. "We of the League believe that many of these men of large means need only to be instructed in the Bible teaching concerning the stewardship of wealth, in order to bring them to the consecration of vast amounts to such ends as are proposed by the League" (Daniel S. Gregory, "The Aims and Methods of the American Bible League," *BST* 3 [June 1906]: 451).

10. See Blaisdell, "Matrix of Reform, 13–44.

11. Alexander McGill, "Deaconesses," *Princeton Review* 1 (1880): 283, 287; for Warfield's views, see *Minutes of the General Assembly* (New York, 1890), 119–21;

Minutes of the General Assembly (New York, 1893), 170. Despite denominational endorsement, few women entered deaconess orders, a relatively low status occupation. See Boyd and Brackenridge, *Presbyterian Women in America*, 112–14.

12. Benjamin Warfield, "Paul on Women Speaking in the Church," *Presbyterian* 15 July 1920, 8–9.

13. *History of Woman Suffrage*, ed. Stanton et al., 1:7.

14. Kraditor, *Ideas of the Woman Suffrage Movement*, 76; Smylie, "*Woman's Bible* and the Spiritual Crisis."

15. *Woman's Bible*, 16, 26–27.

16. Smylie, "*Woman's Bible* and the Spiritual Crisis," 314–15.

17. Gage, *Woman, Church, and State*, 234–35.

18. *Woman's Bible*, 173.

19. *History of Woman Suffrage*, ed. Stanton et al., 1:513, 3:152.

20. Ibid., 4:374; Matilda Gage, "Religious Tyranny," *Ballot Box* 2 (December 1877): 4; Harper, *Life of Susan B. Anthony*, 2:596.

21. Kate Tannatt Woods, "Woman in the Pulpit" in *Transactions of the National Council of Women*, 287; Boardman, *Who Shall Publish the Glad Tidings?* 39. The ties between feminism and the holiness movement have been well documented: see Dayton and Dayton, "Your Daughters Shall Prophesy."

22. *Minutes of the National Woman's Christian Temperance Union*, 39, 41. In I Timothy 5:23, Paul advised Timothy to "no longer drink only water, but [to] take a little wine for the sake of your stomach and your frequent ailments." See Smith, *Revivalism*, 216–18.

23. Lathrap, "Women in the Methodist Church," in *Transactions of the National Council of Women*, 24.

24. F. M. B., "Answer to Dr. Crosby," *Our Union* 15 January 1880, 2; Blake, *Woman's Place Today*, 48–49.

25. Blake, *Woman's Place Today*, 13; Willard, *Woman in the Pulpit*, 47; *Address of Frances E. Willard*, 34.

26. Gilman, *His Religion and Hers*, 92–93; Mencken, *In Defense of Women*, 184.

27. James H. Brookes, "Inspiration," *Truth* 21 (April 1895): 197; John Kernighan, "The Interpretation of Scripture," *Truth* 21 (September 1895): 451.

28. Wilkin, *Prophesying of Women*, 245, 323–24.

29. See, e.g., "Taking the Bible 'Literally,' " *MBIM* 23 (January 1923): 191–92; Graham Gilmer, "Should Christian Women Speak or Lead in Prayer in Our Churches?" *MBIM* 27 (January 1928): 223–24; Grant Stroh, "Practical and Perplexing Questions," *MBIM* 21 (September 1920): 21.

30. Finley D. Jenkins, "The Self-Destruction of the Movement to License and Or-

dain Women," *Presbyterian* 27 March 1930, 27; Ethelbert D. Warfield, "May Women Be Ordained in the Presbyterian Church?" *Presbyterian* 14 November 1929, 6.

31. Scofield, *Prophecy Made Plain*, 21–22; Gray, *Great Epochs of Sacred History*, 36, 38.

32. Evans, *Book of Genesis*, 31.

33. Clouser, *Dispensations and Ages of Scripture*, 113.

34. On premillennial dispensationalism, see Sandeen, *The Roots of Fundamentalism*; Marsden, *Fundamentalism and American Culture*, 43–71; Weber, *Living in the Shadow of the Second Coming*.

35. Elizabeth Needham, "Leprosy in Houses," *Truth* 9 (August 1882): 418. See also James Brookes, "At Home with the Lord," *Truth* 3 (December 1876): 5–6.

36. "Editorial," *Watchword* 8 (June 1886): 73.

37. For descriptions of meetings, see "The Prophetic Conference," *Watchword* 1 (December 1878): 40–41; George C. Needham, "Believers' Meeting for Bible Study," *Truth* 9 (September 1882): 467–70.

38. "Bible and Prophetic Conference," *Truth* 12 (November 1886): 562–68; *The Coming and Kingdom of Christ*, 242–49.

39. Magnuson, *Salvation in the Slums*, 112–17.

40. On charismatic arguments supporting women speaking, see, e.g., Andrews, "Restricted Freedom"; and Maria Gordon, "Women as Evangelists," *Northfield Echoes* 1 (1894): 147–51. A recent study of Pentecostal women evangelists and pastors in rural Missouri points out the relatively weak authority of the female itinerants as compared to the recognized authority of a pastor, a role very few, even charismatic, women aspired to. See Lawless, *Handmaidens of the Lord*, 89–110.

41. *Scofield Reference Bible*, ed. Scofield, notes to Gen. 3:14, p. 9. See also, e.g., J. M. Stifler, "The Second Coming and Christian Doctrine," in *Addresses on the Second Coming of Our Lord*, 166–67; Clarence Larkin, *Dispensational Truth, or God's Plan and Purpose in the Ages* (Philadelphia, 1924), 32–34, 149–50.

42. Stifler, "The Five-Fold Gospel," *OH* 5 (August–September 1898): 97; see also Stifler, "Second Coming and Christian Doctrine," 166.

43. Needham, *Woman's Ministry*, 11.

44. John F. Kendall, "The Family," *Truth* 11 (March 1885): 184. See also Gray, *Christian Workers' Commentary on the Old and New Testaments*, 372.

45. Dayton, "Introduction," to *Holiness Tracts*, viii–x.

46. See, e.g., Pierson, "God's Word to Women," *Northfield Echoes* 3 (1896): 252–63; A. J. Gordon, "The Ministry of Women," *Missionary Review of the World* 7 (December 1894): 910–21.

47. Gordon, "Shall Women Prophesy?" *Watchword* 8 (January 1887): 250; Gordon, "Twofold Fulfillment of Prophecy," *Watchword* 5 (September 1883): 267–68. See also A.

R. Fausset, "The Promised Blessing of the Latter Rain," *Watchword* 5 (August 1883): 248–52.

48. James Brookes, "Ministry of Women," *Truth* 21 (February 1895): 89. This dispute pointed to a later fracturing among dispensationalists over the meaning of Acts 2. Ultradispensationalists, or "Bullingerists," (after spokesman Ethelbert W. Bullinger) believed that all of the events in Acts, until the twenty-eighth chapter, belonged to a transitional period before the Jews had ceded their role in salvation history to the Gentile church. Ultradispensationalists therefore do not practice water baptism or the Lord's Supper because they believe both sacraments belong to that previous dispensation.

49. Whittle, "Daily Scripture Readings," *Record of Christian Work* 11 (October 1892): 315; Needham, *Woman's Ministry*, 7, 21. See also Arno C. Gaebelein, "Notes on Prophecy to the Jews," *OH* 13 (July 1906): 50.

50. Arno C. Gaebelein, "The Acts of the Apostles," *OH* 14 (November 1907): 320–21; Gaebelein, *Healing Question*, 81; Gaebelein, "What Is This?" *OH* 27 (August 1920): 77–78. See also F. C. Jennings, "The Pentecostal Movement and the Standard of Truth," *OH* 17 (January 1921): 410–18.

51. D. W. Whittle, "Daily Scripture Readings," *Record of Christian Work* 11 (October 1892): 357; Brookes, "Woman's Vote a Disappointment," *Truth* 21 (March 1895): 121. See also Kernighan, "The Interpretation of Scripture," 450–51.

52. "Women in Politics," *Truth* 21 (January 1895): 6; "Woman Suffrage," *Watchman* 7 (March 1895): 1–2.

53. Trumbull, *Prophecy's Light on Today*, 122.

54. See, e.g., Isaac Wylie, "A Word of Warning to Women," *Watchword* 14 (September–October 1894): 258–59; "Religion Enough to Hurt," *Truth* 9 (October 1882): 486–89.

55. "Infidelity among Women," *Truth* 12 (August 1886): 387. See also Gray, *Great Epochs of Sacred History*, 69.

56. James Orr, "The Virgin Birth of Christ," in *Fundamentals*, 1:11. Orr suggested, and many other writers have followed his lead, that the Virgin Birth explained Paul's curious statement in I Timothy 2:15 that women "shall be saved in childbearing." The child in question was the divine son himself.

57. Gaebelein, "Acts of the Apostles," *OH* 14 (August 1907): 85–86. Compare with Maude Royden, "A Woman's View of the Virgin Birth," *Christian Century* 20 October 1921, 12–15.

58. Blackstone, *Jesus Is Coming*, 96.

59. George F. Guille, "Isaac and Rebekah," in *The Coming and Kingdom of Christ*, 216; Massee, "Intercessory Prayer for a World-Wide Revival," in *God Hath Spoken*, 56.

60. Needham, *Woman's Ministry*, 52; Brookes, "Question Drawer," *Truth* 6 (December 1879): 29.

61. Arno Gaebelein, "Studies in Zechariah," *OH* 5 (May 1899): 389. See, e.g.,

Brookes, "The Parable of the Leaven," *Truth* 4 (June 1876): 289–97; Brookes, "The Parable of the Net," *Truth* 6 (September 1878): 436; L. W. Munhall, "Leaven," *OH* 5 (August–September 1898): 89–90.

62. Gaebelein, "Revelation. Chapter XIV," *OH* 19 (June 1913): 723–38.

63. Massee, "The Old-Fashioned Woman," n.d., J. C. Massee Papers.

64. On Blanchard and Wheaton College, see, e.g., "Helen M. Gougar," *Christian Cynosure* 31 (May 1888): 8; Townsley, *A Pilgrim Maid*; Mary Dorsett, "And the Ladies of the College," *Wheaton Alumni* (February 1987): 4–7.

65. Marsden, *Fundamentalism and American Culture*, 43, 47.

66. See Hassey, *No Time for Silence*, 84–86, 105–10; Needham, *Woman's Ministry*.

67. Gray, *Great Epochs of Sacred History*, 75–78.

68. "God's Word on Femininity," *MBIM* 31 (June 1931): 486; E. Myers Knoth, "Woman's Rebellion *and* Its Consequences," *MBIM* 34 (October 1933): 55.

69. Harry Ironside, "Characteristics of the Last Days," *Pilot* 27 (July 1947): 297, 316; Sarah Foulkes Moore, "Eve Is Again Listening to the Voice of the Serpent," *SL* 15 July 1949, 6–7.

70. This theme is more fully discussed in chapter 4. Larkin, *Dispensational Truth*, 150.

Chapter Three

1. Friedman, "New Woman"; Daniel Scott Smith, "The Dating of the American Sexual Revolution: Evidence and Interpretation," in *The American Family in Social-Historical Perspective*, ed. Michael Gordon (New York: St. Martin's Press, 1978), 426–38; Fass, *Damned and the Beautiful*.

2. Helen Barrett Montgomery, "The New Opportunity for Baptist Women," *Watchman-Examiner* 26 July 1923, 950.

3. Virginia Lieson Brereton, "United and Slighted: Women as Subordinated Insiders," in *Between the Times*, ed. Hutchison, 147–48. See also Bendroth, "Women and Missions." Walter Hillis also presents evidence for economic and social sources of "status anxiety" among fundamentalist leaders. See Hillis, "Social and Religious Factors in the Fundamentalist-Modernist Schism among Baptists in North America, 1895–1934" (Ph.D. diss., University of Pittsburgh, 1974).

4. See Boyd and Brackenridge, *Presbyterian Women in America*; Verdesi, *In But Still Out*.

5. Mrs. Max (Nellie) Aszmann to Lucy H. Dawson, 10 August 1922, Presbyterian Historical Society, Philadelphia, Penn.

6. Clement MacAfee, "Women and Official Church Life," *Presbyterian Banner* 16 (January 1930): 32.

7. Bennett, *Status of Women*, 14. See Verdesi, *In But Still Out*.

8. Warfield, "Paul on Women Speaking in Church," *Presbyterian* 15 July 1920, 8–9; "Paul's Teaching about Women," ibid., 4.

9. See, e.g., William H. Bates, "Paul (and Others) on Women Speaking in the Church," ibid., 9–10; Wallace MacGowan, "A Word about Women Speaking in the Church," ibid., 11, 26; F. L. Hitchcock, "Shall Women Be Ordained as Elders and Deacons?" ibid., 2 September 1920, 7; A. Mackenzie Lamb, "The Ecclesiastical Rank of Women," ibid., 9 September 1920, 8–9.

10. Mark A. Mathews, "Why Women in the Pulpit?" *Presbyterian* 16 January 1930, 7; Macartney, "Shall We Ordain Women as Ministers and Elders?" ibid., 7 November 1929, 8.

11. Warfield, "May Women Be Ordained in the Presbyterian Church?" ibid., 14 November 1929, 5; John R. Stevenson "Views and Voices: Ordination of Women," ibid., 3 April 1930, 27.

12. Finley Jenkins, "The Self-Destruction of the Movement to License and Ordain Women," *Presbyterian* 27 March 1930, 27.

13. For a conservative account of Speer's role, see Stonehouse, *J. Gresham Machen*, 469–92. Speer was an outspoken advocate of equality for women in the church; his views are found in a recorded discussion, "Conference of the General Council with Fifteen Representative Women at the Fourth Presbyterian Church, Chicago, Ill., November 22, 1928," Presbyterian Historical Society.

14. Macartney, "Shall We Ordain Women as Ministers and Elders?" 7.

15. Euclid Philips, "Woman's Place in the Church," *Presbyterian* 16 September 1930, 10. See also George W. Brown, "Fears on the Woman Question," *Presbyterian Banner* 20 February 1930, 11–12.

16. See account in Stonehouse, *J. Gresham Machen*, 469–92.

17. "Mrs. Buck Resigns; Board Accepts with 'Deep Regret' " *Christianity Today* 4 (May 1933): 34–36.

18. John Roach Straton, "Why I Am Cutting Loose from the Apostate Ecclesiastical Baptist Machine Though I Am a Better Baptist Than Ever Before," sermon preached at Calvary Baptist Church, 29 October 1926, 10, John Roach Straton Papers.

19. "What Should We Do in the Present Denominational Situation?" *Religious Searchlight* 15 May 1922; Tulga, *Foreign Missions Controversy*.

20. Tulga, "The Northern Baptist Convention and the New Testament: A Commentary on Convention Politics," unpublished manuscript in Glen B. Ewell Papers.

21. Tulga, "The National Baptist Convention and the New Testament."

22. Anna C. Swain to John W. Bradbury, 17 June 1946. On the bottom of her letter to Bradbury, editor of the conservative *Watchman-Examiner*, Swain added a note in her own hand that "*his* letter to me when I was elected was the only letter regretting a "woman" president." Bradbury's letter was not found in her correspon-

dence. Anna Canada Swain to Minnie Crosby, 21 October 1946, Anna Canada Swain Papers.

William Bell Riley also characterized the struggle in Minnesota as one between a "small minority of Liberals, especially operative in the Twin City Union and Women's organization" and "the overwhelming majority of Conservative churches" (Riley, *Bolsheviki Aspects of the Northern Baptist Convention* [Chicago: Fundamentalist Fellowship of the NBC, 1945?], 6).

23. Hill, *The World Their Household*; Notes from Fundamentalist League Executive Committee Meeting, 30 August–3 September 1925, J. C. Massee Papers. See also Carpenter and Shenk, eds., *Earthen Vessels*.

24. Harriet Eynon Williams, "A Laywoman Expresses Her Views," *Presbyterian* 22 February 1923, 17; Flora Cameron Burr, "The Veiled Lady of Corinth," *Presbyterian Banner* 22 May 1930, 28.

25. Calkins, *Follow Those Women: Church Women in the Ecumenical Movement* (New York: National Council of Churches, 1961), 19.

26. Mabelle Rae Le Grand to Mrs. Leslie Swain and Dr. Jesse Wilson, 4 November 1943, Anna Canada Swain Papers.

27. "Editorial Comment," *Northern Baptist World-Times* 27 February 1944, 5. For fundamentalist response, see, e.g., "What the Women Believe," *Watchman-Examiner* 9 March 1944, 231; "Baptists and Theology," *Watchman-Examiner* 23 March 1944, 271; Clarence S. Roddy, "The Need for Theology," *Watchman-Examiner* 7 September 1944, 876–77.

28. "The Baptist Bible Union of America," *Baptist* 7 October 1922, 1110; [Frank Goodchild], *Twenty Questions: What, Why and How* (New York: General Committee on Fundamentalism in the Northern Baptist Convention, 1924).

29. Lucy Peabody, "A Convention or an Adventure," *Watchman-Examiner* 20 September 1928, 1210; "Over-Organized," *Christian Fundamentalist* 2 (December 1928): 20.

30. Cattan, *Lamps Are for Lighting*, 111–12.

31. Peabody, "The Bible and Women," *Record of Christian Work* 45 (March 1926): 194–97.

32. "Shall We Have Peace?" *Christian Fundamentals in School and Church* 8 (October–December 1926): 8. See also Peabody, "A Woman's Criticism of the Laymen's Report," *Missionary Review of the World* 45 (January 1933): 39–42.

33. Henry, *For Such a Time as This*, 42, 126–29.

34. "Program of the 14th Annual Convention of the WCFA," *Christian Fundamentalist* 4 (May 1931): 5.

35. "New Officers of the Christian Fundamentals Association," *Christian Fundamentals in School and Church* 5 (July–September 1923): 28–29. On Gray, see, e.g., "Personals," *Christian Fundamentalist* 1 (June 1928): 10; Mrs. Carl R. Gray, "Today's Problems of Children and Parents," *SST* 22 October 1938, 754–55, 770.

36. "Officers of the WCFA," *KB* 28 (March 1937): 90. Mrs. Sheperd, widely known

for her public resignation from the board of the Young Women's Christian Association, when it became too liberal for her convictions, was actively courted by Machen and his associates for financial aid to the nascent Westminister Theological Seminary. See his correspondence, J. Gresham Machen to Paul Woolley, 10 June 1930; Winifred M. Griffith Thomas to J.G.M., 29 August 1929, Ida Goepp Pierson to J.G.M., 9 June 1930, J. Gresham Machen Papers.

37. Macartney, *Ancient Wives and Modern Husbands*; and Riley, *Wives of the Bible*. Compare with, e.g., *Notable Women of Olden Time* (Philadelphia: American Sunday School Union, 1852).

38. J. C. Massee, "Women Attend Special Meeting," 30 January 1931, a reprinted excerpt from a standard sermon on "The Old Fashioned vs. the New Woman," J. C. Massee Papers; Macartney, *Way of a Man with a Maid*, 62.

39. Maude M. Aldrich, "Modern Problems of Womanhood," *WE* (1922): 8. Liberal spokesmen also voiced similar doubts; see, e.g., "What Shall Be Done with the Women?" *Christian Century* 1 April 1920, 6.

40. George Walter Fiske, "Can Religion Come Back to the Home?" *Christian Century* 15 November 1927, 1486–87; "The Modernist's Quest for God," *Atlantic Monthly* 137 (September 1926): 228; Fosdick, "The Dangers of Modernism," *Harpers Magazine* 152 (March 1926): 407. See also J. D. Jones, "Spiritual Effeminacy" *Baptist* 21 October 1922, 1179.

41. Quoted in Carter, *Another Part of the Twenties*, 53–54.

42. Bartholomew, "The Full Work of the Ministry," *WE* (1930): 21–22.

43. Earle V. Pierce, "Introduction," in *Dynamic of a Dream*, Marie Acomb Riley, 11; Giboney and Potter, *Life of Mark A. Matthews*, 94–95; "Dr. Straton No Eccentric, But Normal, Says Wife," *New York Evening Journal* 31 May 1928; Austen K. DeBlois, "John Roach Straton: An Appreciation," *Baptist* 30 November 1929, 1484.

44. A. William Lewis, "The Investment of Manhood," *BC* 34 (July 1929): 384; Kennedy, "Quit You Like Men, Be Strong," *BC* 30 (March 1924): 134; "Notes and Comments," *BC* 30 (March 1924): 141.

45. [Gaebelein], "Good Bye Darwinism," *OH* 28 (March 1922): 552; Riley, "She-Men, or How Some Become Sissies," sermon preached at First Baptist Church, Minneapolis, Minn., 30 September 1934, William Bell Riley Papers.

46. Kennedy, "Characteristics of the Destructive Rationalist," *BC* 30 (July 1924): 355; "God's Young Men," *Baptist Bulletin* 5 (October 1939): 18.

47. Elizabeth Knauss, *The Conflict: A Narrative Based on the Fundamentalist Movement* (Los Angeles: Bible Institute of Los Angeles, 1923).

48. *A Call to Arms!* (Executive Commitee of Baptist Bible Union of North America, n.d.), ABHS.

49. R. T. Ketcham, *The Answer* (Chicago: General Association of Regular Baptists, 1950), 50–51; "Important Changes at Waterloo," *Baptist Bulletin* 4 (July–August 1938): 7. Of course, liberals also charged that fundamentalism amounted to a

"monstrous assertion of ecclesiastical authority" (Robert Hastings Nichols, "Fundamentalism in the Presbyterian Church," *Journal of Religion* 5 [January 1925]: 35).

50. Laws, "The Supernatural," *Watchman-Examiner* 8 November 1923, 1432.

51. "What Is Modernism?" *Presbyterian* 20 October 1927, 4.

52. "The Aridity of Liberalism," ibid., 22 April 1926, 7; "The Background of Religious Experience," ibid., 13 October 1927, 5.

53. Laws, "Christianity's Distinguishing Characteristics," *Watchman-Examiner* 3 May 1923, 549; Eastburg, "A Self Discovery," *Christian Fundamentalist* 4 (November 1930): 185; George R. Straton, "The Passing of 'Miss Kitty,'" *Progressive Thinker* 21 December 1929. William Bell Riley's voluminous clipping file, in his personal papers, also contained numerous articles on psychic healing.

54. J. Gresham Machen to John W. Porten, 15 September 1930, J. Gresham Machen Papers; William L. Pettingill, "Unbelief is Unscientific," *Revelation* 1 (May 1931): 151. A 1936 article by Harry Rimmer described the "highly organized system of government" of the supernatural world in amazing detail (Rimmer, "The Borderland of the Supernatural," *Christian Faith and Life* 42 [July 1936]: 191–98).

55. Gaebelein, "Herod and Pilate Became Friends," *Revelation* 2 (September 1932): 364; Paul H. Holsinger, "Has the Y.W.C.A. Adopted a Modernistic Program?" *BC* 34 (September 1928): 493.

56. Charles R. Scoville, "Restoring Old Evangelistic Fervor," *WE* (1927): 212.

57. "Moral Decay through Subservience to Foreign Fashions in Women's Dress," unpublished sermon, John Roach Straton Papers; Gaebelein, "The March of Emancipation," *OH* 28 (November 1921): 304.

58. John Snape, "Women Smokers," *Watchman-Examiner* 3 January 1929, 10; "Massee Hits Girl Smoking," unid. clipping, 30 January 1931, Box 8, J. C. Massee Papers. The Methodist Board of Temperance also produced tracts against "This Cloud of Feminine Smoke" and "Why Girls Should Not Smoke."

59. "Maude Royden, Cigarette Smoker and Theological Liberal," *Christian Fundamentalist* 1 (March 1928): 14.

60. Massee, "Should Girls Smoke? Sermon by Dr. Massee," 22 March 1925, J. C. Massee Papers.

61. "Bobbed Hair," *Grace and Truth* 11 (June 1924): 226. This remained a consistent theme in fundamentalist literature: see, e.g., Homer Rodeheaver, "Five Reasons Why Women Should Not Smoke," *SST* 2 March 1940, 174–75; William James Robinson, "King Nicotene and His Women Thralls," *MM* 47 (September 1946): 19, 66.

62. "More concerning Women's Dress," *MBIM* 31 (October 1930): 64; A. R. Funderburk, "The Word of God on Women's Dress," *MBIM* 22 (January 1922): 759.

63. "Man's Moral Machinery," *KB* (December 1920): 1143; Funderburk, "The Word of God on Women's Dress," 759.

64. "Concerning Women's Dress," *MBIM* 30 (August 1930): 577; Robert G. Flood and Jerry B. Jenkins, *Teaching the Word, Reaching the World* (Chicago: Moody Bible Institute, 1985), 61; see photographs in Bernard R. DeRemer, *Moody Bible Institute: A Pictoral History* (Chicago: Moody Press, 1960), 31, 47, 63, 102, passim.

65. A. Z. Conrad to Dr. Plumb, 4 February 1905, Congregational Historical Society, Boston, Mass.

66. On Riley, see "Discontinuing This Magazine," *Christian Fundamentalist* 6 (September–October 1932): 34; C. Allyn Russell, "Mark Allison Matthews: Seattle Fundamentalist and Civic Reformer," *Journal of Presbyterian History* 57 (Spring 1979): 446–61; DeBlois, "John Roach Straton: An Appreciation," 1484. On Massee, see "Preachers You Hear on the Radio," n.d., J. C. Massee Papers.

67. Smith, *A Watchman on the Wall*, 55, 164–65; Smith wrote of Houghton that "sometimes his countenance would have a dark, overcast, purplish hue, and at other times, when suffering great pain, his whole face would turn pale, sometimes almost white" (*Watchman on a Wall* [1951], reprinted in *Enterprising Fundamentalism*, ed. Carpenter, 164). Mel Larson, *God's Man in Manhattan: The Biography of William Ward Ayer* (Grand Rapids, Mich.: Eerdmans, 1950), reprinted in *Enterprising Fundamentalism*, ed. Carpenter, 106.

68. Macartney, *Way of a Man with a Maid*, 137; "Dr. R. A. Torrey in His Home: An Address by the Rev. R. A. Torrey, Jr.," *MBIM* (October 1929): 68.

69. Rothman, *Woman's Proper Place*, chapter 5; Clyde Griffen, "Reconstructing Masculinity," in *Meanings for Manhood*, ed. Carnes and Griffen, 201.

70. Weber, *Living in the Shadow of the Second Coming*, 128–57; Trollinger, *God's Empire*, 62–82.

71. Marsden, *Fundamentalism and American Culture*, 205.

Chapter Four

1. Carpenter, "Fundamentalist Institutions"; Samuel Kincheloe, *Research Memorandum on Religion in the Depression* (New York, 1937; reprint, Westwood, Conn.: Greenwood Press, 1970), 7–8. I am indebted to Michael Hamilton for many of the themes included in this chapter. See his forthcoming article, "Women, Public Ministry, and American Fundamentalism."

2. "Christian Workers," *Pilot* 6 (April 1921): 56; "Secretaries Speak," *Pilot* 27 (February 1947): 150.

3. G. Allen Fleece, "Ambition from Above," *WE* (1943): 87; Bob Jones, "God's Program," *WE* (1940): 113.

4. Lillyan Anderson, "Wanted—Some Real Men," *Pilot* 10 (April 1930): 196.

5. Norma B. Randolph, "If I Don't Marry . . . " *HIS* 9 (November 1948): 1. See also Chafe, *American Woman*, 48–65.

6. See, e.g., Brereton, "United and Slighted: Women as Subordinated Insiders," in *Between the Times*, ed. Hutchison, 143–67; *Interim Report of the Study on the*

Life and Work of Women in the Church (Geneva, Switz.: World Council of Churches, 1948), 27; Barbara Brown Zikmund, "Women and the Churches" in *Altered Landscapes*, ed. Lotz, 125–39.

7. Lewis, *God's Ideal Woman*, 11, 22, 25.

8. "... Now Mrs. Allan MacMullen!" *SL* 1 July 1949, 6.

9. Lynd and Lynd, *Middletown*, 354.

10. A. R. Clippinger, "Ministerial Equations," *WE* (1937): 54.

11. William Bell Riley, "Is Christianity Womanish?" sermon preached at First Baptist Church, Minneapolis, Minn., n.d., Willam Bell Riley Papers; Walden Howard, "Are You Man or Molly-Coddle?" *MM* 48 (July 1948): 793–94.

12. David Allen, "On the Extermination of Mr. Milktoast Christian," *HIS* (July 1945): 13; Rice, "Men and Their Sins," *SL* 26 December 1947, 2.

13. P. F. Hamilton, "Harry E. Ketcham, Evangelist," *Baptist Bulletin* 4 (March 1939): 9.

14. Rice, "Football: Is It a Sin to Play or Attend?" *SL* 27 October 1939, 3.

15. Matthews, "What Is the Supreme Need of the Church?" *KB* 21 (February 1930): 71–72; Dodd, "The Call of the Christian Minister," *WE* (1937): 91.

16. Rice, "And He Gave... Some Evangelists," *SL* 19 January 1940, 1–3; Rice, "Evangelistic Preaching," *SL* 20 September 1940, 1–4. In 1940 Rice left his Dallas church to become a full-time evangelist.

17. Riley, "Let Us Help You," *Pilot* 11 (December 1930): 92.

18. Mrs. Gilbert H. Johnson, "The Preacher's Wife," *MM* 48 (January 1948): 334; George B. Walton, "The Minister's Wife," *Pilot* 19 (October 1938): 22.

19. Lindsell, *Park Street Prophet*, 43–44; Riley, "Managing Church Troubles," *KB* 26 (March 1935): 85. Although most fundamentalist pastors preferred wives who kept to the sidelines, some shared their work effectively. During World War II it was not unknown for a wife to fill her absent husband's church pulpit. Navy chaplain Gerald Morgan recounted his wife's preaching career with obvious pride. Other women, like radio broadcaster Charles Fuller's wife Grace, acquired national reputations alongside their husbands. Grace's segment on the "Old Fashioned Revival Hour," in which she read and answered personal letters from listeners, was one of the most popular parts of the broadcast. See " 'Mrs. Preacher' by her Husband, Chaplain (1st Lt.) Gerald R. Morgan," *MM* 46 (March 1946): 466; Wright, *Old Fashioned Revival Hour*, 401.

20. William B. Crowe, "What Are We Talking About? Or the Place of Preaching in the Church of Today," *WE* (1929): 43.

21. "Loyalty to the Laity," *KB* (July 1923): 675.

22. On the development of businessmen's clubs, see, e.g., "Winona Year Book Program," (Winona Lake, Ind., 1921), 19; Boyd W. Hargreaves to Association of Businessmen's Evangelistic Clubs, 12 March 1931, William A. Sunday Papers, 1–40. Nearly all of the Billy Sunday clubs were located in the South. See also Paul Rood,

"The Ministry of Laymen," *KB* (March 1936): 82. On LeTourneau, see, e.g., "In Business for God," *MM* 50 (October 1950): 74–75, 119; "R. G. LeTourneau, Soul-Winning Big Business Man," *SL* 12 April 1940, 1, 3.

23. See, e.g., "Christian Business Men Schedule Convention," *Pilot* 32 (October 1951): 9; "Months of Preparation to Be Climaxed as Graham Campaign Opens in Washington," *Pilot* 32 (January 1952): 116.

24. C. B. Hedstrom, "Pay Day—Some Day," *SL* 4 August 1939, 1; Grunigen quoted in "In Business for God," 119.

25. Grunigen quoted in "The Pew Speaks to the Pulpit," *KB* (April 1936): 122.

26. See Watt, *Transforming Faith*, 50–67.

27. "LeTourneau, "God Needs Laymen," *WE* (1945): 205; Roger W. Babson, "The Minister's Job," *Christian Faith and Life* 43 (April 1937): 151. On laymen's activities, see "Loyalty to the Laity," 675–76; Almin G. Swanson, "Laymen and Fundamentalism," *Christian Fundamentalist* 4 (August 1930): 60–63; Winifred Tuft, "A Soul-Winning Men's Class," *SST* 10 February 1934, 84; Craig Massey, "Points for Part-Time Preachers," *MM* 50 (February 1950): 392, 444; David C. Wilcox, "Christian Laymen's Activities," *MM* 46 (February 1946): 345.

28. Rice, "The Reproach of Being a Fundamentalist," *SL* 22 March 1935, 1–4; Riley, "What's the Matter with the Church?" *KB* (September 1920): 822–24.

29. Randall Balmer, "Evangelicals, Public Discourse, and American Culture," paper presented to Center for the Study of Religion and American Culture, Indianapolis, 4 April 1992.

30. Massee, "God's Answer to Modern Programs of Righteousness," *WE* (1920): 129.

31. David S. Kennedy, "Christianity and Woman," *BC* 32 (June–July 1926): 309–10; "A Christian Worker among Women," *Pilot* 11 (May 1931): 231; "Bible Questions Answered," *SL* 3 August 1945, 8. See, e.g., a talk by Grace Saxe on the Book of Ruth, which describes "how gladly [God] receives and restores a repentant backslider" ("The Book of Ruth," *WE* [1930]: 253–58).

32. C. W. Foley, "The Place of Woman," *Pilot* 12 (January 1933): 127. See, e.g., "Question Box," *OH* 52 (March 1946): 630.

33. "Taking the Bible 'Literally,' " *MBIM* 23 (January 1923): 191–92; Riley, "Women in the Ministry," *Christian Fundamentalist* 1 (May 1928): 21. See also Graham Gilmer, "Should Christian Women Speak or Lead in Prayer in Our Churches?" ibid., 27 (January 1928): 223–24; Grant Stroh, "Practical and Perplexing Questions," ibid., 21 (January 1920): 21. By the early 1930s, Riley's views on women had grown far more conservative. See his sermon on "The Ways of Women in Unsexing Themselves," 23 September 1934, William Bell Riley Papers.

34. Arno C. Gaebelein, "What Is This?" *OH* 27 (August 1920): 77; Ralph E. Hone, "Should Women Preach?" *Grace and Truth* 17 (February 1939): 36.

35. Haldeman, *Signs of the Times*, 193; Ockenga, "The Ideal Mother," *Christian Faith and Life* 37 (January 1931): 38.

36. "The Interdenominational Association of Evangelists," Winona Bible Conference records, Grace College and Seminary, Winona Lake, Ind. Thirteen of the forty-two women were listed with their husbands; many of them were probably soloists or musicians.

37. Straton's article is found in Hassey, *No Time for Silence*, appendix 11. See also Blumhofer, "Footlights, Flappers and the Sawdust Trail." Utley was featured at the Winona Bible Conference in 1927. See Utley, "Wanted: A Workshop," *WE* (1927): 242–54. For Straton's relationship with Utley, see correspondence in John Roach Straton Papers.

38. Rice, *Bobbed Hair, Bossy Wives, and Women Preachers*, 58–59. Rice departed strongly from the more permissive attitudes of other northern fundamentalists, arguing against any form of public speaking for women, even against their leading "mixed" Bible classes.

39. Brereton, *From Sin to Salvation*, 88.

40. M. A. Leger, "A Message to Women," *Alliance Weekly* 17 September 1927, 612–13.

41. "25th Anniversary of the Bible Institute of Los Angeles," *KB* 21 (November 1930): 502–3; "Euodia—A Great Work among Los Angeles School Girls," *KB* 22 (June 1931): 247–48. See also Hassey, *No Time for Silence*, 25–27.

42. "BIOLA Bible Women," *KB* 28 (June 1937): 208.

43. Mrs. Ralph Campbell, "Our Neighborhood Bible Classes," *SST* 16 April 1932, 210; Faith Coxe Bailey, "Texas Grows a Giant Bible Class," *MM* 55 (1955): 17–19, 43.

44. Sanders, *Council Torchbearer*, 10. See also Parker, *Billy Sunday Meetings*, 32–33, 42.

45. Edna Louise Asher Case, taped interview. Scattered records indicate that in 1938 the group included roughly 1,000 members. See annual reports in William A. Sunday Papers, Box 2–55. Most were from small cities in Virginia, Ohio, West Virginia, and Indiana.

46. Sanders, *Council Torchbearer*, 11, 19.

47. Evans, *Wright Vision*, 104–5.

48. "She Hath Done What She Could," *Pilot* 20 (December 1939): 93; Mrs. Carl R. Gray, "Today's Problems of Children and Parents," *SST* 22 October 1938, 754; Mrs. W. F. Barnum, "A Busy Woman's Sunday-School Broadcasting," *SST* 14 April 1923, 235.

49. Heidebrecht, "Educational Legacy of Lois and Mary LeBar," 14–15.

50. Hunt and Hunt, *For Christ and the University*, 96–99.

51. Dorothy Jean Furnish, "Women in Religious Education: Pioneers for Women in Professional Ministry," in *Women and Religion in America*, vol. 3: *1900–1968*, ed. Ruether and Keller, 310–38.

52. Baldwin and Benson, *Henrietta Mears*; Roe, ed., *Dream Big*.

53. Heidebrecht, "The Educational Legacy of Lois and Mary LeBar."

54. "Class of 1933: Fifty Golden Years, 1933–1983, A Record of God's Faithfulness," William Bell Riley Papers.

55. Evans, *Wright Vision*, 33–45; Elizabeth Evans, taped interview; Rose Phillips, personal interview with author.

56. See Nathan R. Wood, "Report of Recent Work of Gordon Students in Rural Fields," 12 May 1934, President's Office Files, 1Dg3, Gordon College archives, Wenham, Mass.

57. "Missionaries on Platform at Los Angeles, Convention," *Christian Fundamentalist* 4 (July 1930): 10; Joel A. Carpenter, "Propagating the Faith Once Delivered," in *Earthen Vessels*, ed. Carpenter, 109; "Ministers, Missionaries, and Licensed Ministers of the G.A.R.B.," *Baptist Bulletin* 15 (August 1949): 33–46. The list also included 3 ordained women, 216 licensed men (and 5 women), 6 women in Christian education, and 255 male missionaries, 107 who were unmarried. The lopsided numbers of single women missionaries in twentieth-century fundamentalist organizations reflected a long-standing feminine dominance in missionary enterprises. By the early twentieth century, independent women's groups boasted a membership of more than three million women, and an overwhelming majority on the mission fields. See Ruth Tucker, "Women in Missions," in *Earthen Vessels*, ed. Carpenter, 251–80.

58. A 1979 survey of women in missions examined thirty-six mission boards related to the Evangelical Foreign Missions Association and Interdenominational Foreign Mission Association and found only one with equal numbers of men and women. Most had less than a third women, and four were entirely male. See Olson, "Understanding Women's Role in Missions Today"; Tucker, "Female Mission Strategists," 76; pamphlet distributed by Christians for Biblical Equality, Inver Grove Heights, Minn.

59. Riley, *Pastoral Problems*, 165–67.

60. Ellis, "Social and Religious Factors," 233. See also Bendroth, "Search for 'Woman's Role.' "

61. Zoe Anne Alford, taped interview.

62. Brown quoted in "Missions—A Man's Job," *Pilot* 15 (May 1935): 234.

63. "A Men's Missionary League," *Pilot* 15 (May 1935): 211. On the facing page of the first article, the *Pilot* reprinted extracts from A. J. Gordon's famous defense of women missionaries' right to speak.

64. Rosell, *Challenging Youth for Christ*, 80, 83; Donald E. Nelson, "Missions Militant," *Pilot* 29 (September 1949): 369.

65. Ockenga, *Church God Blesses*, 34; Donald Nelson, "But There Must Be Some Men in Your Country..." *Pilot* 30 (May 1950): 255.

66. Zoe Anne Alford, "Wheaton Graduate Chapel, October 27, 1958," in Zoe Anne Alford Papers; Ruth Hege, letter to "Mid Missions: Reflections of God's Faithfulness," *Baptist Bulletin* 15 (February 1950): 24.

67. "59 New Churches Received at the 19th Annual Conference," *Baptist Bulletin* 16 (July 1950): 5, 10.

68. W. S. Hottel, "Uniform Sunday-School Lessons," *Pilot* 15 (September 1935): 313; Roy T. Brumbaugh, "Career Women's Number Will Never Be Legion," *Christian Beacon* 14 September 1950, 3.

69. Buswell, "Why I Believe in Theology," *WE* (1932): 29.

70. Sandeen, *Roots of Fundamentalism*, 241–43. See also Trollinger, *God's Empire*, 108.

71. Board of Trustees, Gordon College of Theology and Missions, Minutes for June 12, 1930, p. 83, Trustees Minutes, Box 1, Book 4, Gordon College Archives, Wenham, Mass.; *Gordon News-Letter*, no. 26 (November 1931): 1.

72. *Gordon News-Letter*, no. 1 (October 1922): 3; Nathan R. Wood, "Report of Recent Work of Gordon Students in Rural Fields," 4–6, Gordon College Archives; Rose Phillips interview.

73. "President's Report to Trustees, Alumni and Friends of Gordon College and Gordon Divinity School, 1944," p. 1, President's Office Publications, 1917– , Gordon College Archives, Wenham, Mass. See also Waldron-Stains, "Evangelical Women."

74. "Further Developments," *Pilot* 15 (July 1935): 274.

75. "Commencement, 1941," *Pilot* 21 (July 1941): 300–301. Most women seminarians graduated with either Th.G. degrees, designed for students without high school diplomas, or master's degrees in religious education.

76. Trollinger, *God's Empire*, 108–50.

77. Marsden, *Reforming Fundamentalism*, 123–28; author interview with Helen Clark MacGregor.

78. "Accreditation Self-Study," in Faculty Minutes, 1 May 1947, pp. 31–32, and Faculty Minutes, 13 May 1949, p. 165, Gordon College Archives, Wenham, Mass.

79. See *Northwestern Scroll, 1938*, 88, 96, 100; William Bell Riley Papers.

80. Powers, *Henrietta Mears Story*, 29; Billy Graham cited in Roe, ed., *Dream Big*, 197–98, frontispiece.

81. Heidebrecht, "Legacy of Lois and Mary LeBar," 24–43.

82. Elizabeth Evans interview transcript, 16–18.

83. "Constitution and By-Laws, Women's Fellowship of the NAE," CN# 44, 1–6.

84. "Minutes of the Mid-Year Meeting of the Executive Committee of the Women's Fellowship of the NAE, October 12, 1953," CN# 44, 1–6; "Minutes of the Meetings of the Women's Fellowship, Chicago, April 15–19, 1952," 1–2, 4; CN# 44, 1–6; all in Billy Graham Center Archives.

85. "Girls' Problems of Today," *SST* 3 March 1934, 138, 145; "How 'Mother' Green Takes Care of Her Family," *SST* 30 July 1932, 399–400; "Edith Norton's Triumphant Life," *SST* 15 August 1936, 537–38.

86. Rice, "Men and Their Sins," 2.

87. "Women Preachers," *Eternity* 7 (May 1956): 11; Hollingsworth cited in Hunt, *For Christ and the University*, 424n.24; "Echoes from Cleveland," *Baptist Bulletin* 15 (July 1949): 4–5.

88. Kenneth Wuest, "The Headship of the Man," *MM* 56 (January 1956): 35.

Chapter Five

1. See Watt, *Transforming Faith*, 84–91. Fascination with eschatology of course continued. See Boyer, *When Time Shall Be No More*.

2. Ironside, "The Ministry of Women," *OH* 56 (May 1950): 653–58.

3. See, e.g., W. Erskine Blackburn, "The Mother Love of God," *WE* (1928): 33–40.

4. Massee, "The Old Fashioned Home," *WE* (1931): 112; Sweazy, "The Christian American Home," *Baptist Bulletin* 10 (May 1945): 8. See also William Bell Riley, "The Ideal Family," *Pilot* 10 (October 1929): 10–12.

5. L. W. S., "The Christian Home," *Presbyterian Guardian* 7 (January 1940): 73; Jones, "The Battlements of the House," *WE* (1920): 258–59.

6. Darrow quoted in Hofstadter, *Anti-Intellectualism*, 127; Massee, "The Old Fashioned Home," 114; McQuilkin, "The Lesson as a Whole," *SST* 8 October 1932, 527;

7. Biederwolf, "Shall Communists Rule in America?" *WE* (1936): 11; Gilbert, "The Modern Assault on the Home," *Pilot* 19 (January 1939): 113.

8. Lee, "The Influence of a Christian Home," *SL* 2 January 1942, 4. See also G. B. Young, "The Ideal Mother," *KB* 21 (May 1930): 231–33; "A Christian Mother," *SST* 23 April 1938, 297, 303.

9. Mel Larson, *God's Man in Manhattan: The Biography of William Ward Ayer* (Grand Rapids, Mich.: Zondervan, 1950; reprint, New York: Garland Publishing, 1988), 23–48.

10. Macartney, *Making of a Minister*, 14, 38. See also Tarr, *Shields of Canada*, 23–24; Smith, *A Watchman on the Wall*.

11. Mrs. Carl R. Gray, "Today's Problems of Children and Parents," *SST* 22 October 1938, 754.

12. Ibid., 754; "Keeping Our Homes Christian," *SST* 6 June 1936, 394.

13. Lucretia Kays Hanson, "Leading Our Children to Christ," *SST* 7 December 1940, 986–87; Katharine Polk, "The Fruits of Early Training," *SST* 1 October 1938, 694. See also Adeline F. Webb, "Making a Christian Home for Our Ten Children," *SST* 16 November 1940, 924–25.

14. "When Christ Is Lord of the Home, by a Christian Mother," *SST* 27 April 1940, 339.

15. Lizzie Wallace Childs, "Training Children for the King," *SST* 30 March 1940, 256.

16. "Girls' Problems of To-Day, Discussed by Aunt Mary," *SST* 7 August 1948, 682, 696.

17. Webb, "Making a Christian Home for Our Ten Children," 924–25.

18. Mary L. Miles, "My Baby: From One Mother to Another," *SST* 6 March 1948, 210.

19. "Entrusting Our Children to God: By a Christian Mother," 314. See also "Two Mothers—and Christ," *SST* 2 May 1936, 307; "A Mother Discusses Humility," *SST* 4 May 1940, 353–54.

20. "Our Mothers," *Pilot* 15 (May 1935): 211; Frank Gaebelein, "A Message for Each Day," *OH* 41 (November 1934): 311; "Mother's Day," *Christian Beacon* 7 May 1936, 4.

21. Rice, "Rebellious Wives and Slacker Husbands," *SL* 22 July 1938, 1, 3, 4; Hankins, "The Father's Responsibility," *SL* 30 October 1942, 1–2, 4.

22. Rice, "Men and Their Sins," *SL* 26 December 1947, 2; Rice, "Father, Mother, Home, and Heaven," *SL* 9 August 1946, 4.

23. Rice, "Bringing Up Children," *SL* 21 August 1936, 1–4; Rice, "The Bible on Child Correction and Discipline," *SL* 22 March 1940, 1–4; Rice, "Whipping Children," *SL* 11 May 1945, 1–3, 7.

24. Hankins, "The Father's Responsibility," 2; Rice, "The Bible on Child Correction and Discipline," 1–4; Rice, "Bringing Up Children," 3.

25. Rice, "Bringing Up Children," 3.

26. Rice, "The Bible on Child Correction and Discipline," 4; Bill Rice, "Should It Be Illegal to Spank Children?" *SL* 11 February 1949, 7. See also "Spank Your Children," *Revelation* 2 (November 1932): 450–51.

27. Hankins, "Father's Responsibility," 1.

28. Walden Howard, "What Right Has a Woman?" *MM* 48 (May 1948): 633; Sweazy, "The Christian American Home," *Baptist Bulletin* 11 (October 1945): 8. See also Angela Dantuma, "If I Were a Mother," *MM* 46 (May 1945): 478–79.

29. Seeley et al., *Crestwood Heights*, 167, 220.

30. Bacmeister, *All in the Family* (New York, 1951), quoted in Scudder, *Family in Christian Perspective*, 12; Ernest R. Mowrer, "The Family in Suburbia," in *Suburban Community*, ed. Dobriner, 156–58.

31. Ehrenreich, *Hearts of Men*; Arthur F. Schlesinger, Jr., "The Crisis of Masculinity," in *The Politics of Hope* (Boston, 1963), 23–246; Diggins, *Proud Decades*, 211–19.

32. "Report of the National Family Life Committee," *Journal of the General Conference of the Methodist Church* (1956): 1853–55; Wynn cited in *Proceedings of the North American Conference on Church and Family*, ed. Elizabeth Steel Genné and William Henry Genné, (New York: National Council of Churches, 1961), 36.

33. Wynn cited in *Proceedings of the North American Conference on Church and Family*, 36–37.

34. "Marriage—A Career?" *HIS* 5 (January 1945): 5–7.

35. Luci Deck Shaw, "Finding Time for God's Best," *MM* 55 (January 1955): 22; Marjorie McShane, "Around the Fireside," *Baptist Bulletin* 8 (January 1948): 8; David R. Enlow, "Ministries on Your Doorstep," *MM* 60 (October 1959): 20–23.

36. Luetta Kiel, "Just a Housewife... What Can I Do?" *MM* 55 (June 1955): 14–15.

37. Faith Coxe Bailey, "Meet Ruth Graham," *MM* 55 (January 1955): 20–21, 23.

38. "Spiritual Clinic by Pastor 'Mac,' " *Pilot* 35 (October 1955): 29; Armerding, "Parental Intercession," *MM* 46 (May 1945): 477.

39. Ryrie, "Is Your Home Scriptural?" *Bibliotheca Sacra* 109 (October–December 1952): 346–52.

40. Ayer, "Beauty for Ashes," *WE* (1947): 30–41.

41. Weber, *Living in the Shadow of the Second Coming*, 177–203; Marsden, *Reforming Fundamentalism*.

42. Bieber, "The End of the Lord," *WE* (1937): 34.

43. Barnhouse, "When God Laughs," in *Unveiling the Future: Twelve Prophetic Messages*, ed. T. Richard Dunham (Findlay, Ohio: Fundamental Truth Publishing, 1934), 105; Rogers, "The Sovereign Claims of God in Relation to Divine Prophecy," in *The Sure Word of Prophecy: Report on the New York Congress on Prophecy... 1942*, ed. John W. Bradbury (New York: Revell, 1943), 17.

44. Chafer, "The Doctrine of Sin," *Bibliotheca Sacra* 92 (January–March 1935): 8; Buswell, *Sin and Atonement*, 31–32.

45. Bauman, "Is Dispensationalism in the Christian's Bible," *WE* (1937): 40–41. See also Ironside, *Lamp of Prophecy*, 37.

46. Harold John Ockenga, "The Pin-Up Girl of a King," sermon preached at Park Street Church, 17 December 1944, p. 3, Park Street Church Records.

47. World Council of Churches, *Interim Report on the Life and Work of Women in the Church* (Geneva, Switz.: World Council of Churches, 1948); Margaret Frakes, "Women's Status in the Churches: A Summary of the Report to the Atlantic City Convention of United Church Women," *Christian Century* 14 October 1953, 1164–66. See also Cavert, *Women in American Church Life*; Wyker, *Church Women in the Scheme of Things*. Fundamentalists and neo-evangelicals either ignored or resisted the progress of women's ordination. See, e.g., "Women as Ministers," *Baptist Bulletin* 22 (July 1956): 5; Elton M. Eenigenburg, "The Ordination of Women," *Christianity Today* 27 April 1959, 15–16.

48. "Why We Grow So Fast," *SL* 25 May 1945, 7.

49. "No Sunday School Literature but the Bible," *SL* 19 October 1934, 1, 3. See also "100 Men Wanted 9.45 A.M. Sunday in Pastor's Adult Mixed Class," *SL* 29

March 1935, 1. Rice's wife was also an accomplished Bible teacher who led a class of young women. See advertisement, *SL* 30 November 1934, 1.

50. "Wide Interest in New Book by the Editor," *SL* 2 January 1942, 1, 3; advertisement in *SL* 11 June 1943, 3; "Wife Tells of Rich Blessings through 'Bobbed Hair, Bossy Wives, Women Preachers,' " *SL* 4 December 1942, 3. The personal ethics of northern and southern fundamentalists sometimes came into conflict, as Rice noted the relatively lax attitudes of the latter on feminine cosmetics, and the northern practice of "mixed bathing," a practice he vehemently opposed; see Rice, "Mixed Bathing: Right or Wrong?" *SL* 1 July 1949, 1. Rice's influence reflects the growing involvement of Southerners, especially Baptists, in the fundamentalist movement, initially a northern, urban coalition. His allies, Bob Jones, Sr., and Bob Jones, Jr., came from Southern Methodist stock and fostered a rising generation of fundamentalist and neo-evangelical leaders at Bob Jones University. See Rice, "Southern Baptists, Hail!" *SL* 12 May 1950, 1–2.

51. Fitzwater, *Woman*, 30–31.

52. Ibid., 82–84.

53. Ryrie, *Place of Women in the Church*, 68.

54. Ibid., 80.

55. "Women as Ministers," *Baptist Bulletin* 22 (July 1956): 5. The discussion was not exclusive to fundamentalists; conservatives in a variety of traditions adopted increasingly restrictive teaching. Lutherans, for example, adopted an "order of creation" theology in response to the World Council of Churches' study on women and the translation and American publication of Zerbst, *Office of Woman in the Church*. See Schroeder, "Orders of Creation."

56. "Except the Lord Build...," *MM* 50 (June 1950): 688; G. Coleman Luck, "New Books," *MM* 50 (May 1950): 654; advertisement, *SL* 15 March 1946, 8.

57. "Spiritual Clinic by Pastor 'Mac,' " *Pilot* 34 (December 1954): 12.

58. Advertisement in *SST* 2 October 1948, 867.

59. See Scanzoni, "Great Chain of Being"; Hofstadter, *Anti-Intellectualism*, 119n.1.

60. See Billy Sunday, "Women's Sermon," n.d., William A. Sunday Papers, 10–5.

61. John R. Rice, "Editor Visits Bob Jones College," *SL* 8 June 1945, 5.

62. Rice, "Is Dancing Necessarily Wrong and Hurtful for Christians?" *SL* 29 July 1949, 2. See also Lowry, *A Virtuous Woman*, 57–58.

63. "Questions about Immodest Dress Answered," *SL* 3 June 1949, 3.

64. "Young People, Petting, and the Scarlet Sin," *SL* 19 February 1943, 1, 2, 4.

65. "Girls' Problems of Today," *SST* 3 April 1948, 314.

66. Wuest, "The Adornment of the Christian Woman," *MM* 40 (May 1940): 481; Woods, "The Principles of Christian Modesty," *HIS* 8 (March 1948): 3–4; Jones,

"The Woman in the Case," *SL* 16 August 1946, 4. These were not new themes in fundamentalist literature. See, e.g., "Man's Moral Machinery," *KB* (December 1920): 1143; Leora M. Blanchard, "Bathsheba—A Study of An Immodest Woman," *MBIM* 21 (May 1921): 396–97; D. L. Peters, "The Preservation of American Womanhood," *MBIM* 31 (January 1931): 253–54; A. Z. Conrad, "Eternal Vigilance the Price of Decency," *Christian Faith and Life* 40 (October 1934): 241–44.

67. [Name withheld], "I Don't Give Testimonials, But...," *HIS* 19 (June 1959): 4–5.

68. "Happily Unmarried, By a Girl Who Is," *HIS* 5 (February 1945): 21–23. See also the huffy reply from a male reader who wrote that as head of the home, men were entitled to "a little respect" ("Readers Say—Happily Unmarried," *HIS* 5 [April 1945]: 2).

69. "Girls' Problems of Today," *SST* 20 October 1934, 667; *SST* 7 March 1936, 161–62; *SST* 23 May 1936, 367–68; *SST* 16 April 1938, 286. This was not a new theme. See, e.g., "Unequally Yoked," *Watchman* 28 July 1904, 11–12; "The N.W.B.S. as a Matrimonial Recruiting Station," *Pilot* 6 (April 1921): 64. On submitting to non-Christian husbands, see, e.g., John Henry Bennetch, "Exegetical Studies in I Peter," *Bibliotheca Sacra* 100 (April–June 1943): 265; Harold J. Ogilvie, "A Help Meet for Man," *MM* 46 (March 1946): 448; "Spiritual Clinic by Pastor 'Mac,' " *Pilot* 34 (November 1954): 21.

70. "Girls' Problems of Today," *SST* 15 December 1934, 820–21; Dorothy Watts, "A Woman's Point of View," *HIS* 18 (March 1958): 33.

71. Finkelhor, "Common Features of Family Abuse," 17–28. See also Alsdurf and Alsdurf, *Battered into Submission*.

72. Rice, "Rebellious Wives and Slacker Husbands," 4; "Spiritual Clinic by Pastor 'Mac,' " *Pilot* 34 (November 1954): 21.

Epilogue

1. On neo-evangelicalism, see Marsden, *Reforming Fundamentalism*, 153–54; Carl F. H. Henry, *The Uneasy Conscience of Modern Fundamentalism* (Grand Rapids, Mich.: Eerdmans, 1948; reprint, New York: Garland Publishing, 1988); Harold J. Ockenga, "The New Evangelicalism," *Park Street Spire* (February 1958). Note that neo-evangelicals, and indeed many fundamentalists, called themselves simply "evangelicals," a misleading identification that does not take into account other conservative denominations, or groups within mainstream denominations that are largely unaffected by the fundamentalist phenomenon.

2. Watt, *Transforming Faith*, 119–36.

3. Donald Bloesch, *The Evangelical Renaissance* (Grand Rapids, Mich.: Eerdmans, 1973), 25.

4. "Mother Church's Daughters: Distaff Dissent," *Christianity Today* 5 June 1970, 37–38.

5. Letha Scanzoni, "Woman's Place: Silence or Service," *Eternity* 17 (February 1966): 14–16. This was not, of course, the first mention of the subject among neo-evangelicals. See Russell Prohl, *Women in the Church* (Grand Rapids, Mich.: Eerdmans, 1957), a book decidedly before its time.

6. "Letters—Women in the Church," *Eternity* 17 (April 1966): 3.

7. Letha Scanzoni, "Elevating Marriage to Partnership," *Eternity* 19 (July 1968) 11–14. Author interview with Letha Dawson Scanzoni, 12 March 1992; Nancy Hardesty to Letha Scanzoni, 13 May 1968, provided to author by L. D. S.

8. Author interview with Nancy Hardesty, 2 February 1992; Ronald Sider, ed., *The Chicago Declaration* (Carol Stream, Ill.: Creation House, 1974).

9. "First at the Cradle, Last at the Cross," *Christianity Today* 16 March 1973, 622–23.

10. Roy Larson, "Evangelism God's 'Truth in Action,' " *Chicago Sun-Times* 7 December 1974. See also "Another Step for Social Concern," *MM* (February 1975): 8–9.

11. Rufus Jones to Jay Wells, 10 February 1975, Evangelicals for Social Action papers, CN#37, 3–16, Billy Graham Center Archives, Wheaton, Ill. See also Quebedeaux, *Worldly Evangelicals*, 121–26.

12. "Poll Puts Women First," *Eternity* 26 (December 1975): 44.

13. The "Wesleyan quadrilateral" of biblical interpretation takes into account Scripture, tradition, reason, and experience. See Gabriel Fackre, *The Christian Story*, vol. 2 (Grand Rapids, Mich.: Eerdmans, 1985), 96. Walter C. Hobbs, "Jesus and Women in a Male-Dominated Society," *Eternity* 24 (January 1973): 17–20; Gerard T. Sheppard, "Biblical Hermeneutics: The Academic Language of Evangelical Identity," *Union Seminary Review Quarterly* 32 (Winter 1977): 81–94; Letha Scanzoni, "The Feminists and the Bible," *Christianity Today* 2 February 1973, 442–45. Attempts by evangelical feminists to forge connections with the holiness movement were relatively common. See Dayton and Dayton, "Your Daughters Shall Prophesy," 67–92.

14. Elton M. Eenigenburg, "The Ordination of Women," *Christianity Today* 27 April 1959, 15–16. Other popular treatments also followed, or rejected, strict Calvinist reasoning. See, e.g., George W. Knight III, *The Role Relationship of Men and Women: New Testament Teaching* (Chicago: Moody Press, 1985); Susan Foh, *Women and the Word of God: A Response to Biblical Feminism* (Phillipsburg, N.J.: Presbyterian and Reformed, 1980); Aida Bescancon Spencer, *Beyond the Curse: Women Called to Ministry* (Nashville: Thomas Nelson, 1985).

Parallels between arguments over women's role and the ethics of slavery in the antebellum period are striking. Abolitionists often relativized Paul's apparent support for slavery and appealed to the egalitarian implications of Galatians 3:28. Proslavery apologists, particularly Charles Hodge, rested their arguments on the existence of hierarchy in the created order. See, e.g., Charles Hodge, "The Bible Argument on Slavery," in *Cotton Is King* (Augusta, Ga., 1860), 841–72; "Harper on Slavery," in *The Pro-Slavery Argument* (Philadelphia, 1853); Frederick Augustus Ross, *Slavery Ordained of God* (New York, 1859); Thornton Stringfellow, *Slavery: Its Origin, Nature, and History* (Alexandria, Va., 1860); George Armstrong, *The Christian Doctrine of Slavery* (New York, 1857).

15. H. Wayne House, "Paul, Women, and Contemporary Evangelical Feminism," *Bibliotheca Sacra* 136 (January–March 1979): 40–53; Harold Lindsell, "Egalitarianism and Scriptural Infallibility," *Christianity Today* 26 March 1976, 693–94. See also A. Duane Litfin, "Evangelical Feminism: Why Traditionalists Reject It," *Bibliotheca Sacra* 136 (July–September 1979): 258–71.

16. Alexander, "Are Women People?" 31; John Alexander, "A Conversation With Virginia Mollenkott," *The Other Side* (May–June 1976): 75. See also Virginia Ramey Mollenkott, "Evangelicalism: A Feminist Perspective," *Union Seminary Quarterly Review* 32 (Winter 1977): 95–103.

17. Marsden, *Reforming Fundamentalism*, 280–82.

18. Mollenkott, "Evangelicalism: A Feminist Perspective," 95–103; Walter C. Hobbs, "Jesus and Women in a Male-Dominated Society," 20.

19. Margaret N. Barnhouse, "ERA: Fairness or Fraud?" *Eternity* 26 (November 1975): 29–30; Elisabeth Elliot Leitch, "Feminism or Femininity?" *Cambridge Fish* 5 (Winter 1975–1976): 6. See also Elisabeth Elliot [Leitch], "Why I Oppose the Ordination of Women," *Christianity Today* 6 June 1975, 878–82.

20. Bockelman, *Bill Gothard*, 117.

21. Patricia Gundry, *Heirs Together* (Grand Rapids, Mich.: Zondervan, 1980), 44.

22. Stacey, *Brave New Families*, 53–63.

23. Mike Yorkey and Peb Jackson, "Finding New Friends on the Block," *Focus on the Family* 16 (June 1992): 2–4; Rolf Zettersten, "When a Man Doesn't Keep a Promise," ibid., 14.

24. Dobson quoted in "Making Sense of the Men's Movement," *Focus on the Family* 16 (June 1992): 4; Dalbey quoted in Yorkey and Jackson, "Finding New Friends," 2.

Selected Bibliography

Researching fundamentalist history necessarily involves studying the careers of prominent individuals. Published biographies and autobiographies of fundamentalist and neo-evangelical leaders are readily accessible, and manuscript collections, including those of Billy Sunday, John Roach Straton, J. C. Massey, and William Bell Riley offer a wealth of largely untapped material, even though their correspondence is often unavailable.

Reaching beyond the experiences of prominent individuals poses greater difficulties, however. The popular fundamentalist press is a necessary and valuable resource, but these journals and magazines can simply reflect the views of the men who owned and edited them. Yet the influence and importance of these published sources is without question, and they provide many incidental announcements of institutional activities and developments that can be pieced together effectively (see, for example, William Vance Trollinger, *God's Empire: William Bell Riley and Midwestern Fundamentalism* (Madison: University of Wisconsin Press, 1990).

Published expressions about women and gender roles were often influenced by their social and institutional context; for example, Presbyterian conservatives mounting resistance both to women's ordination and to the authority of the General Assembly were much more vocal in expressing negative attitudes than were Bible institutes and conferences, and other entrepreneurial institutions eager to attract women as clientele or financial supporters. In these institutions, attitudes about gender emerge in more subtle expressions of language and descriptions of activities where men and women met together or separately. Material from the Winona Lake Bible Conferences, contained at Grace Theological Seminary in Winona Lake, Indiana, was very useful in this respect. The same is true for archival material on Bible institutes, available at a number of different sites (see, for example, the bibliographic essay in Virginia Lieson Brereton, *Training God's*

Army: The American Bible School, 1880–1940 (Bloomington, Ind.: Indiana University Press, 1990), 197–208.)

Books, Pamphlets, and Articles

Address of Frances E. Willard, President of the Woman's National Council of the United States. Washington, D.C., 1891.

Addresses on the Second Coming of Our Lord. Pittsburgh: W. W. Waters, 1896.

Alexander, John. "Are Women People?" In *What You Should Know about Women's Lib*, ed. Mirian G. Moran. New Canaan, Conn.: Keats Publishing Company, 1974.

Alsdurf, James, and Phyllis Alsdurf. *Battered into Submission: The Tragedy of Wife Abuse in the Christian Home.* Downers Grove, Ill.: InterVarsity Press, 1989.

Ammerman, Nancy. *Bible Believers: Fundamentalists in the Modern World.* New Brunswick, N.J.: Rutgers University Press, 1987.

Andrews, Leslie A. "Restricted Freedom: A. B. Simpson's View of Women." In *Birth of a Vision*, ed. David F. Hartzfeld and Charles Nienkirchen. Regina, Sask.: His Dominion, 1986.

Andrews, William. *Sisters of the Spirit: Three Black Women's Autobiographies of the Nineteenth Century.* Bloomington: Indiana University Press, 1986.

Baldwin, Ethel May, and David V. Benson. *Henrietta Mears and How She Did It!* Glendale, Calif.: Gospel Light Publications, 1966.

Balmer, Randall. "Evangelicals, Public Discourse, and American Culture." Paper presented to Center for the Study of Religion and American Culture, Indianapolis, 4 April 1992.

Bell, Marion L. *Crusade in the City: Revivalism in Nineteenth-Century Philadelphia.* Lewisburg: Bucknell University Press, 1978.

Bendroth, Margaret Lamberts. "Fundamentalism and Femininity: Points of Encounter between Religious Conservatives and Women, 1919–1935." *Church History* 61 (June 1992): 221–33.

———. "The Search for 'Woman's Role' in American Evangelicalism, 1930–1980." In *Evangelicalism and Modern America*, ed. George Marsden. Grand Rapids, Mich.: Eerdmans, 1984.

———. "Women and Missions: Conflict and Changing Roles in the Presbyterian Church in the United States of America, 1870–1935." *Presbyterian History* 65 (Spring 1987): 49–59.

Bennett, M. Katharine. *The Status of Women in the Presbyterian Church in the United States of America, with Reference to Other Denominations.* Philadelphia, 1929.

Blackstone, William. *Jesus Is Coming.* Chicago: Fleming H. Revell, 1908. Reprint. New York: Garland Publishing, 1988.

Blaisdell, Charmarie Jenkins. "The Matrix of Reform: Women in the Lutheran and Calvinist Movements." In *Triumph over Silence: Women in Protestant History*, ed. Richard L. Greaves. Westport, Conn.: Greenwood Press, 1985.

Blake, Lillie Devereaux. *Woman's Place Today; Four Lectures, in Reply to the Lenten Lectures on "Woman" by the Rev. Morgan Dix.* New York: J. W. Lovell, 1883.

Blumhofer, Edith. "Footlights, Flappers, and the Sawdust Trail." Paper presented at American Society of Church History, December 1991.

Boardman, Mary. *Who Shall Publish the Glad Tidings?* Boston, 1875.

Bockelman, Wilfred. *Bill Gothard: The Man and His Ministry, an Evaluation.* Santa Barbara, Calif.: Quill Publications, 1976.

Bordin, Ruth. *Frances Willard.* Chapel Hill: University of North Carolina Press, 1986.

Boyd, Lois A. "Shall Women Speak? Confrontation in the Church, 1876." *Journal of Presbyterian History* 56 (Winter 1976): 281–94.

Boyd, Lois A., and R. Douglas Brackenridge. *Presbyterian Women in America: Two Centuries of a Quest for Status.* Westport, Conn.: Greenwood Press, 1983.

Boyer, Paul. *When Time Shall Be No More: Prophecy Belief in Modern American Culture.* Cambridge, Mass.: Harvard University Press, 1992.

Brereton, Virginia Lieson. *From Sin to Salvation: Stories of Women's Conversions, 1800 to the Present.* Bloomington: Indiana University Press, 1991.

———. *Training God's Army: The American Bible School, 1880–1940.* Bloomington: Indiana University Press, 1990.

Buswell, J. Oliver. *Sin and Atonement.* Grand Rapids, Mich.: Zondervan, 1937.

Bynum, Caroline Walker, et al., eds. *Gender and Religion: On the Complexity of Symbols.* Boston: Beacon Press, 1986.

Carnes, Mark. *Secret Ritual and Manhood in Victorian America.* New Haven: Yale University Press, 1989.

Carnes, Mark, and Clyde Griffen, eds. *Meanings for Manhood: Constructions of Masculinity in Victorian America.* Chicago: University of Chicago Press, 1990.

Carpenter, Joel. "Fundamentalist Institutions and the Rise of Evangelical Protestantism, 1929–1942." *Church History* 49 (1980): 62–75.

———, ed. *Enterprising Fundamentalism: Two Second Generation Leaders.* New York: Garland Publishing, 1988.

Carpenter Joel, and Wilbert Shenk, eds. *Earthen Vessels: American Evangelicals and Foreign Missions, 1880–1980.* Grand Rapids, Mich.: Eerdmans, 1990.

Carter, Paul A. *Another Part of the Twenties.* New York: Columbia University Press, 1977.

Cattan, Louise A. *Lamps Are for Lighting.* Grand Rapids, Mich.: Eerdmans, 1972.

Cavert, Inez. *Women in American Church Life.* New York: Friendship Press, 1949.

Chafe, William H. *The American Woman: Her Changing Social, Economic, and Political Roles, 1920–1970.* New York: Oxford University Press, 1972.

Christ and Glory: Addresses Delivered at the New York Prophetic Conference. Ed. A. C. Gaebelein. New York: Our Hope Publishing, 1918.

Clouser, G. B. M. *Dispensations and Ages of Scripture.* New York: F. E. Fitch, 1903.

The Coming and Kingdom of Christ, a Stenographic Report of the Prophetic Bible Conference Held at Moody Bible Institute. Chicago: Bible Institute Colportage Association, 1914. Reprint. New York: Garland Publishing, 1988.

Daniels, W. H., ed. *Moody: His Words, Works, and Workers.* New York: Nelson and Phillips, 1877.

Davenport, Henry, ed. *Dwight L. Moody: His Life and Labors.* New York, 1899.

Dayton, Donald. "Introduction" to *Holiness Tracts Defending the Ministry of Women.* New York: Garland Publishing, 1985.

———. "The Social and Political Conservatism of Modern American Evangelicalism: A Preliminary Search for the Reasons." *Union Seminary Quarterly Review* 32 (Winter 1977): 71–80.

Dayton, Donald, and Robert K. Johnston, eds. *The Variety of American Evangelicalism.* Downers Grove, Ill.: InterVarsity Press, 1991.

Dayton, Lucille, and Donald H. Dayton. "Your Daughters Shall Prophesy: Feminism in the Holiness Movement." *Methodist History* 14 (January 1976): 67–92.

DeBerg, Betty. *Ungodly Women: Gender and the First Wave of American Fundamentalism.* Minneapolis: Fortress Press, 1990.

DeSwart Gifford, Caroline, ed. *The Debate in the Methodist Episcopal Church over Laity Rights for Women.* New York: Garland Publishing, 1987.

Diggins, John Patrick. *The Proud Decades: America in War and Peace, 1941–1960.* New York: Norton, 1988.

Dobriner, William M., ed. *The Suburban Community.* New York: G. P. Putnam's Sons, 1958.

Dorsett, Lyle. *Billy Sunday and the Redemption of Urban America.* Grand Rapids, Mich.: Eerdmans, 1991.

Dorsett, Mary. "And the Ladies of the College." *Wheaton Alumni* (February 1987): 4–7.

Douglas, Ann C. *The Feminization of American Culture.* New York: Alfred A. Knopf, 1977.

Eaton, Grace R. *A Heroine of the Cross: Sketches in the Life and Work of Miss Joanna P. Moore.* N.p., n.d.

Ehrenreich, Barbara. *Hearts of Men: American Dreams and the Flight from Commitment.* Garden City, N.Y.: Anchor Books, 1983.

Ehrenreich, Barbara, and Deirdre English. *For Her Own Good: 150 Years of Experts' Advice to Women*. New York: Anchor Books, 1978.

Ellis, Walter. "Social and Religious Factors in the Fundamentalist-Modernist Schisms among Northern Baptists in North America, 1895–1914." Ph.D. diss., University of Pittsburgh, 1974.

Epstein, Barbara Leslie. *The Politics of Domesticity*. Middletown, Conn.: Wesleyan University Press, 1981.

Evans, Elizabeth. *The Wright Vision: The Story of the New England Fellowship*. Lanham, Md.: University Press of America, 1986.

Evans, William. *The Book of Genesis*. New York: Fleming H. Revell, 1916.

Executive Committee of the Baptist Bible Union of North America. *A Call to Arms*. N.p., n.d.

Fass, Paula. *The Damned and the Beautiful: American Youth in the 1920s*. New York: Oxford University Press, 1977.

Filene, Peter. *Him/Her/Self: Sex Roles in Modern America*. Baltimore: Johns Hopkins University Press, 1986.

Finkelhor, David. "Common Features of Family Abuse." In *The Dark Side of Families: Current Family Violence Research*, ed. David Finkelhor, Richard J. Gelles, Gerard T. Totaling, and Murray A. Straus. New York: Sage, 1983.

Fishburn, Janet Forsythe. *The Fatherhood of God and the Victorian Family*. Philadelphia: Fortress Press, 1981.

Fitzgerald, Frances. *Cities on a Hill: A Journey through Contemporary American Culture*. New York: Simon and Schuster, 1986.

———. "Reflections on Jim and Tammy." *New Yorker* 23 April 1990, 45–87.

Fitzwater, P. B. *Woman: Her Mission, Position, and Ministry*. Grand Rapids, Mich.: Eerdmans, 1950.

Friedman, Estelle. "The New Woman: Changing Views of Women in the 1920s." *Journal of American History* 61 (September 1974): 372–93.

———. "Separatism as Strategy: Female Institution Building and American Feminism, 1870–1930," *Feminist Studies* 5 (Fall 1979): 512–29.

Fry, Luther. *The United States Looks at Its Churches*. New York: Institute of Social and Religious Research, 1930.

The Fundamentals. Chicago: Testimony Publishing, 1910.

Gaebelein, A. C. *Half a Century*. New York: Our Hope, ca. 1930. Reprint. New York: Garland Publishing, 1988.

———. *The Healing Question*. New York: Our Hope, 1925.

Gage, Matilda Jocelyn. *Woman, Church, and State*. Chicago: Charles H. Kerr, 1893. Reprint. Watertown, Mass.: Persephone Press, 1980.

Genné, Elizabeth Steel, and William Henry Genné, eds. *Proceedings of the North American Conference on Church and Family.* New York: National Council of Churches, 1961.

Getz, Gene. *MBI: The Story of Moody Bible Institute.* Chicago: Moody Press, 1969.

Giboney, Ezra P., and Agnes M. Potter. *The Life of Mark A. Matthews.* Grand Rapids, Mich.: Eerdmans, 1948.

Gilman, Charlotte Perkins. *His Religion and Hers: A Study of the Faith of Our Fathers and the Work of Our Mothers.* New York, 1923. Reprint. Westport, Conn.: Hyperion Press, 1976.

Ginzberg, Lori. *Women and the Work of Benevolence.* New Haven: Yale University Press, 1992.

God Hath Spoken: Twenty-Five Addresses Delivered at the World Conference on Christian Fundamentals. Philadelphia: Philadelphia Bible Conference Committee, 1919. Reprint. New York: Garland Publishing, 1988.

Gray, James M. *Bible Problems Explained.* New York: Fleming H. Revell, 1913. Reprint. New York: Garland Publishing, 1988.

———. *Christian Workers' Commentary on the Old and New Testaments.* New York: Fleming H. Revell, 1915. Reprint. New York: Garland Publishing, 1988.

———. *Great Epochs of Sacred History.* New York: Fleming H. Revell, 1910.

Haldeman, I. M. *The Signs of the Times,* 8th ed. New York: F. E. Fitch, 1929.

Hamilton, Michael. "Women, Public Ministry, and American Fundamentalism, 1920–1950." *Religion and American Culture* [forthcoming].

Harper, Ida Husted. *The Life of Susan B. Anthony.* 2 vols. Indianapolis: Howen-Merrill, 1908.

Hassey, Janette. *No Time for Silence: Evangelical Women in Public Ministry around the Turn of the Century.* Grand Rapids, Mich.: Zondervan, 1986.

Hatch, Nathan. *The Democratization of American Christianity.* New Haven: Yale University Press, 1989.

Heidebrecht, Paul. "The Educational Legacy of Lois and Mary LeBar." Unpublished paper, 1991.

Henry, James O. *For Such a Time as This: A History of the Independent Fundamental Churches in America.* Westchester, Ill.: Independent Fundamental Churches in America, 1983.

Hill, Patricia. *The World Their Household: The American Woman's Foreign Mission Movement and Cultural Transformation, 1870–1920.* Ann Arbor: University of Michigan Press, 1985.

History and Minutes of the National Council of Women of the United States, ed. Louise Barnum Robbins. Boston, 1898.

History of Woman Suffrage. Ed. Elizabeth Cady Stanton, Susan B. Anthony, Matilda J. Gage. 4 vols. Reprint. New York: Arno Press, 1969.

Hofstadter, Richard. *Anti-Intellectualism in American Life*. New York: Vantage Books, 1963.

Hogeland, Ronald. "Charles Hodge, the Association of Gentlemen and Ornamental Womanhood." *Journal of Presbyterian History* 53 (Fall 1975): 239–55.

Horton, Isabelle. *The Builders: A Story of Faith and Works*. Chicago, 1910.

Hunt, Keith, and Gladys Hunt. *For Christ and the University: The Story of InterVarsity Christian Fellowship, 1940–1990*. Downers Grove, Ill.: InterVarsity Press, 1991.

Hunter, James Davison. *American Evangelicalism: Conservative Religion and the Quandary of Modernity*. New Brunswick, N.J.: Rutgers University Press, 1983.

———. *Culture Wars: The Struggle to Define America*. New York: Basic Books, 1991.

———. *Evangelicalism: The Coming Generation*. Chicago: University of Chicago Press, 1987.

Hutchison, William R., ed. *Between the Times: The Travail of the Protestant Establishment in America, 1900–1960*. Cambridge: Cambridge University Press, 1989.

Interim Report on the Study on the Life and Work of Women in the Church. Geneva, Swit.: World Council of Churches, 1948.

Ironside, Harry A. *The Lamp of Prophecy*. Grand Rapids, Mich.: Zondervan, 1940.

Kane, Thomas. *All About Winona: Winona Assembly and Summer School Association, Its History, Methods, and Future*. Winona Lake, Ind., 1904.

Ketcham, Robert T. *The Answer*. Chicago: General Association of Regular Baptists, 1950.

Kraditor, Aileen. *Ideas of the Woman Suffrage Movement, 1890–1920*. New York: Columbia University Press, 1967.

Larkin, Clarence. *Dispensational Truth*. Philadelphia: Rev. Clarence Larkin Est., 1924.

Lawless, Elaine. *Handmaidens of the Lord: Pentecostal Women Preachers and Traditional Religion*. Philadelphia: University of Pennsylvania Press, 1988.

Lewis, Clifford. *God's Ideal Woman*. Grand Rapids, Mich.: Zondervan, 1941.

Light on Prophecy: A Coordinated, Constructive Teaching; Proceedings and Addresses at Philadelphia Prophetic Conference. New York: Christian Herald Bible House, 1918.

Lindsell, Harold. *Park Street Prophet: A Life of Harold John Ockenga*. Wheaton, Ill.: Van Kampen Press, 1951. Reprint. New York: Garland Publishing, 1988.

Lotz, David W., ed. *Altered Landscapes: Christianity in America, 1935–1985*. Grand Rapids, Mich.: Eerdmans, 1989.

Loveland, Anne C. "Domesticity and Religion in the Antebellum Period: The Career of Phoebe Palmer." *Historian* 39 (May 1977): 455–71.

Lowry, Oscar. *A Virtuous Woman: Sex in Relation to the Christian Life*, 10th ed. Grand Rapids, Mich.: Zondervan, 1943.

Lynd, Robert, and Helen Lynd. *Middletown: A Study in American Culture*. New York: Harcourt and Brace, 1929.

Macartney, Clarence E. *Ancient Wives and Modern Husbands*. Nashville: Cokesbury Press, 1934.

———. *The Making of a Minister*, ed. J. Clyde Henry. Great Neck, N.Y.: Channel Press, 1961.

———. *The Way of a Man with a Maid*. Nashville: Cokesbury Press, 1931.

Magnuson, Norris. *Salvation in the Slums: Evangelical Social Work, 1865–1920*. 1977. Reprint. Grand Rapids, Mich.: Baker Book House, 1990.

Marsden, George. *Fundamentalism and American Culture: The Shaping of Twentieth-Century Evangelicalism*. New York: Oxford University Press, 1980.

———. *Reforming Fundamentalism: Fuller Seminary and the New Evangelicalism*. Grand Rapids, Mich.: Eerdmans, 1987.

Melder, Keith. *Beginnings of Sisterhood: The American Woman's Rights Movement, 1800–1850*. New York: Schocken Books, 1977.

Mencken, D. L. *In Defense of Women*. New York, 1918. Reprint. New York: Octagon Books, 1977.

Merriam, Edmund F. *A History of American Baptist Missions*. Philadelphia: American Baptist Publication Society, 1900.

Minutes of the General Assembly of the Presbyterian Church. New York, 1890, 1893.

Minutes of the National Woman's Christian Temperance Union at the Ninth Annual Meeting, 1882. Brooklyn: Woman's Christian Temperance Union, 1882.

Moody, Dwight L. *Great Joy: Sermons and Prayer Meeting Talks Delivered in the Chicago Tabernacle*. New York: E. B. Treat, 1877.

Moore, R. Laurence. *Religious Outsiders and the Makings of Americans*. New York: Oxford University Press, 1986.

Myers, Cortland. *Why Men Do Not Go to Church*. New York: Funk and Wagnalls, 1899.

Needham, Elizabeth. *Woman's Ministry*. New York: Fleming H. Revell, 1895.

Niebuhr, Richard, and Daniel D. Williams, eds. *The Ministry in Historical Perspective*. New York: Harper and Row, 1956.

Noll, Mark. *Between Faith and Criticism: Evangelicals, Scholarship, and the Bible in America*. San Francisco: Harper and Row, 1986.

Ockenga, Harold J. *The Church God Blesses*. Pasadena: Fuller Missions Fellowship and Park Street Church Board of Missions, 1959.

———. *Women Who Made Bible History*. 1940. Reprint. Grand Rapids, Mich.: Zondervan, 1962.

Olson, Virgil. "Understanding Women's Role in Missions Today: An Executive's View." Paper presented at Evangelical Foreign Missionary Association conference, Orlando, Fla., 6 March 1979. Billy Graham Center Archives, Wheaton, Ill., CN# 165, 35–12.

Palmer, Phoebe. *The Promise of the Father; Or a Neglected Specialty of the Last Days.* Boston: W. C. Palmer, 1859.

Parker, Mac. *Billy Sunday Meetings.* Tampa, Fla.: Tribune Press, 1919.

Pierson, Arthur T. *The Modern Mission Century Viewed as a Cycle of Divine Working.* New York: Baker and Taylor, 1901.

Pink, Walter. *Gleanings in Genesis.* Chicago: Moody Press, 1922.

Powers, Barbara H. *The Henrietta Mears Story.* New York: Fleming H. Revell, 1947.

Presbyterian Brotherhood: Report of the First Convention, Held at Indianapolis, 1906. Philadelphia: Presbyterian Board of Publication, 1907.

Presbyterian Brotherhood: Report of the Second Convention, Held at Cincinnati, 1907. Philadelphia: Presbyterian Board of Publication, 1908.

Quebedeaux, Richard. *The Worldly Evangelicals.* San Francisco: Harper and Row, 1978.

———. *The Young Evangelicals: Revolution in Orthodoxy.* New York: Harper and Row, 1974.

Rice, John R. *Bobbed Hair, Bossy Wives, and Women Preachers.* Wheaton, Ill.: Sword of the Lord Publishers, 1941. Reprint. New York: Garland Publishing, 1988.

Riley, Marie Acomb. *The Dynamic of a Dream.* Grand Rapids, Mich.: Eerdmans, 1938.

Riley, William Bell. *Pastoral Problems.* New York: Fleming H. Revell, 1936.

———. *Wives of the Bible: A Cross-Section of Femininity.* Grand Rapids, Mich.: Zondervan, 1938.

Robinson, Margaret Blake. *A Reporter at Moody's.* Chicago: Bible Institute Colportage Association, 1900.

Roe, Earl, ed. *Dream Big! The Henrietta Mears Story.* Ventura, Calif.: Regal Books, 1990.

Rosell, Merv. *Challenging Youth for Christ.* Grand Rapids, Mich.: Zondervan, 1945.

Rothman, Sheila. *Woman's Proper Place: A History of Changing Ideals and Practices, 1870 to the Present.* New York: Basic Books, 1978.

Rotundo, E. Anthony. "Body and Soul: Changing Ideals of American Middle-Class Manhood, 1770–1920." *Journal of Social History* 16 (1983): 23–35.

Ruether, Rosemary Radford, and Rosemary Skinner Keller, eds. *Women and Religion in America*, vol. 3: *1900–1968.* San Francisco: Harper and Row, 1986.

Russell, C. Allyn. *Voices of American Fundamentalism: Seven Biographical Studies.* Philadelphia: Westminster Press, 1976.

Ryan, Mary. *Cradle of the Middle Class: The Family in Oneida, New York, 1790–1865.* Cambridge, Eng.: Cambridge University Press, 1981.

Ryrie, Charles C. *The Place of Women in the Church.* Chicago: Moody Press, 1958.

Sandeen, Ernest, R. *The Roots of Fundamentalism: British and American Millenarianism.* Chicago: University of Chicago Press, 1970.

Sanders, Lena S. *The Council Torchbearer: A Tribute to Mrs. Virginia Asher.* Roanoke, Va.: Virginia Asher Businesswoman's Bible Council, 1936.

Scanzoni, Letha. "The Great Chain of Being and the Chain of Command." *Reformed Journal* 26 (October 1976): 14–18.

Scanzoni, Letha, and Nancy Hardesty. *All We're Meant to Be: A Biblical Approach to Women's Liberation.* Waco, Tex.: Word Books, 1974.

Schroeder, Edward H. "The Orders of Creation—Some Reflections on the History and Place of the Term in Systematic Theology." *Concordia Theological Monthly* 43 (March 1972): 165–78.

Scofield Reference Bible. Ed. C. I. Scofield. New York: Pickering and Inglis, 1917.

Scofield, C. I. *Prophecy Made Plain.* Glasgow and London: Pickering and Inglis, n.d.

Scudder, C. W. *The Family in Christian Perspective.* Nashville: Broadman Press, 1962.

Seeley, John R., et al. *Crestwood Heights: A Study of the Culture of Suburban Life.* New York: Basic Books, 1956.

Sennett, Richard. *Families against the City: Middle Class Homes of Industrial Chicago.* Cambridge, Mass.: Harvard University Press, 1970.

Sizer, Sandra. *Gospel Hymns and Social Religion: The Rhetoric of Nineteenth-Century Revivalism.* Philadelphia: Temple University Press, 1978.

Smith, Timothy L. *Revivalism and Social Reform.* New York: Harper and Row, 1965.

Smylie, James H. "The *Woman's Bible* and the Spiritual Crisis." *Soundings* 59 (Fall 1976): 305–28.

Spretnak, Charlene. "The Christian Right's 'Holy War' against Feminism." In *The Politics of Women's Spirituality*, ed. Charlene Spretnak. Garden City, N.Y.: Anchor Press, 1982.

Stacey, Judith. *Brave New Families: Stories of Domestic Upheaval in Late Twentieth Century America.* New York: Basic Books, 1991.

Stonehouse, Ned. *J. Gresham Machen: A Biographical Memoir.* Grand Rapids, Mich.: Eerdmans, 1954.

Straton, Hillyer Hawthorn. "The Bible Teaching concerning the Place of Woman in the Modern Church." Th.M. thesis, Eastern Baptist Theological Seminary, 1929.

The Sure Word of Prophecy: Report on the New York Congress on Prophecy, 1942. Ed. John W. Bradbury. New York: Fleming H. Revell, 1943.

Tarr, Leslie K. *Shields of Canada.* Grand Rapids: Baker Books, 1967.

Townsley, Frances. *A Pilgrim Maid: The Self-Told Story of Frances E. Townsley.* Butler, Ind.: L. H. Higley, 1908.

Transactions of the National Council of Women in the United States. ed. Rachel Foster Avery. Philadelphia, 1891.

Trollinger, William Vance. *God's Empire: William Bell Riley and Midwestern Fundamentalism.* Madison: University of Wisconsin Press, 1990.

Trumbull, Charles. *Prophecy's Light on Today*. New York: Fleming H. Revell, 1937. Reprint. New York: Garland Publishing, 1988.

Tucker, Ruth. "Female Mission Strategists: A Historical and Contemporary Perspective." Pamphlet distributed by Christians for Biblical Equality, Inver Grove Heights, Minn.

Tulga, Chester E. *The Foreign Missions Controversy in the Northern Baptist Convention, 1919–1949*. Chicago: Conservative Baptist Fellowship, 1950.

—————. "The Northern Baptist Convention and the New Testament." Glen B. Ewell Papers, American Baptist Historical Society, Rochester, N.Y.

Unveiling the Future: Twelve Prophetic Messages. Ed. T. Richard Dunham. Findley, Ohio: Fundamental Truth Publishing, 1934.

Verdesi, Elizabeth H. *In But Still Out: Women in the Church*. Philadelphia: Westminster Press, 1973.

Victor, Frances F. *The Women's War with Whiskey; or Crusading in Portland*. Portland, Oreg., 1874.

The Victorious Christ: Messages from Conferences Held by the Victorious Life Testimony in 1922. Philadelphia: Sunday-School Times, 1923.

The Victorious Life. Philadelphia: Board of Managers of the Victorious Life Conference, 1918.

Victory in Christ. Princeton: Board of Managers of the Princeton Conference, 1916.

Wacker, Grant. "The Holy Spirit and the Spirit of the Age in American Protestantism, 1880–1919." *Journal of American History* 72 (June 1985): 45–62.

Waldron-Stains, Candace. "Evangelical Women: From Feminist Reform to Silent Femininity." *debarim* 3 (1978–1979): 57–73.

Watt, David Harrington. *A Transforming Faith: Explorations of Twentieth-Century American Evangelicalism*. New Brunswick, N.J.: Rutgers University Press, 1991.

Weber, Timothy P. *Living in the Shadow of the Second Coming: American Premillennialism, 1875–1982*. Chicago: University of Chicago Press, 1987.

Wiebe, Richard. *The Search for Order, 1877–1920*. New York: Hill and Wang, 1967.

Wilkin, G. F. *The Prophesying of Women: A Popular and Practical Exposition of the Bible Doctrine*. Chicago: Fleming H. Revell, 1895.

Willard, Frances. *Glimpses of Fifty Years*. Chicago: Woman's Temperance Publishing Association and H. J. Smith, 1889.

—————. *Woman and Temperance*. 6th ed. Evanston, Ill.: Woman's Christian Temperance Union, 1897.

—————. *Woman in the Pulpit*. Chicago, 1889. Reprint. Washington, D.C.: Zenger Publishing, 1978.

Wills, Garry. *Under God: Religion and American Politics*. New York: Simon and Schuster, 1990.

Winona: Its Activities and Attractions. Winona Lake, Ind., 1906.

Woman's Bible. Ed. Elizabeth Cady Stanton et al. Reprint. New York: Arno Press, 1974.

Wright, J. Elwyn. *The Old Fashioned Revival Hour and the Broadcasters.* Boston: Fellowship Press, 1940. Reprint. New York: Garland Publishing, 1988.

Wyker, Mossie Allman. *Church Women in the Scheme of Things.* St. Louis: Bethany Press, 1953.

Zerbst, Fritz. *The Office of Woman in the Church: A Study in Practical Theology.* St. Louis: Concordia Publishing House, 1955.

Periodicals

Alliance Weekly, Christian and Missionary Alliance, 1887–

The Baptist, Northern Baptist Convention, 1920–1933 (merged into *Christian Century* in 1933)

Baptist Bulletin, General Association of Regular Baptists, 1935–

Bibliotheca Sacra, Pittsburgh-Xenia Theological Seminary, 1844–1933; Evangelical Theological Seminary, Dallas, Tex. (later Dallas Theological Seminary), 1934–

Christian Beacon, edited by Carl McIntire for the Bible Presbyterian Church, 1936–

Christian Cynosure, founded by Jonathan Blanchard for the National Christian Association, 1868–

Christian Faith and Life, 1930–1939 (previously *Bible Student,* 1900–1903; *Bible Student and Teacher,* 1904–1913; and *Bible Champion* 1913–1930)

Christianity Today, Orthodox Presbyterian Church, Philadelphia, 1930–1949; nondenominational evangelical, Carol Stream, Ill., 1956–

Eternity, Philadelphia, 1950– (previously *Revelation,* edited by Donald Grey Barnhouse, 1931–1950)

HIS, InterVarsity Christian Fellowship, 1941–

King's Business, Bible Institute of Los Angeles, 1910–

Missionary Review of the World, Princeton, N.J., 1878–1939

Moody Monthly, Chicago, Ill., 1938– (previously *Institute Tie,* 1900–1910; *Christian Workers' Magazine,* 1910–1920; *Moody Bible Institute Monthly,* 1920–1938)

Our Hope, edited by Arno C. Gaebelein, 1894–1957, and absorbed by *Eternity* in 1957

Pilot, edited by Willam Bell Riley and an organ of his Northwestern schools, Minneapolis, Minn. (previously *Christian Fundamentalist,* 1927–1932, a merger of *Christian Fundamentals in School and Church,* 1918–1927, and *School and Church,* 1918–1920; *Pilot,* 1920–1943, became *Northwestern Pilot,* 1943–1956)

Presbyterian, Philadelphia, 1831–1948

Record of Christian Work, 1881–1933 (absorbed *Northfield Echoes*, 1894–1903, and *Watchword*, 1878–1921)

Sunday-School Times, Philadelphia, 1859–1966

Sword of the Lord, edited by John R. Rice, Murphreesboro, Tenn., 1934–

Truth; or Testimony for Christ, edited by James H. Brookes, St. Louis, Mo., 1874–1897

Union Signal, Woman's Christian Temperance Union, 1883–1903 (previously *Woman's Temperance Union*, 1875–1877; *Our Union*, 1878–1882)

Watchman-Examiner, edited by Baptists Curtis Lee Laws and John W. Bradbury, 1913–1970 (previously *Watchman*, 1876–1913, and merged with *Examiner*)

Winona Echoes, Winona Lake Bible Conference, Winona Lake, Ind., 1902–1947

Manuscript Collections

Zoe Anne Alford Papers, Billy Graham Center Archives, Wheaton, Ill.

Evangelicals for Social Action Papers, Billy Graham Center Archives, Wheaton, Ill.

Glen B. Ewell Papers, American Baptist Historical Society, Rochester, N.Y.

J. Gresham Machen Papers, Westminster Theological Seminary, Chestnut Hill, Penn.

J. C. Massee Papers, American Baptist Historical Society, Rochester, N.Y.

National Association of Evangelicals, Billy Graham Center Archives, Wheaton, Ill.

Park Street Church Records, Park Street Church and Congregational Historical Society, Boston, Mass.

William Bell Riley Papers, Northwestern College, Roseville, Minn.

John Roach Straton Papers, American Baptist Historical Society, Rochester, N.Y.

William A. Sunday Papers, Billy Graham Center Archives, Wheaton, Ill.

Anna Canada Swain Papers, American Baptist Historical Society, Rochester, N.Y.

Winona Lake Bible Conference Papers, Grace College and Theological Seminary, Winona Lake, Ind.

Nathan Wood Papers, Gordon College Archives, Wenham, Mass.

Interviews

Alford, Zoe Anne. Taped interview, Billy Graham Center Archives, Wheaton, Ill., CN# 177.

Case, Edna Louise Asher. Taped interview, Billy Graham Center Archives, Wheaton, Ill., CN# 196.

Evans, Elizabeth. Taped interview, 8 October 1984, Billy Graham Center Archives, Wheaton, Ill., CN# 279.

Hardesty, Nancy S. Telephone interview with author, 24 February 1992.

Howe, Alison and Kenneth. Former associates of William Bell Riley, personal interview with author, Minneapolis, 19 November 1991.

MacGregor, Helen Clark. Fuller graduate, personal interview with author, Brewster, Mass., 7 September 1991.

Phillips, Rose. Associate of Nathan Wood, personal interview with author, Cambridge, Mass., 4 March 1992.

Scanzoni, Letha Dawson. Telephone interview with author, 12 March 1992.

Woods, Irene. Associate of William Bell Riley, personal interview with author, Roseville, Minn., 21 November 1991.

Index